TWO CREATIVE TRADITIONS IN ENGLISH POETRY

TWO CREATIVE TRADITIONS
IN ENGLISH POETRY

Edited by
SEYMOUR M. PITCHER, 1906 –   ed.
JOSEPH E. BAKER, 1905 –
WILBUR L. SCHRAMM, 1907 –

with an introduction by
NORMAN FOERSTER

Granger Index Reprint Series

BOOKS FOR LIBRARIES PRESS
FREEPORT, NEW YORK

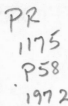

First Published 1939
Reprinted 1972

Library of Congress Cataloging in Publication Data

Pitcher, Seymour Maitland, 1906–   ed.
    Two creative traditions in English poetry.
                    21 cm
    (Granger index reprint series)
    Reprint of the 1939 ed.
    1. English poetry (Collections) I. Baker, Joseph
Ellis, 1905–   joint ed. II. Schramm, Wilbur Lang,
1907–   joint ed. III. Title.
PR1175.P58 1972   821'.008   72–450
ISBN 0–8369–6367–9

PRINTED IN THE UNITED STATES OF AMERICA
BY
NEW WORLD BOOK MANUFACTURING CO., INC.
HALLANDALE, FLORIDA 33009

INTRODUCTION

However it may be elsewhere, in America we have based our hopes for the future on democracy and science. We believe in the dignity of man and we believe in the inquiring mind. Facing the future in a creative spirit, we propose to develop these two faiths and to make them vital in the life of the nation.

If this twofold creed of ours were merely the result of a century and a half of national experience, it might well be fragile and temporary. But it was not "made in America," nor was it created suddenly in modern times. Its strength—and hence our strength—lies in the fact that it springs from two very old traditions, deeply expressive of human nature, which essentially formed that Western civilization of which America is a part. Hebraism and Hellenism they were named by Matthew Arnold, who declared that "between these two points of influence moves our world." Broadly speaking, Hebraism stands for character, right acting; Hellenism stands for intelligence, right thinking. A recent writer, Sir R. W. Livingstone, has described the role of these two traditions as follows: "The essential life of the modern world, its chief creating and animating forces, come from two countries, Palestine and Greece (for convenience I shall group Christianity and Judaism together and not attempt to analyze their differences). Suppose these countries had never been, take away their contributions, and what we mean by Europe would not exist. He who knows Palestine and Greece knows the germ of four-fifths or more of Western civilization, and has seen its animating and sustaining forces in their simplest and purest form."

That "dignity of man" to which we often refer so glibly—what do we mean by it? Our answer is likely to be vague indeed, perilously vague it may be said, for a vague conception is always in danger of being swept aside by one that has a sharper fighting edge. Before attempting a more resolute reply we might well review the history of the idea, and its richest expressions in life, as far back as its origin in Greece, where the dignity of man was very real, and in Christianity, which proclaimed on definite grounds the dignity of *each* man. Plainly, the democratic dogma of the dignity of man is a development out of the traditions of Hebraism and Hellenism. As for the inquiring mind, which for us today is usually the scientific mind, let us remember that science is not a new human enterprise that may easily succumb to distortion or suppression by hysterical political forces, but a normal working of the human mind which was well established by the ancient Greeks and which has triumphed over many obstacles in the course of its long history. If at the present time democracy and science, the professed bases of our civilization, are not altogether safe, it may well be because our faith in them has been allowed to grow vague and unmeaning, because our faith in them needs renewal at the source. By means of such a renewal we should be able to rise above the present tendency to think of democracy as merely an instrument for giving every man a better chance in a materialistic society and of science as merely an instrument for providing convenience of living.

To the modern reader, in a time when economic and political confusion is matched by intellectual and spiritual confusion, nothing could be more stimulating to

Introduction

clarity than a fresh effort to understand the old sustaining forces of our Western civilization in their simplest and purest form: the Old Testament and Homer (the Bible of the Hebrews and the Bible of the Greeks), which may be thought of as together forming our older testament or dispensation, and then the newer testament or dispensation, the New Testament and the great ages of Athens and Rome. These are our source, available to our uses today in unsurpassed literary expression. The Middle Ages that followed were of course above all ages of Christian faith, but the Christian tradition was already vitally blended with the Hellenic in the philosophy of St. Augustine and St. Thomas Aquinas and in the poetry of Dante. When the Renaissance came, it restored the many-sidedness of the pagan world, but the two traditions of Greece and Palestine were widely and variously fused by such men as Erasmus, More, and Milton. To this point the traditions were highly creative. Since the seventeenth century, however, the religious tradition has on the whole markedly declined in vitality, and perhaps the same must be said of the humanistic tradition except for one strand of it, the scientific. More than at any time since the seventeenth century, democracy and science are today on the defensive. Can they survive alone? Will it not be necessary to include in the "dignity of man" a humane or religious connotation? Will it not be necessary to widen the task of the "inquiring mind" by including philosophic reflection?

While a serious effort to bring the light of the two great traditions to bear upon our modern problems is scarcely characteristic of our schools and colleges, it is being increasingly undertaken in institutions of higher learning. There is a growing inclination to seek an understanding of "the wisdom of the ages" by means of the great books, such ancient books as the epics of Homer, the tragedies of Sophocles, the *Republic* of Plato, the Bible; such medieval works as the *Divine Comedy* of Dante and Chaucer's *Troilus and Criseyde*. With the Renaissance came a flowering of national literature in Italy, in Spain, in France, and also in England—fortunately for us

> . . . who speak the tongue
> That Shakespeare spake.

From the Renaissance onward, the student of English poetry may see how the old traditions of Palestine and Greece, sometimes apart from each other, sometimes organically united, reappear in new creations in most of the great writers and often in their longer, more sustained works: in Spenser (*The Faerie Queene*), in Milton (*Paradise Lost*), in Dryden, in Pope (of whose translation of the *Iliad* Bentley said, "a pretty poem, Mr. Pope, but you must not call it Homer"), in Keats, in Shelley, in Tennyson, in Browning, in Swinburne, poets and poetry so diverse as to indicate the endless suggestive power of the old traditions, the ever novel uses to which genius could put their doctrine, spirit, symbols, and forms.

This is equally true of the shorter poems in our language; in them also, from the Renaissance to our own day, is revealed again and again, in unpredictably fresh versions, the infinite fecundity of Hebraism and Hellenism. It is the object of the present collection, the first of the kind, to bring together a rich selection of these shorter poems scattered through three hundred years of English literature. It is expected that it will be used, ordinarily by classes in English literature, along with the study of the sources themselves, ancient and medieval.

Introduction

So studied, it will take on a resonance and interest not to be expected when studied alone.

Inevitably perhaps, the collection has many limitations. Not all the poems have highest poetic merit. Though generous, the collection is far from comprehensive. Some periods of English poetry are represented more fully than others; thus it seemed desirable to subordinate the pseudo-classical age as being essentially Latinate and to emphasize the nineteenth century as being more Greek, though sometimes in a distorted manner. The arrangement is not always strictly chronological, because it seemed useful to bring together certain poems closely related in subject. By further grouping—by following a sequence of related poems—the reader may consider the poems derivative from Homer, Greek tragedy, Plato and Greek thought, Greek art, the Greek ideal in general, and, similarly, the poems derivative from the Old Testament, the New Testament, Catholicism, Anglicanism, and Protestantism. The selection was made largely on the basis of allusion; that is, poems were included if they touched directly upon concrete images and themes drawn from the two traditions, as, for example, Milton's "On the Morning of Christ's Nativity" or Tennyson's "Ulysses," where the influence is manifest. Had an attempt been made to represent the hidden influence of ancient ideas and attitudes, which permeates almost the whole of our literature, this book would have expanded virtually into a general anthology of English poetry. It is not such a voluminous work; but one may venture to say of it that it presents a higher average of art, a greater richness and depth of feeling and thought, than any other collection of short poems that might be made on an equally definite principle.

NORMAN FOERSTER

CONTENTS

[xi]

Contents

[xii]

Contents

Contents

GREEK THEMES

ULYSSES AND THE SIREN

Sir. Come, worthy Greek, Ulysses, come,
    Possess these shores with me;
    The winds and seas are troublesome,
    And here we may be free.
      Here may we sit and view their toil
    That travail on the deep,
    And joy the day in mirth the while,
    And spend the night in sleep.

Ulys. Fair nymph, if fame or honor were
    To be attained with ease,
    Then would I come and rest with thee,
    And leave such toils as these.
      But here it dwells, and here must I
    With danger seek it forth;
    To spend the time luxuriously
    Becomes not men of worth.

Sir. Ulysses, O be not deceived
    With that unreal name;
    This honor is a thing conceived,
    And rests on others' fame.

Begotten only to molest
Our peace, and to beguile
The best thing of our life, our rest,
And give us up to toil.

Ulys. Delicious nymph, suppose there were
Nor honor nor report,
Yet manliness would scorn to wear
The time in idle sport.
   For toil doth give a better touch,
To make us feel our joy;
And ease finds tediousness, as much
As labor, yields annoy.

Sir. Then pleasure likewise seems the shore
Whereto tends all your toil,
Which you forgo to make it more,
And perish oft the while.
   Who may disport them diversly,
Find never tedious day,
And ease may have variety
As well as action may.

Ulys. But natures of the noblest frame
These toils and dangers please,
And they take comfort in the same
As much as you in ease,
   And with the thoughts of actions past
Are recreated still;
When pleasure leaves a touch at last
To show that it was ill.

[4]

SAMUEL DANIEL

Sir. That doth opinion only cause
That's out of custom bred,
Which makes us many other laws
Than ever nature did.

  No widows wail for our delights,
Our sports are without blood;
The world, we see, by warlike wights
Receives more hurt than good.

Ulys. But yet the state of things require
These motions of unrest,
And these great spirits of high desire
Seem born to turn them best,

  To purge the mischiefs that increase
And all good order mar;
For oft we see a wicked peace
To be well changed for war.

Sir. Well, well, Ulysses, then I see
I shall not have thee here,
And therefore I will come to thee,
And take my fortunes there.

  I must be won that cannot win,
Yet lost were I not won;
For beauty hath created been
T'undo, or be undone.

SAMUEL DANIEL

L'ALLEGRO

Hence, loathèd Melancholy,
    Of Cerberus and blackest Midnight born,
In Stygian cave forlorn,
    'Mongst horrid shapes, and shrieks, and sights unholy!
Find out some uncouth cell,
    Where brooding Darkness spreads his jealous wings,
And the night raven sings;
    There under ebon shades, and low-browed rocks,
As ragged as thy locks,
    In dark Cimmerian desert ever dwell.
But come thou Goddess fair and free,
In heaven y-clep'd Euphrosyne,
And by men, heart-easing Mirth,
Whom lovely Venus at a birth
With two sister Graces more,
To ivy-crownèd Bacchus bore;
Or whether (as some sager sing)
The frolic wind that breathes the spring,
Zephyr with Aurora playing,
As he met her once a Maying;
There on beds of violets blue,
And fresh-blown roses washed in dew,
Filled her with thee a daughter fair,
So buxom, blithe, and debonair.

[6]

Haste thee, Nymph, and bring with thee
Jest, and youthful Jollity,
Quips, and Cranks, and wanton Wiles,
Nods, and Becks, and wreathèd Smiles,
Such as hang on Hebe's cheek,
And love to live in dimple sleek;
Sport that wrinkled Care derides,
And Laughter holding both his sides.
Come, and trip it as you go,
On the light fantastic toe;
And in thy right hand lead with thee
The mountain nymph, sweet Liberty;
And if I give thee honour due,
Mirth, admit me of thy crew,
To live with her, and live with thee,
In unreprovèd pleasures free.
To hear the lark begin his flight,
And singing startle the dull night,
From his watch-tower in the skies,
Till the dappled dawn doth rise;
Then to come in spite of sorrow,
And at my window bid good morrow,
Through the sweet-briar, or the vine,
Or the twisted eglantine:
While the cock with lively din
Scatters the rear of darkness thin,
And to the stack, or the barn-door,
Stoutly struts his dames before,
Oft listening how the hounds and horn
Cheerly rouse the slumb'ring morn,
From the side of some hoar hill,
Through the high wood echoing shrill:

Some time walking, not unseen,
By hedge-row elms, on hillocks green,
Right against the eastern gate,
Where the great sun begins his state,
Robed in flames, and amber light,
The clouds in thousand liveries dight;
While the ploughman near at hand
Whistles o'er the furrowed land,
And the milkmaid singeth blithe,
And the mower whets his scythe,
And every shepherd tells his tale
Under the hawthorn in the dale.
Straight mine eye hath caught new pleasures
Whilst the landscape round it measures;
Russet lawns, and fallows gray,
Where the nibbling flocks do stray,
Mountains, on whose barren breast
The lab'ring clouds do often rest;
Meadows trim with daisies pied,
Shallow brooks, and rivers wide.
Towers and battlements it sees
Bosomed high in tufted trees,
Where perhaps some Beauty lies,
The Cynosure of neighb'ring eyes.
Hard by, a cottage-chimney smokes,
From betwixt two agèd oaks,
Where Corydon and Thyrsis met,
Are at their savoury dinner set
Of herbs, and other country messes,
Which the neat-handed Phillis dresses;
And then in haste the bower she leaves,
With Thestylis to bind the sheaves;

Or, if the earlier season lead,
To the tanned haycock in the mead,
Sometimes with secure delight
The upland hamlets will invite,
When the merry bells ring round,
And the jocund rebecks sound
To many a youth, and many a maid,
Dancing in the chequered shade;
And young and old come forth to play
On a sunshine holiday,
Till the live-long daylight fail;
Then to the spicy nut-brown ale,
With stories told of many a feat,
How fairy Mab the junkets eat;
She was pinched and pulled, she said,
And he by Friar's lanthorn led,
Tells how the drudging Goblin sweat,
To earn his cream-bowl duly set,
When in one night, ere glimpse of morn,
His shadowy flail hath threshed the corn,
That ten day-lab'rers could not end;
Then lies him down the lubber fiend,
And stretched out all the chimney's length,
Basks at the fire his hairy strength,
And crop-full out of doors he flings,
Ere the first cock his matin rings.
Thus done the tales, to bed they creep,
By whispering winds soon lulled asleep.
Towered cities please us then,
And the busy hum of men,
Where throngs of knights and barons bold
In weeds of peace high triumphs hold,

With store of ladies, whose bright eyes
Rain influence, and judge the prize
Of wit, or arms, while both contend
To win her grace, whom all commend.
There let Hymen oft appear
In saffron robe, with taper clear,
And pomp, and feast, and revelry,
With mask, and antique pageantry,
Such sights as youthful poets dream
On summer eves by haunted stream.
Then to the well-trod stage anon,
If Jonson's learnèd sock be on,
Or sweetest Shakespeare, Fancy's child,
Warble his native wood-notes wild.

   And ever against eating cares,
Lap me in soft Lydian airs,
Married to immortal verse,
Such as the meeting soul may pierce,
In notes, with many a winding bout
Of linkèd sweetness long drawn out,
With wanton heed and giddy cunning,
The melting voice through mazes running,
Untwisting all the chains that tie
The hidden soul of harmony;
That Orpheus' self may heave his head
From golden slumber on a bed
Of heaped Elysian flowers, and hear
Such strains as would have won the ear
Of Pluto, to have quite set free
His half regained Eurydice.

   These delights if thou canst give,
Mirth, with thee I mean to live.   JOHN MILTON

IL PENSEROSO

Hence, vain deluding joys,
  The brood of folly without father bred,
How little you bestead,
  Or fill the fixèd mind with all your toys!
Dwell in some idle brain,
  And fancies fond with gaudy shapes possess,
As thick and numberless
  As the gay motes that people the sunbeams,
Or likest hovering dreams
  The fickle pensioners of Morpheus' train,
But hail thou Goddess, sage and holy,
  Hail divinest Melancholy,
Whose saintly visage is too bright
To hit the sense of human sight,
And therefore to our weaker view
O'erlaid with black, staid Wisdom's hue;
Black, but such as in esteem
Prince Memnon's sister might beseem,
Or that starred Ethiop queen that strove
To set her beauty's praise above
The Sea-Nymphs, and their powers offended:
Yet thou art higher far descended;
Thee bright-haired Vesta, long of yore,
To solitary Saturn bore;

His daughter she (in Saturn's reign,
Such mixture was not held a stain).
Oft in glimmering bowers and glades
He met her, and in secret shades
Of woody Ida's inmost grove,
While yet there was no fear of Jove.
Come, pensive Nun, devout and pure,
Sober, steadfast, and demure,
All in a robe of darkest grain,
Flowing with majestic train,
And sable stole of cyprus lawn,
Over thy decent shoulders drawn.
Come, but keep thy wonted state,
With even step, and musing gait,
And looks commercing with the skies,
Thy rapt soul sitting in thine eyes:
There held in holy passion still,
Forget thyself to marble, till
With a sad, leaden, downward cast
Thou fix them on the earth as fast:
And join with thee calm Peace, and Quiet,
Spare Fast, that oft with gods doth diet,
And hears the Muses in a ring
Aye round about Jove's altar sing:
And add to these retired Leisure,
That in trim gardens takes his pleasure;
But first, and chiefest, with thee bring
Him that yon soars on golden wing,
Guiding the fiery-wheelèd throne,
The Cherub Contemplation;
And the mute Silence hist along,
'Less Philomel will deign a song,

In her sweetest, saddest plight,
Smoothing the rugged brow of night,
While Cynthia checks her dragon yoke,
Gently o'er the accustomed oak;
Sweet bird, that shunn'st the noise of folly,
Most musical, most melancholy!
Thee, chauntress, oft the woods among
I woo, to hear thy even-song;
And missing thee, I walk unseen
On the dry smooth-shaven green,
To behold the wandering moon,
Riding near her highest noon,
Like one that had been led astray
Through the heav'n's wide pathless way;
And oft, as if her head she bowed,
Stooping through a fleecy cloud.
Oft on a plat of rising ground,
I hear the far-off curfew sound,
Over some wide-watered shore,
Swinging slow with sullen roar;
Or if the air will not permit,
Some still removèd place will fit,
Where glowing embers through the room
Teach light to counterfeit a gloom,
Far from all resort of mirth,
Save the cricket on the hearth,
Or the bellman's drowsy charm,
To bless the doors from nightly harm.
Or let my lamp at midnight hour
Be seen in some high lonely tower,
Where I may oft out-watch the Bear,
With thrice-great Hermes, or unsphere

The spirit of Plato, to unfold
What worlds, or what vast regions hold
The immortal mind, that hath forsook
Her mansion in this fleshly nook:
And of those Demons that are found
In fire, air, flood, or under ground,
Whose power hath a true consent
With planet, or with element.
Sometimes let gorgeous tragedy
In sceptred pall come sweeping by,
Presenting Thebes, or Pelops' line,
Or the tale of Troy divine,
Or what (though rare) of later age
Ennobled hath the buskined stage.
But, O sad Virgin, that thy power
Might raise Musæus from his bower,
Or bid the soul of Orpheus sing
Such notes as warbled to the string,
Drew iron tears down Pluto's cheek,
And made Hell grant what love did seek.
Or call up him that left half told
The story of Cambuscan bold,
Of Camball, and of Algarsife,
And who had Canace to wife,
That owned the virtuous ring and glass,
And of the wondrous horse of brass,
On which the Tartar king did ride;
And if aught else great bards beside
In sage and solemn tunes have sung,
Of tourneys and of trophies hung,
Of forests, and enchantments drear,
Where more is meant than meets the ear.

Thus Night oft see me in thy pale career,
Till civil-suited Morn appear,
Not tricked and frounced as she was wont
With the Attic boy to hunt,
But kerchefed in a comely cloud,
While rocking winds are piping loud,
Or ushered with a shower still,
When the gust hath blown his fill,
Ending on the rustling leaves,
With minute drops from off the eaves.
And when the sun begins to fling
His flaring beams, me, Goddess, bring
To archèd walks of twilight groves,
And shadows brown that Sylvan loves
Of pine, or monumental oak,
Where the rude axe with heavèd stroke
Was never heard the Nymphs to daunt,
Or fright them from their hallowed haunt.
There in close covert by some brook,
Where no profaner eye may look,
Hide me from day's garish eye,
While the bee with honied thigh,
That at her flowery work doth sing,
And the waters murmuring
With such consort as they keep,
Entice the dewy-feathered sleep;
And let some strange mysterious dream
Wave at his wings in airy stream
Of lively portraiture displayed,
Softly on my eyelids laid.
And as I wake, sweet music breathe
Above, about, or underneath,

Sent by some Spirit to mortals good,
Or the unseen Genius of the wood,
But let my due feet never fail
To walk the studious cloister's pale,
And love the high embowèd roof,
With antic pillars massy proof,
And storied windows richly dight,
Casting a dim religious light:
There let the pealing organ blow,
To the full voiced quire below,
In service high, and anthems clear,
As may with sweetness, through mine ear,
Dissolve me into ecstasies,
And bring all heav'n before mine eyes.
And may at last my weary age
Find out the peaceful hermitage,
The hairy gown and mossy cell,
Where I may sit and rightly spell
Of every star that heav'n doth show,
And every herb that sips the dew;
Till old experience do attain
To something like prophetic strain.
These pleasures, Melancholy, give,
And I with thee will choose to live.

JOHN MILTON

ATHENS THE EYE OF GREECE

From *Paradise Regained—Book IV*

Be famous then

By wisdom; as thy empire must extend,
So let extend thy mind o'er all the world
In knowledge, all things in it comprehend:
All knowledge is not couched in Moses' law,
The Pentateuch, or what the prophets wrote;
The Gentiles also know, and write, and teach
To admiration, led by nature's light;
And with the Gentiles much thou must converse,
Ruling them by persuasion as thou mean'st.
Without their learning, how wilt thou with them,
Or they with thee, hold conversation meet?
How wilt thou reason with them? how refute
Their idolisms, traditions, paradoxes?
Error by his own arms is best evinced.
Look once more, ere we leave this specular mount,
Westward, much nearer by south-west, behold
Where on the Ægean shore a city stands,
Built nobly, pure the air, and light the soil,
Athens the eye of Greece, mother of arts
And eloquence, native to famous wits,

Or hospitable, in her sweet recess,
City or suburban, studious walks and shades;
See there the olive grove of Academe,
Plato's retirement, where the Attic bird
Trills her thick-warbled notes the summer long;
There flow'ry hill Hymettus with the sound
Of bees' industrious murmur oft invites
To studious musing; there Ilissus rolls
His whispering stream; within the walls then view
The schools of ancient sages; his who bred
Great Alexander to subdue the world:
Lyceum there, and painted Stoa next.
There thou shalt hear and learn the secret power
Of harmony, in tones and numbers hit
By voice or hand, and various-measured verse,
Æolian charms and Dorian lyric odes,
And his who gave them breath, but higher sung,
Blind Melesigenes, thence Homer called,
Whose poem Phœbus challenged for his own.
Thence what the lofty grave tragedians taught
In chorus or iambick, teachers best
Of moral prudence, with delight received,
In brief sententious precepts, while they treat
Of fate, and chance, and change in human life;
High actions and high passions best describing.
Thence to the famous orators repair,
Those ancient, whose resistless eloquence
Wielded at will that fierce democraty,
Shook the Arsenal, and fulmined over Greece,
To Macedon, and Artaxerxes' throne.
To sage philosophy next lend thine ear,
From heav'n descended to the low-rooft house

Of Socrates; see there his tenement,
Whom, well inspired, the oracle pronounced
Wisest of men; from whose mouth issued forth
Mellifluous streams that watered all the schools
Of Academics old and new, with those
Surnamed Peripatetics, and the sect
Epicurean, and the Stoic severe;
These here revolve, or, as thou lik'st, at home,
Till time mature thee to a kingdom's weight;
These rules will render thee a king complete
Within thyself, much more with empire joined.

JOHN MILTON

ALEXANDER'S FEAST;
OR, THE POWER OF MUSIC

A SONG IN HONOUR OF ST. CECILIA'S DAY: 1697

I

'TWAS at the royal feast for Persia won
    By Philip's warlike son:
  Aloft in awful state
  The godlike hero sate
    On his imperial throne.
His valiant peers were placed around;
Their brows with roses and with myrtles bound:
(So should desert in arms be crowned.)
The lovely Thais, by his side,
Sate like a blooming Eastern bride,
    In flower of youth and beauty's pride.
    Happy, happy, happy pair!
      None but the brave,
      None but the brave,
    None but the brave deserves the fair.

CHORUS
    Happy, happy, happy pair!
      None but the brave,
      None but the brave,
    None but the brave deserves the fair.

II

Timotheus placed on high
    Amid the tuneful quire,
With flying fingers touched the lyre:
    The trembling notes ascend the sky,
    And heavenly joys inspire.
    The song began from Jove,
    Who left his blissful seats above,
    (Such is the power of mighty love.)
    A dragon's fiery form belied the god:
    Sublime on radiant spires he rode,
    When he to fair Olympia pressed:
    And while he sought her snowy breast,
    Then round her slender waist he curled,
And stamped an image of himself, a sovereign of
    the world.
    The listening crowd admire the lofty sound,
    A present deity, they shout around;
    A present deity, the vaulted roofs rebound:
        With ravished ears
        The monarch hears,
        Assumes the god,
        Affects to nod,
And seems to shake the spheres.

CHORUS

        With ravished ears
        The monarch hears,
        Assumes the god,
        Affects to nod,
    And seems to shake the spheres.

III

The praise of Bacchus then the sweet musician sung,
  Of Bacchus ever fair, and ever young.
    The jolly god in triumph comes;
    Sound the trumpets, beat the drums;
      Flushed with a purple grace
      He shows his honest face:
Now give the hautboys breath; he comes, he comes.
  Bacchus ever fair and young,
    Drinking joys did first ordain;
  Bacchus' blessings are a treasure,
  Drinking is the soldier's pleasure;
    Rich the treasure,
    Sweet the pleasure,
  Sweet is pleasure after pain.

CHORUS

    Bacchus' blessings are a treasure,
    Drinking is the soldier's pleasure;
      Rich the treasure,
      Sweet the pleasure,
    Sweet is pleasure after pain.

IV

Soothed with the sound the king grew vain;
  Fought all his battles o'er again;
And thrice he routed all his foes, and thrice he slew
    the slain.
  The master saw the madness rise,
  His glowing cheeks, his ardent eyes;
And while he heaven and earth defied,

[22]

Changed his hand, and checked his pride.
  He chose a mournful Muse,
  Soft pity to infuse;
He sung Darius great and good,
  By too severe a fate,
Fallen, fallen, fallen, fallen,
  Fallen from his high estate,
And weltering in his blood;
Deserted at his utmost need
By those his former bounty fed;
On the bare earth exposed he lies,
With not a friend to close his eyes.
With downcast looks the joyless victor sate,
  Revolving in his altered soul
    The various turns of chance below;
  And, now and then, a sigh he stole,
    And tears began to flow.

CHORUS

  Revolving in his altered soul
    The various turns of chance below;
  And, now and then, a sigh he stole,
    And tears began to flow.

V

The mighty master smiled to see
That love was in the next degree;
'Twas but a kindred-sound to move,
For pity melts the mind to love.
  Softly sweet, in Lydian measures,
  Soon he soothed his soul to pleasures,

[23]

War, he sung, is toil and trouble;
Honour but an empty bubble;
      Never ending, still beginning,
      Fighting still, and still destroying:
        If the world be worth thy winning,
      Think, O think it worth enjoying:
        Lovely Thais sits beside thee,
        Take the good the gods provide thee.

The many rend the skies with loud applause;
So Love was crowned, but Music won the cause.
  The prince, unable to conceal his pain,
    Gazed on the fair
    Who caused his care,
  And sighed and looked, sighed and looked,
  Sighed and looked, and sighed again;
At length, with love and wine at once oppressed,
The vanquished victor sunk upon her breast.

CHORUS

  The prince, unable to conceal his pain,
    Gazed on the fair
    Who caused his care,
  And sighed and looked, sighed and looked,
  Sighed and looked, and sighed again;
At length, with love and wine at once oppressed,
The vanquished victor sunk upon her breast.

VI

Now strike the golden lyre again;
A louder yet, and yet a louder strain.
Break his bands of sleep asunder,
And rouse him, like a rattling peal of thunder.

Hark, hark, the horrid sound
  Has raised up his head;
  As awaked from the dead,
And amazed, he stares around.
  Revenge, revenge, Timotheus cries,
    See the Furies arise;
    See the snakes that they rear,
    How they hiss in their hair,
And the sparkles that flash from their eyes!
    Behold a ghastly band,
    Each a torch in his hand!
Those are Grecian ghosts, that in battle were slain,
      And unburied remain
      Inglorious on the plain:
      Give the vengeance due
      To the valiant crew.
Behold how they toss their torches on high,
  How they point to the Persian abodes,
And glittering temples of their hostile gods.
The princes applaud with a furious joy;
And the king seized a flambeau with zeal to destroy;
    Thais led the way,
    To light him to his prey,
And, like another Helen, fired another Troy.

CHORUS

And the king seized a flambeau with zeal to destroy;
    Thais led the way,
    To light him to his prey,
And, like another Helen, fired another Troy.

[25]

VII

Thus long ago,
Ere heaving bellows learned to blow,
While organs yet were mute,
Timotheus, to his breathing flute
And sounding lyre,
Could swell the soul to rage, or kindle soft desire.
At last divine Cecilia came,
Inventress of the vocal frame;
The sweet enthusiast, from her sacred store,
Enlarged the former narrow bounds,
And added length to solemn sounds,
With Nature's mother-wit, and arts unknown before.
Let old Timotheus yield the prize,
Or both divide the crown:
He raised a mortal to the skies;
She drew an angel down.

GRAND CHORUS

At last divine Cecilia came,
Inventress of the vocal frame;
The sweet enthusiast, from her sacred store,
Enlarged the former narrow bounds,
And added length to solemn sounds,
With Nature's mother-wit, and arts unknown before.
Let old Timotheus yield the prize,
Or both divide the crown:
He raised a mortal to the skies;
She drew an angel down.

JOHN DRYDEN

KNOW THYSELF

From *An Essay on Man—Epistle II*

Know then thyself, presume not God to scan;
The proper study of mankind is Man.
Placed on this isthmus of a middle state,
A being darkly wise, and rudely great:
With too much knowledge for the sceptic side,
With too much weakness for the stoic's pride,
He hangs between; in doubt to act or rest,
In doubt to deem himself a god or beast;
In doubt his mind or body to prefer,
Born but to die, and reasoning but to err;
Alike in ignorance, his reason such
Whether he thinks too little or too much:
Chaos of thought and passion, all confused;
Still by himself abused, or disabused;
Created half to rise, and half to fall;
Great lord of all things, yet a prey to all;
Sole judge of truth, in endless error hurled:
The glory, jest, and riddle of the world!

ALEXANDER POPE

HOMER

From *An Essay on Criticism—Part I*

You, then, whose judgment the right course would
    steer,
Know well each ancient's proper character;
His fable, subject, scope in every page;
Religion, country, genius of his age:
Without all these at once before your eyes,
Cavil you may, but never criticize.
Be Homer's works your study and delight,
Read them by day, and meditate by night;
Thence form your judgment, thence your maxims bring,
And trace the Muses upward to their spring.
Still with itself compar'd, his text peruse;
And let your comment be the Mantuan Muse.
    When first young Maro in his boundless mind
A work t' outlast immortal Rome design'd,
Perhaps he seem'd above the Critic's law,
And but from Nature's fountains scorn'd to draw:
But when t' examine ev'ry part he came,
Nature and Homer were, he found, the same.
Convinc'd, amaz'd, he checks the bold design;
And rules as strict his labour'd work confine,

As if the Stagirite o'erlook'd each line.
Learn hence for ancient rules a just esteem;
To copy nature is to copy them.
   Some beauties yet no Precepts can declare,
For there's a happiness as well as care.
Music resembles Poetry, in each
Are nameless graces which no methods teach,
And which a master-hand alone can reach.
If, where the rules not far enough extend,
(Since rules were made but to promote their end)
Some lucky Licence answer to the full
Th' intent propos'd, that Licence is a rule.
Thus Pegasus, a nearer way to take,
May boldly deviate from the common track;
From vulgar bounds with brave disorder part,
And snatch a grace beyond the reach of art,
Which without passing thro' the judgment, gains
The heart, and all its end at once attains.
In prospects thus, some objects please our eyes,
Which out of nature's common order rise,
The shapeless rock, or hanging precipice.
Great Wits sometimes may gloriously offend,
And rise to faults true Critics dare not mend.
But tho' the Ancients thus their rules invade,
(As Kings dispense with laws themselves have made)
Moderns, beware! or if you must offend
Against the precept, ne'er transgress its End;
Let it be seldom, and compell'd by need;
And have, at least, their precedent to plead.
The Critic else proceeds without remorse,
Seizes your fame, and puts his laws in force.
   I know there are, to whose presumptuous thoughts

Those freer beauties, ev'n in them, seem faults.
Some figures monstrous and mis-shap'd appear,
Consider'd singly, or beheld too near,
Which, but proportion'd to their light, or place,
Due distance reconciles to form and grace.
A prudent chief not always must display
His pow'rs in equal ranks, and fair array,
But with th' occasion and the place comply,
Conceal his force, nay seem sometimes to fly.
Those oft are stratagems which errors seem,
Nor is it Homer nods, but we that dream.

Still green with bays each ancient Altar stands,
Above the reach of sacrilegious hands;
Secure from Flames, from Envy's fiercer rage,
Destructive War, and all-involving Age.
See, from each clime the learn'd their incense bring!
Hear, in all tongues consenting Pæans ring!
In praise so just let ev'ry voice be join'd,
And fill the gen'ral chorus of mankind.
Hail, Bards triumphant! born in happier days;
Immortal heirs of universal praise!
Whose honours with increase of ages grow,
As streams roll down, enlarging as they flow;
Nations unborn your mighty names shall sound,
And worlds applaud that must not yet be found!
Oh may some spark of your celestial fire,
The last, the meanest of your sons inspire,
(That on weak wings, from far, pursues your flights;
Glows while he reads, but trembles as he writes)
To teach vain Wits a science little known,
T' admire superior sense, and doubt their own!

ALEXANDER POPE

TO THE MUSES

WHETHER on Ida's shady brow
   Or in the chambers of the East,
The chambers of the Sun, that now
   From ancient melody have ceased;

Whether in heaven ye wander fair,
   Or the green corners of the earth,
Or the blue regions of the air
   Where the melodious winds have birth;

Whether on crystal rocks ye rove,
   Beneath the bosom of the sea,
Wandering in many a coral grove;
   Fair Nine, forsaking Poetry;

How have you left the ancient love
   That bards of old enjoy'd in you!
The languid strings do scarcely move,
   The sound is forced, the notes are few.

WILLIAM BLAKE

LAODAMIA

"WITH sacrifice before the rising morn
Vows have I made by fruitless hope inspired;
And from the infernal Gods, 'mid shades forlorn
Of night, my slaughtered Lord have I required:
Celestial pity I again implore;—
Restore him to my sight—great Jove, restore!"

So speaking, and by fervent love endowed
With faith, the Suppliant heavenward lifts her hands;
While, like the sun emerging from a cloud,
Her countenance brightens—and her eye expands;
Her bosom heaves and spreads, her stature grows;
And she expects the issue in repose.

O terror! what hath she perceived?—O joy!
What doth she look on?—whom doth she behold?
Her Hero slain upon the beach of Troy?
His vital presence? his corporeal mould?
It is—if sense deceive her not—'tis He!
And a God leads him, wingèd Mercury!

Mild Hermes spake—and touched her with his wand
That calms all fear; "Such grace hath crowned thy prayer,

Laodamía! that at Jove's command
Thy Husband walks the paths of upper air:
He comes to tarry with thee three hours' space;
Accept the gift, behold him face to face!"

Forth sprang the impassioned Queen her Lord to clasp;
Again that consummation she essayed;
But unsubstantial Form eludes her grasp
As often as that eager grasp was made.
The Phantom parts—but parts to re-unite,
And re-assume his place before her sight.

"Protesiláus, lo! thy guide is gone!
Confirm, I pray, the vision with thy voice:
This is our palace,—yonder is thy throne;
Speak, and the floor thou tread'st on will rejoice.
Not to appal me have the gods bestowed
This precious boon; and blest a sad abode."

"Great Jove, Laodamía! doth not leave
His gifts imperfect:—Spectre though I be,
I am not sent to scare thee or deceive;
But in reward of thy fidelity.
And something also did my worth obtain;
For fearless virtue bringeth boundless gain.

"Thou knowest, the Delphic oracle foretold
That the first Greek who touched the Trojan strand
Should die; but me the threat could not withhold:
A generous cause a victim did demand;
And forth I leapt upon the sandy plain;
A self-devoted chief—by Hector slain."

"Supreme of Heroes—bravest, noblest, best!
Thy matchless courage I bewail no more,
Which then, when tens of thousands were deprest
By doubt, propelled thee to the fatal shore;
Thou found'st—and I forgive thee—here thou art—
A nobler counsellor than my poor heart.

"But thou, though capable of sternest deed,
Wert kind as resolute, and good as brave;
And he, whose power restores thee, hath decreed
Thou shouldst elude the malice of the grave:
Redundant are thy locks, thy lips as fair
As when their breath enriched Thessalian air.

"No Spectre greets me,—no vain Shadow this;
Come, blooming Hero, place thee by my side!
Give, on this well-known couch, one nuptial kiss
To me, this day, a second time thy bride!"
Jove frowned in heaven: the conscious Parcæ threw
Upon those roseate lips a Stygian hue.

"This visage tells thee that my doom is past:
Nor should the change be mourned, even if the joys
Of sense were able to return as fast
And surely as they vanish. Earth destroys
Those raptures duly—Erebus disdains:
Calm pleasures there abide—majestic pains.

"Be taught, O faithful Consort, to control
Rebellious passion: for the Gods approve
The depth, and not the tumult, of the soul;
A fervent, not ungovernable, love.
Thy transports moderate; and meekly mourn
When I depart, for brief is my sojourn—"

"Ah wherefore?—Did not Hercules by force
Wrest from the guardian Monster of the tomb
Alcestis, a reanimated corse,
Given back to dwell on earth in vernal bloom?
Medea's spells dispersed the weight of years,
And Æson stood a youth 'mid youthful peers.

"The Gods to us are merciful—and they
Yet further may relent: for mightier far
Than strength of nerve and sinew, or the sway
Of magic potent over sun and star,
Is love, though oft to agony distrest,
And though his favourite seat be feeble woman's breast.

"But if thou goest, I follow—" "Peace!" he said,—
She looked upon him and was calmed and cheered;
The ghastly colour from his lips had fled;
In his deportment, shape, and mien, appeared
Elysian beauty, melancholy grace,
Brought from a pensive though a happy place.

He spake of love, such love as Spirits feel
In worlds whose course is equable and pure;
No fears to beat away—no strife to heal—
The past unsighed for, and the future sure;
Spake of heroic arts in graver mood
Revived, with finer harmony pursued;

Of all that is most beauteous—imaged there
In happier beauty; more pellucid streams,
An ampler ether, a diviner air,
And fields invested with purpureal gleams;
Climes which the sun, who sheds the brightest day
Earth knows, is all unworthy to survey.

[35]

Yet there the Soul shall enter which hath earned
That privilege by virtue.—"Ill," said he,
"The end of man's existence I discerned,
Who from ignoble games and revelry
Could draw, when we had parted, vain delight,
While tears were thy best pastime, day and night;

"And while my youthful peers before my eyes
(Each hero following his peculiar bent)
Prepared themselves for glorious enterprise
By martial sports,—or, seated in the tent,
Chieftains and kings in council were detained;
What time the fleet at Aulis lay enchained.

"The wished-for wind was given:—I then revolved
The oracle, upon the silent sea;
And, if no worthier led the way, resolved
That, of a thousand vessels, mine should be
The foremost prow in pressing to the strand,—
Mine the first blood that tinged the Trojan sand.

"Yet bitter, oft-times bitter, was the pang
When of thy loss I thought, belovèd Wife!
On thee too fondly did my memory hang,
And on the joys we shared in mortal life,—
The paths which we had trod—these fountains, flowers;
My new-planted cities, and unfinished towers.

"But should suspense permit the Foe to cry,
'Behold they tremble!—haughty their array,
Yet of their number no one dares to die?'
In soul I swept the indignity away:
Old frailties then recurred:—but lofty thought,
In act embodied, my deliverance wrought.

• [36]

"And Thou, though strong in love, art all too weak
In reason, in self-government too slow;
I counsel thee by fortitude to seek
Our blest re-union in the shades below.
The invisible world with thee hath sympathised;
Be thy affections raised and solemnised.

"Learn, by a mortal yearning, to ascend—
Seeking a higher object. Love was given,
Encouraged, sanctioned, chiefly for that end;
For this the passion to excess was driven—
That self might be annulled: her bondage prove
The fetters of a dream opposed to love."—

Aloud she shrieked! for Hermes reappears!
Round the dear Shade she would have clung—'tis vain:
The hours are past—too brief had they been years;
And him no mortal effort can detain:
Swift, toward the realms that know not earthly day,
He through the portal takes his silent way,
And on the palace-floor a lifeless corse she lay.

Thus, all in vain exhorted and reproved,
She perished; and, as for a wilful crime,
By the just Gods whom no weak pity moved,
Was doomed to wear out her appointed time,
Apart from happy Ghosts, that gather flowers
Of blissful quiet 'mid unfading bowers.

—Yet tears to human suffering are due;
And mortal hopes defeated and o'erthrown
Are mourned by man, and not by man alone,
As fondly he believes.—Upon the side

Of Hellespont (such faith was entertained)
A knot of spiry trees for ages grew
From out the tomb of him for whom she died;
And ever, when such stature they had gained
That Ilium's walls were subject to their view,
The trees' tall summits withered at the sight;
A constant interchange of growth and blight!

WILLIAM WORDSWORTH

THE WORLD IS TOO MUCH
WITH US

THE world is too much with us: late and soon,
    Getting and spending, we lay waste our powers.
Little we see in nature that is ours;
We have given our hearts away, a sordid boon!
This sea that bares her bosom to the moon,
The winds that will be howling at all hours,
And are up-gathered now like sleeping flowers;
For this, for everything, we are out of tune;
It moves us not.—Great God! I'd rather be
A pagan suckled in a creed outworn;
So might I, standing on this pleasant lea,
Have glimpses that would make me less forlorn;
Have sight of Proteus rising from the sea;
Or hear old Triton blow his wreathéd horn.

WILLIAM WORDSWORTH

THE ISLES OF GREECE

From *Don Juan—Canto III*

I

The isles of Greece, the isles of Greece!
    Where burning Sappho loved and sung,
Where grew the arts of war and peace,
    Where Delos rose, and Phœbus sprung!
Eternal summer gilds them yet,
But all, except their sun, is set.

II

The Scian and the Teian muse,
    The hero's harp, the lover's lute,
Have found the fame your shores refuse:
    Their place of birth alone is mute
To sounds which echo further west
Than your sires' "Islands of the Blest."

III

The mountains look on Marathon—
    And Marathon looks on the sea;
And musing there an hour alone,
    I dream'd that Greece might still be free;
For standing on the Persians' grave,
I could not deem myself a slave.

IV

A king sate on the rocky brow
   Which looks o'er sea-born Salamis;
And ships, by thousands, lay below,
   And men in nations;—all were his!
He counted them at break of day—
And when the sun set where were they?

V

And where are they? and where art thou,
   My country? On thy voiceless shore
The heroic lay is tuneless now—
   The heroic bosom beats no more!
And must thy lyre, so long divine,
Degenerate into hands like mine?

VI

'Tis something, in the dearth of fame,
   Though link'd among a fetter'd race,
To feel at least a patriot's shame,
   Even as I sing, suffuse my face;
For what is left the poet here?
For Greeks a blush—for Greece a tear.

VII

Must *we* but weep o'er days more blest?
   Must *we* but blush?—Our fathers bled.
Earth! render back from out thy breast
   A remnant of our Spartan dead!
Of the three hundred grant but three,
To make a new Thermopylæ!

[41]

VIII

What, silent still? and silent all?
   Ah! no;—the voices of the dead
Sound like a distant torrent's fall,
   And answer, "Let one living head,
But one arise,—we come, we come!"
'Tis but the living who are dumb.

IX

In vain—in vain: strike other chords;
   Fill high the cup with Samian wine!
Leave battles to the Turkish hordes,
   And shed the blood of Scio's vine!
Hark! rising to the ignoble call—
How answers each bold Bacchanal!

X

You have the Pyrrhic dance as yet;
   Where is the Pyrrhic phalanx gone?
Of two such lessons, why forget
   The nobler and the manlier one?
You have the letters Cadmus gave—
Think ye he meant them for a slave?

XI

Fill high the bowl with Samian wine!
   We will not think of themes like these!
It made Anacreon's song divine:
   He served—but served Polycrates—
A tyrant; but our masters then
Were still, at least, our countrymen.

XII

The tyrant of the Chersonese
  Was freedom's best and bravest friend;
That tyrant was Miltiades!
  Oh! that the present hour would lend
Another despot of the kind!
Such chains as his were sure to bind.

XIII

Fill high the bowl with Samian wine!
  On Suli's rock, and Parga's shore,
Exists the remnant of a line
  Such as the Doric mothers bore;
And there, perhaps, some seed is sown,
The Heracleidan blood might own.

XIV

Trust not for freedom to the Franks—
  They have a king who buys and sells;
In native swords, and native ranks,
  The only hope of courage dwells:
But Turkish force, and Latin fraud,
Would break your shield, however broad.

XV

Fill high the bowl with Samian wine!
  Our virgins dance beneath the shade—
I see their glorious black eyes shine;
  But gazing on each glowing maid,
My own the burning tear-drop laves,
To think such breasts must suckle slaves.

[43]

XVI

Place me on Sunium's marbled steep,
  Where nothing, save the waves and I,
May hear our mutual murmurs sweep;
  There, swan-like, let me sing and die:
A land of slaves shall ne'er be mine—
Dash down yon cup of Samian wine!

GEORGE GORDON, LORD BYRON

ON FIRST LOOKING INTO
CHAPMAN'S HOMER

Much have I travell'd in the realms of gold,
    And many goodly states and kingdoms seen;
  Round many western islands have I been
Which bards in fealty to Apollo hold.
Oft of one wide expanse had I been told
    That deep-brow'd Homer ruled as his demesne;
  Yet did I never breathe its pure serene
Till I heard Chapman speak out loud and bold:
Then felt I like some watcher of the skies
    When a new planet swims into his ken;
Or like stout Cortez when with eagle eyes
    He star'd at the Pacific—and all his men
Look'd at each other with a wild surmise—
    Silent, upon a peak in Darien.

JOHN KEATS

TO MAIA

MOTHER of Hermes! and still youthful Maia!
    May I sing to thee
As thou wast hymned on the shores of Baiæ?
    Or may I woo thee
In earlier Sicilian? or thy smiles
Seek as they once were sought, in Grecian isles,
By bards who died content on pleasant sward,
    Leaving great verse unto a little clan?
O, give me their old vigour, and unheard
    Save of the quiet Primrose, and the span
        Of heaven and few ears,
Rounded by thee, my song should die away
        Content as theirs,
Rich in the simple worship of a day.

JOHN KEATS

PROCESSION OF BACCHUS

From *Endymion—Book IV*

Beneath my palm trees, by the river side,
    I sat a weeping: in the whole world wide
There was no one to ask me why I wept,—
        And so I kept
Brimming the water-lilly cups with tears
        Cold as my fears.

"Beneath my palm trees, by the river side,
I sat a weeping: what enamour'd bride,
Cheated by shadowy wooer from the clouds,
        But hides and shrouds
Beneath dark palm trees by a river side?

"And as I sat, over the light blue hills
There came a noise of revellers: the rills
Into the wide stream came of purple hue—
        'Twas Bacchus and his crew!
The earnest trumpet spake, and silver thrills
From kissing cymbals made a merry din—
        'Twas Bacchus and his kin!
Like to a moving vintage down they came,
Crown'd with green leaves, and faces all on flame;

All madly dancing through the pleasant valley,
    To scare thee, Melancholy!
O then, O then, thou wast a simple name!
And I forgot thee, as the berried holly
By shepherds is forgotten, when, in June,
Tall chestnuts keep away the sun and moon:—
    I rush'd into the folly!

"Within his car, aloft, young Bacchus stood,
Trifling his ivy-dart, in dancing mood,
    With sidelong laughing;
And little rills of crimson wine imbrued
His plump white arms, and shoulders, enough white
    For Venus' pearly bite:
And near him rode Silenus on his ass,
Pelted with flowers as he on did pass
    Tipsily quaffing.

"Whence came ye, merry Damsels! whence came ye!
So many, and so many, and such glee?
Why have ye left your bowers desolate,
    Your lutes, and gentler fate?—
'We follow Bacchus! Bacchus on the wing,
    A conquering!
Bacchus, young Bacchus! good or ill betide,
We dance before him thorough kingdoms wide:—
Come hither, lady fair, and joined be
    To our wild minstrelsy!'

"Whence came ye, jolly Satyrs! whence came ye!
So many, and so many, and such glee?
Why have ye left your forest haunts, why left
    Your nuts in oak-tree cleft?—

'For wine, for wine we left our kernel tree;
For wine we left our heath, and yellow brooms,
    And cold mushrooms;
For wine we follow Bacchus through the earth;
Great God of breathless cups and chirping mirth!—
Come hither, lady fair, and joined be
    To our mad minstrelsy!'

"Over wide streams and mountains great we went,
And, save when Bacchus kept his ivy tent,
Onward the tiger and the leopard pants,
    With Asian elephants:
Onward these myriads—with song and dance,
With zebras striped, and sleek Arabians' prance,
Web-footed alligators, crocodiles,
Bearing upon their scaly backs, in files,
Plump infant laughers mimicking the coil
Of seamen, and stout galley-rowers' toil:
With toying oars and silken sails they glide,
    Nor care for wind and tide.

"Mounted on panthers' furs and lions' manes,
From rear to van they scour about the plains;
A three days' journey in a moment done:
And always, at the rising of the sun,
About the wilds they hunt with spear and horn,
    On spleenful unicorn.

"I saw Osirian Egypt kneel adown
    Before the vine-wreath crown!
I saw parch'd Abyssinia rouse and sing
    To the silver cymbals' ring!

[49]

I saw the whelming vintage hotly pierce
      Old Tartary the fierce!
 The kings of Inde their jewel-sceptres vail,
And from their treasures scatter pearled hail;
Great Brahma from his mystic heaven groans,
      And all his priesthood moans;
Before young Bacchus' eye-wink turning pale.—
Into these regions came I following him,
Sick hearted, weary—so I took a whim
To stray away into these forests drear
      Alone, without a peer:
And I have told thee all thou mayest hear."

JOHN KEATS

ON SEEING THE ELGIN
MARBLES

My spirit is too weak—mortality
   Weighs heavily on me like unwilling sleep,
  And each imagin'd pinnacle and steep
Of godlike hardship, tells me I must die
Like a sick Eagle looking at the sky.
   Yet 'tis a gentle luxury to weep
   That I have not the cloudy winds to keep,
Fresh for the opening of the morning's eye.
Such dim-conceived glories of the brain
   Bring round the heart an undescribable feud;
So do these wonders a most dizzy pain,
   That mingles Grecian grandeur with the rude
Wasting of old Time—with a billowy main—
   A sun—a shadow of a magnitude.

JOHN KEATS

ON A GRECIAN URN

I

Thou still unravish'd bride of quietness,
  Thou foster-child of silence and slow time,
Sylvan historian, who canst thus express
  A flowery tale more sweetly than our rhyme:
What leaf-fring'd legend haunts about thy shape
  Of deities or mortals, or of both,
    In Tempe or the dales of Arcady?
  What men or gods are these? What maidens loth?
What mad pursuit? What struggle to escape?
    What pipes and timbrels? What wild ecstasy?

II

Heard melodies are sweet, but those unheard
  Are sweeter; therefore, ye soft pipes, play on;
Not to the sensual ear, but, more endear'd,
  Pipe to the spirit ditties of no tone:
Fair youth, beneath the trees, thou canst not leave
  Thy song, nor ever can those trees be bare;
    Bold Lover, never, never canst thou kiss,
Though winning near the goal—yet, do not grieve;
  She cannot fade, though thou hast not thy bliss,
    For ever wilt thou love, and she be fair!

III

Ah, happy, happy boughs! that cannot shed
　Your leaves, nor ever bid the Spring adieu;
And, happy melodist, unwearied,
　For ever piping songs for ever new;
More happy love! more happy, happy love!
　For ever warm and still to be enjoy'd,
　　For ever panting, and for ever young;
All breathing human passion far above,
　That leaves a heart high-sorrowful and cloy'd,
　　A burning forehead, and a parching tongue.

IV

Who are these coming to the sacrifice?
　To what green altar, O mysterious priest,
Lead'st thou that heifer lowing at the skies,
　And all her silken flanks with garlands drest?
What little town by river or sea shore,
　Or mountain-built with peaceful citadel,
　　Is emptied of this folk, this pious morn?
And, little town, thy streets for evermore
　Will silent be; and not a soul to tell
　　Why thou art desolate, can e'er return.

V

O Attic shape! Fair attitude! with brede
　Of marble men and maidens overwrought,
With forest branches and the trodden weed;
　Thou, silent form, dost tease us out of thought
As doth eternity: Cold Pastoral!
　When old age shall this generation waste,

Thou shalt remain, in midst of other woe
Than ours, a friend to man, to whom thou say'st,
"Beauty is truth, truth beauty,"—that is all
Ye know on earth, and all ye need to know.

JOHN KEATS

TO PSYCHE

Goddess! hear these tuneless numbers, wrung
  By sweet enforcement and remembrance dear,
And pardon that thy secrets should be sung
    Even into thine own soft-conched ear:
Surely I dreamt to-day, or did I see
    The winged Psyche with awaken'd eyes?
I wander'd in a forest thoughtlessly,
    And, on the sudden, fainting with surprise,
Saw two fair creatures, couched side by side
    In deepest grass, beneath the whisp'ring roof
    Of leaves and trembled blossoms, where there ran
        A brooklet, scarce espied:

'Mid hush'd, cool-rooted flowers, fragrant-eyed,
    Blue, silver-white, and budded Tyrian,
They lay calm-breathing on the bedded grass;
    Their arms embraced, and their pinions too;
    Their lips touch'd not, but had not bade adieu,
As if disjoined by soft-handed slumber,
And ready still past kisses to outnumber
    At tender eye-dawn of aurorean love:
        The winged boy I knew;
    But who wast thou, O happy, happy dove?
        His Psyche true!

O latest born and loveliest vision far
  Of all Olympus' faded hierarchy!
Fairer than Phoebe's sapphire-region'd star,
  Or Vesper, amorous glow-worm of the sky;
Fairer than these, though temple thou hast none,
    Nor altar heap'd with flowers;
Nor virgin-choir to make delicious moan
    Upon the midnight hours;
No voice, no lute, no pipe, no incense sweet
  From chain-swung censer teeming;
No shrine, no grove, no oracle, no heat
  Of pale-mouth'd prophet dreaming.

O brightest! though too late for antique vows,
  Too, too late for the fond believing lyre,
When holy were the haunted forest boughs,
  Holy the air, the water, and the fire;
Yet even in these days so far retir'd
  From happy pieties, thy lucent fans,
  Fluttering among the faint Olympians,
I see, and sing, by my own eyes inspir'd.
So let me be thy choir, and make a moan
    Upon the midnight hours;
Thy voice, thy lute, thy pipe, thy incense sweet
  From swinged censer teeming;
Thy shrine, thy grove, thy oracle, thy heat
  Of pale-mouthed prophet dreaming.

Yes, I will be thy priest, and build a fane
  In some untrodden region of my mind,
Where branched thoughts, new grown with pleasant pain,
  Instead of pines shall murmur in the wind:

Far, far around shall those dark-cluster'd trees
   Fledge the wild-ridged mountains steep by steep;
And there by zephyrs, streams, and birds, and bees,
   The moss-lain Dryads shall be lull'd to sleep;
And in the midst of this wide quietness
   A rosy sanctuary will I dress
With the wreath'd trellis of a working brain,
   With buds, and bells, and stars without a name,
With all the gardener Fancy e'er could feign,
   Who breeding flowers, will never breed the same:
And there shall be for thee all soft delight
   That shadowy thought can win,
A bright torch, and a casement ope at night,
   To let the warm Love in!

JOHN KEATS

LAMIA

PART I

Upon a time, before the faery broods
  Drove Nymph and Satyr from the prosperous woods,
Before king Oberon's bright diadem,
Sceptre, and mantle, clasp'd with dewy gem,
Frighted away the Dryads and the Fauns
From rushes green, and brakes, and cowslip'd lawns,
The ever-smitten Hermes empty left
His golden throne, bent warm on amorous theft:
From high Olympus had he stolen light,
On this side of Jove's clouds, to escape the sight
Of his great summoner, and made retreat
Into a forest on the shores of Crete.
For somewhere in that sacred island dwelt
A nymph, to whom all hoofed Satyrs knelt;
At whose white feet the languid Tritons poured
Pearls, while on land they wither'd and adored.
Fast by the springs where she to bathe was wont,
And in those meads where sometime she might haunt,
Were strewn rich gifts, unknown to any Muse,
Though Fancy's casket were unlock'd to choose.
Ah, what a world of love was at her feet!
So Hermes thought, and a celestial heat

Burnt from his winged heels to either ear,
That from a whiteness, as the lilly clear,
Blush'd into roses 'mid his golden hair,
Fallen in jealous curls about his shoulders bare.

From vale to vale, from wood to wood, he flew,
Breathing upon the flowers his passion new,
And wound with many a river to its head,
To find where this sweet nymph prepar'd her secret bed:
In vain; the sweet nymph might nowhere he found,
And so he rested, on the lonely ground,
Pensive, and full of painful jealousies
Of the Wood-Gods, and even the very trees.
There as he stood, he heard a mournful voice,
Such as once heard, in gentle heart, destroys
All pain but pity: thus the lone voice spake:
"When from this wreathed tomb shall I awake!
When move in a sweet body fit for life,
And love, and pleasure, and the ruddy strife
Of hearts and lips! Ah, miserable me!"
The God, dove-footed, glided silently
Round bush and tree, soft-brushing, in his speed,
The taller grasses and full-flowering weed,
Until he found a palpitating snake,
Bright, and cirque-couchant in a dusky brake.

She was a gordian shape of dazzling hue,
Vermilion-spotted, golden, green, and blue;
Striped like a zebra, freckled like a pard,
Eyed like a peacock, and all crimson barr'd;
And full of silver moons, that, as she breathed,
Dissolv'd, or brighter shone, or interwreathed

[59]

Their lustres with the gloomier tapestries—
So rainbow-sided, touch'd with miseries,
She seem'd, at once, some penanced lady elf,
Some demon's mistress, or the demon's self.
Upon her crest she wore a wannish fire
Sprinkled with stars, like Ariadne's tiar:
Her head was serpent, but ah, bitter-sweet!
She had a woman's mouth with all its pearls complete:
And for her eyes: what could such eyes do there
But weep, and weep, that they were born so fair?
As Proserpine still weeps for her Sicilian air.
Her throat was serpent, but the words she spake
Came, as through bubbling honey, for Love's sake,
And thus; while Hermes on his pinions lay,
Like a stoop'd falcon ere he takes his prey.

"Fair Hermes, crown'd with feathers, fluttering light,
I had a splendid dream of thee last night:
I saw thee sitting, on a throne of gold,
Among the Gods, upon Olympus old,
The only sad one; for thou didst not hear
The soft, lute-finger'd Muses chaunting clear,
Nor even Apollo when he sang alone,
Deaf to his throbbing throat's long, long melodious moan.
I dreamt I saw thee, robed in purple flakes,
Break amorous through the clouds, as morning breaks,
And, swiftly as a bright Phœbean dart,
Strike for the Cretan isle; and here thou art!
Too gentle Hermes, hast thou found the maid?"
Whereat the star of Lethe not delay'd
His rosy eloquence, and thus inquired:
"Thou smooth-lipp'd serpent, surely high inspired!

[60]

Thou beauteous wreath, with melancholy eyes,
Possess whatever bliss thou canst devise,
Telling me only where my nymph is fled,—
Where she doth breathe!" "Bright planet, thou hast said,"
Return'd the snake, "but seal with oaths, fair God!"
"I swear," said Hermes, "by my serpent rod,
And by thine eyes, and by thy starry crown!"
Light flew his earnest words, among the blossoms blown.
Then thus again the brilliance feminine:
"Too frail of heart! for this lost nymph of thine,
Free as the air, invisibly, she strays
About these thornless wilds; her pleasant days
She tastes unseen; unseen her nimble feet
Leave traces in the grass and flowers sweet;
From weary tendrils, and bow'd branches green,
She plucks the fruit unseen, she bathes unseen:
And by my power is her beauty veil'd
To keep it unaffronted, unassail'd
By the love-glances of unlovely eyes,
Of Satyrs, Fauns, and blear'd Silenus' sighs.
Pale grew her immortality, for woe
Of all these lovers, and she grieved so
I took compassion on her, bade her steep
Her hair in weïrd syrops, that would keep
Her loveliness invisible, yet free
To wander as she loves, in liberty.
Thou shalt behold her, Hermes, thou alone,
If thou wilt, as thou swearest, grant my boon!"
Then, once again, the charmed God began
An oath, and through the serpent's ears it ran
Warm, tremulous, devout, psalterian.

Ravish'd, she lifted her Circean head,
Blush'd a live damask, and swift-lisping said,
"I was a woman, let me have once more
A woman's shape, and charming as before.
I love a youth of Corinth—O the bliss!
Give me my woman's form, and place me where he is.
Stoop, Hermes, let me breathe upon thy brow,
And thou shalt see thy sweet nymph even now."
The God on half-shut feathers sank serene,
She breath'd upon his eyes, and swift was seen
Of both the guarded nymph near-smiling on the green.
It was no dream; or say a dream it was,
Real are the dreams of Gods, and smoothly pass
Their pleasures in a long immortal dream.
One warm, flush'd moment, hovering, it might seem
Dash'd by the wood-nymph's beauty, so he burn'd;
Then, lighting on the printless verdure, turn'd
To the swoon'd serpent, and with languid arm,
Delicate, put to proof the lythe Caducean charm.
So done, upon the nymph his eyes he bent
Full of adoring tears and blandishment,
And towards her stept: she, like a moon in wane,
Faded before him, cower'd, nor could restrain
Her fearful sobs, self-folding like a flower
That faints into itself at evening hour:
But the God fostering her chilled hand,
She felt the warmth, her eyelids open'd bland,
And, like new flowers at morning song of bees,
Bloom'd, and gave up her honey to the lees.
Into the green-recessed woods they flew;
Nor grew they pale, as mortal lovers do.

Left to herself, the serpent now began
To change; her elfin blood in madness ran,
Her mouth foam'd and the grass, therewith besprent,
Wither'd at dew so sweet and virulent;
Her eyes in torture fix'd, and anguish drear,
Hot, glaz'd, and wide, with lid-lashes all sear,
Flash'd phosphor and sharp sparks, without one cooling
     tear.
The colours all inflam'd throughout her train,
She writh'd about, convulsed with scarlet pain:
A deep volcanian yellow took the place
Of all her milder-mooned body's grace;
And, as the lava ravishes the mead,
Spoilt all her silver mail, and golden brede;
Made gloom of all her frecklings, streaks and bars,
Eclips'd her crescents, and lick'd up her stars:
So that, in moments few, she was undrest
Of all her sapphires, greens, and amethyst,
And rubious-argent: of all these bereft,
Nothing but pain and ugliness were left.
Still shone her crown; that vanish'd, also she
Melted and disappear'd as suddenly;
And in the air, her new voice luting soft,
Cried, "Lycius! gentle Lycius!"—Borne aloft
With the bright mists about the mountains hoar
These words dissolv'd: Crete's forests heard no more.

Whither fled Lamia, now a lady bright,
A full-born beauty new and exquisite?
She fled into that valley they pass o'er
Who go to Corinth from Cenchreas' shore;

And rested at the foot of those wild hills,
The rugged founts of the Peræan rills,
And of that other ridge whose barren back
Stretches, with all its mist and cloudy rack,
South-westward to Cleone. There she stood
About a young bird's flutter from a wood,
Fair, on a sloping green of mossy tread,
By a clear pool, wherein she passioned
To see herself escap'd from so sore ills,
While her robes flaunted with the daffodils.

Ah, happy Lycius!—for she was a maid
More beautiful than ever twisted braid,
Or sigh'd, or blush'd, or on spring-flowered lea
Spread a green kirtle to the minstrelsy:
A virgin purest lipp'd, yet in the lore
Of love deep learned to the red heart's core:
Not one hour old, yet of sciential brain
To unperplex bliss from its neighbour pain;
Define their pettish limits, and estrange
Their points of contact, and swift counterchange;
Intrigue with the specious chaos, and dispart
Its most ambiguous atoms with sure art;
As though in Cupid's college she had spent
Sweet days a lovely graduate, still unshent,
And kept his rosy terms in idle languishment.

Why this fair creature chose so faerily
By the wayside to linger, we shall see;
But first 'tis fit to tell how she could muse
And dream, when in the serpent prison-house,

Of all she list, strange or magnificent:
How, ever, where she will'd, her spirit went;
Whether to faint Elysium, or where
Down through tress-lifting waves the Nereids fair
Wind into Thetis' bower by many a pearly stair;
Or where God Bacchus drains his cups divine,
Stretch'd out, at ease, beneath a glutinous pine;
Or where in Pluto's gardens palatine
Mulciber's columns gleam in far piazzian line.
And sometimes into cities she would send
Her dream, with feast and rioting to blend;
And once, while among mortals dreaming thus,
She saw the young Corinthian Lycius
Charioting foremost in the envious race,
Like a young Jove with calm uneager face,
And fell into a swooning love of him.
Now on the moth-time of that evening dim
He would return that way, as well she knew,
To Corinth from the shore; for freshly blew
The eastern soft wind, and his galley now
Grated the quaystones with her brazen prow
In port Cenchreas, from Egina isle
Fresh anchor'd; whither he had been awhile
To sacrifice to Jove, whose temple there
Waits with high marble doors for blood and incense rare.
Jove heard his vows, and better'd his desire;
For by some freakful chance he made retire
From his companions, and set forth to walk,
Perhaps grown wearied of their Corinth talk:
Over the solitary hills he fared,
Thoughtless at first, but ere eve's star appeared

His phantasy was lost, where reason fades,
In the calm'd twilight of Platonic shades.
Lamia beheld him coming, near, more near—
Close to her passing, in indifference drear,
His silent sandals swept the mossy green;
So neighbour'd to him, and yet so unseen
She stood: he pass'd, shut up in mysteries,
His mind wrapp'd like his mantle, while her eyes
Follow'd his steps, and her neck regal white
Turn'd—syllabling thus, "Ah, Lycius bright,
And will you leave me on the hills alone?
Lycius, look back! and be some pity shown."
He did; not with cold wonder fearingly,
But Orpheus-like at an Eurydice;
For so delicious were the words she sung,
It seem'd he had lov'd them a whole summer long:
And soon his eyes had drunk her beauty up,
Leaving no drop in the bewildering cup,
And still the cup was full,—while he, afraid
Lest she should vanish ere his lip had paid
Due adoration, thus began to adore;
Her soft look growing coy, she saw his chain so sure:
"Leave thee alone! Look back! Ah, Goddess, see
Whether my eyes can ever turn from thee!
For pity do not this sad heart belie—
Even as thou vanishest so shall I die.
Stay! though a Naiad of the rivers, stay!
To thy far wishes will thy streams obey:
Stay! though the greenest woods be thy domain,
Alone they can drink up the morning rain:
Though a descended Pleiad, will not one
Of thine harmonious sisters keep in tune

Thy spheres, and as thy silver proxy shine?
So sweetly to these ravish'd ears of mine
Came thy sweet greeting, that if thou shouldst fade
Thy memory will waste me to a shade:—
For pity do not melt!"—"If I should stay,"
Said Lamia, "here, upon this floor of clay,
And pain my steps upon these flowers too rough,
What canst thou say or do of charm enough
To dull the nice remembrance of my home?
Thou canst not ask me with thee here to roam
Over these hills and vales, where no joy is,—
Empty of immortality and bliss!
Thou art a scholar, Lycius, and must know
That finer spirits cannot breathe below
In human climes, and live: Alas! poor youth,
What taste of purer air hast thou to soothe
My essence? What serener palaces,
Where I may all my many senses please,
And by mysterious sleights a hundred thirsts appease?
It cannot be—Adieu!" So said, she rose
Tiptoe with white arms spread. He, sick to lose
The amorous promise of her lone complain,
Swoon'd, murmuring of love, and pale with pain.
The cruel lady, without any show
Of sorrow for her tender favourite's woe,
But rather, if her eyes could brighter be,
With brighter eyes and slow amenity,
Put her new lips to his, and gave afresh
The life she had so tangled in her mesh:
And as he from one trance was wakening
Into another, she began to sing,
Happy in beauty, life, and love, and every thing,

A song of love, too sweet for earthly lyres,
While, like held breath, the stars drew in their panting
    fires.
And then she whisper'd in such trembling tone,
As those who, safe together met alone
For the first time through many anguish'd days,
Use other speech than looks; bidding him raise
His drooping head, and clear his soul of doubt,
For that she was a woman, and without
Any more subtle fluid in her veins
Than throbbing blood, and that the self-same pains
Inhabited her frail-strung heart as his.
And next she wonder'd how his eyes could miss
Her face so long in Corinth, where, she said,
She dwelt but half retir'd, and there had led
Days happy as the gold coin could invent
Without the aid of love; yet in content
Till she saw him, as once she pass'd him by,
Where 'gainst a column he lent thoughtfully
At Venus' temple porch, 'mid baskets heap'd
Of amorous herbs and flowers, newly reap'd
Late on that eve, as 'twas the night before
The Adonian feast; whereof she saw no more,
But wept alone those days, for why should she adore?
Lycius from death awoke into amaze,
To see her still, and singing so sweet lays;
Then from amaze into delight he fell
To hear her whisper woman's lore so well;
And every word she spake entic'd him on
To unperplex'd delight and pleasure known.
Let the mad poets say whate'er they please
Of the sweets of Faeries, Peris, Goddesses,

There is not such a treat among them all,
Haunters of cavern, lake, and waterfall,
As a real woman, lineal indeed
From Pyrrha's pebbles or old Adam's seed.
Thus gentle Lamia judg'd, and judg'd aright,
That Lycius could not love in half a fright,
So threw the goddess off, and won his heart
More pleasantly by playing woman's part,
With no more awe than what her beauty gave,
That, while it smote, still guaranteed to save.
Lycius to all made eloquent reply.
Marrying to every word a twinborn sigh;
And last, pointing to Corinth, ask'd her sweet,
If 'twas too far that night for her soft feet.
The way was short, for Lamia's eagerness
Made, by a spell, the triple league decrease
To a few paces; not at all surmised
By blinded Lycius, so in her comprized.
They pass'd the city gates, he knew not how,
So noiseless, and he never thought to know.

As men talk in a dream, so Corinth all,
Throughout her palaces imperial,
And all her populous streets and temples lewd,
Mutter'd, like tempest in the distance brew'd,
To the wide-spreaded night above her towers.
Men, women, rich and poor, in the cool hours,
Shuffled their sandals o'er the pavement white,
Companion'd or alone; while many a light
Flared, here and there, from wealthy festivals,
And threw their moving shadows on the walls,

Or found them cluster'd in the corniced shade
Of some arch'd temple door, or dusky colonnade.

Muffling his face, of greeting friends in fear,
Her fingers he press'd hard, as one came near
With curl'd gray beard, sharp eyes, and smooth **bald**
    crown,
Slow-stepp'd, and robed in philosophic gown:
Lycius shrank closer, as they met and past,
Into his mantle, adding wings to haste,
While hurried Lamia trembled: "Ah," said he,
"Why do you shudder, love, so ruefully?
Why does your tender palm dissolve in dew?"—
"I'm wearied," said fair Lamia: "tell me who
Is that old man? I cannot bring to mind
His features:—Lycius! wherefore did you blind
Yourself from his quick eyes?" Lycius replied,
" 'Tis Apollonius sage, my trusty guide
And good instructor; but to-night he seems
The ghost of folly haunting my sweet dreams."

While yet he spake they had arrived before
A pillar'd porch, with lofty portal door.
Where hung a silver lamp, whose phosphor glow
Reflected in the slabbed steps below,
Mild as a star in water; for so new,
And so unsullied was the marble's hue,
So through the crystal polish, liquid fine,
Ran the dark veins, that none but feet divine
Could e'er have touch'd there. Sounds Æolian
Breath'd from the hinges, as the ample span

Of the wide doors disclos'd a place unknown
Some time to any, but these two alone,
And a few Persian mutes, who that same year
Were seen about the markets: none knew where
They could inhabit; the most curious
Were foil'd, who watch'd to trace them to their house:
And but the flitter-winged verse must tell,
For truth's sake, what woes afterwards befel,
'Twould humour many a heart to leave them thus,
Shut from the busy world of more incredulous.

PART II

Love in a hut, with water and a crust,
Is—Love, forgive us!—cinders, ashes, dust;
Love in a palace is perhaps at last
More grievous torment than a hermit's fast:—
That is a doubtful tale from faery land,
Hard for the non-elect to understand.
Had Lycius liv'd to hand his story down,
He might have given the moral a fresh frown,
Or clench'd it quite: but too short was their bliss
To breed distrust and hate, that make the soft voice hiss.
Beside, there, nightly, with terrific glare,
Love, jealous grown of so complete a pair,
Hover'd and buzz'd his wings, with fearful roar,
Above the lintel of their chamber door,
And down the passage cast a glow upon the floor.

For all this came a ruin: side by side
They were enthroned, in the even tide,
Upon a couch, near to a curtaining
Whose airy texture, from a golden string,

Floated into the room, and let appear
Unveil'd the summer heaven, blue and clear,
Betwixt two marble shafts:—there they reposed,
Where use had made it sweet, with eyelids closed,
Saving a tythe which love still open kept,
That they might see each other while they almost slept;
When from the slope side of a suburb hill,
Deafening the swallow's twitter, came a thrill
Of trumpets—Lycius started—the sounds fled,
But left a thought, a buzzing in his head.
For the first time, since first he harbour'd in
That purple-lined palace of sweet sin,
His spirit pass'd beyond its golden bourn
Into the noisy world almost forsworn.
The lady, ever watchful, penetrant,
Saw this with pain, so arguing a want
Of something more, more than her empery
Of joys; and she began to moan and sigh
Because he mused beyond her, knowing well
That but a moment's thought is passion's passing hell.
"Why do you sigh, fair creature?" whisper'd he:
"Why do you think?" returned she tenderly:
"You have deserted me;—where am I now?
Not in your heart while care weighs on your brow:
No, no, you have dismiss'd me; and I go
From your breast houseless: aye, it must be so."
He answer'd, bending to her open eyes,
Where he was mirror'd small in paradise,
"My silver planet, both of eve and morn!
Why will you plead yourself so sad forlorn,
While I am striving how to fill my heart
With deeper crimson, and a double smart?

How to entangle, trammel up and snare
Your soul in mine, and labyrinth you there
Like the hid scent in an unbudded rose?
Aye, a sweet kiss—you see your mighty woes.
My thoughts! shall I unveil them? Listen then!
What mortal hath a prize, that other men
May be confounded and abash'd withal,
But lets it sometimes pace abroad majestical,
And triumph, as in thee I should rejoice
Amid the hoarse alarm of Corinth's voice.
Let my foes choke, and my friends shout afar,
While through the thronged streets your bridal car
Wheels round its dazzling spokes."—The lady's cheek
Trembled; she nothing said, but, pale and meek,
Arose and knelt before him, wept a rain
Of sorrows at his words; at last with pain
Beseeching him, the while his hand she wrung,
To change his purpose. He thereat was stung,
Perverse, with stronger fancy to reclaim
Her wild and timid nature to his aim:
Besides, for all his love, in self despite,
Against his better self, he took delight
Luxurious in her sorrows, soft and new.
His passion cruel grown, took on a hue
Fierce and sanguineous as 'twas possible
In one whose brow had no dark veins to swell.
Fine was the mitigated fury, like
Apollo's presence when in act to strike
The serpent—Ha, the serpent! Certes, she
Was none. She burnt, she lov'd the tyranny,
And, all subdued, consented to the hour
When to the bridal he should lead his paramour.

Whispering in midnight silence, said the youth,
"Sure some sweet name thou hast, though, by my truth,
I have not ask'd it, ever thinking thee
Not mortal, but of heavenly progeny,
As still I do. Hast any mortal name,
Fit appellation for this dazzling frame?
Or friends or kinsfolk on the citied earth,
To share our marriage feast and nuptial mirth?"
"I have no friends," said Lamia, "no, not one;
My presence in wide Corinth hardly known:
My parents' bones are in their dusty urns
Sepulchred, where no kindled incense burns,
Seeing all their luckless race are dead, save me,
And I neglect the holy rite for thee.
Even as you list invite your many guests;
But if, as now it seems, your vision rests
With any pleasure on me, do not bid
Old Apollonius—from him keep me hid."
Lycius, perplex'd at words so blind and blank,
Made close inquiry; from whose touch she shrank,
Feigning a sleep; and he to the dull shade
Of deep sleep in a moment was betray'd.

It was the custom then to bring away
The bride from home at blushing shut of day,
Veil'd, in a chariot, heralded along
By strewn flowers, torches, and a marriage song,
With other pageants: but this fair unknown
Had not a friend. So being left alone,
 (Lycius was gone to summon all his kin)
And knowing surely she could never win

His foolish heart from its mad pompousness,
She set herself, high-thoughted, how to dress
The misery in fit magnificence.
She did so, but 'tis doubtful how and whence
Came, and who were her subtle servitors.
About the halls, and to and from the doors,
There was a noise of wings, till in short space
The glowing banquet-room shone with wide-arched grace.
A haunting music, sole perhaps and lone
Supportress of the faery-roof, made moan
Throughout, as fearful the whole charm might fade.
Fresh carved cedar, mimicking a glade
Of palm and plantain, met from either side,
High in the midst, in honour of the bride:
Two palms and then two plantains, and so on,
From either side their stems branch'd one to one
All down the aisled place; and beneath all
There ran a stream of lamps straight on from wall to wall.
So canopied, lay an untasted feast
Teeming with odours. Lamia, regal drest,
Silently paced about, and as she went,
In pale contented sort of discontent,
Mission'd her viewless servants to enrich
The fretted splendour of each nook and niche.
Between the tree-stems, marble plain at first,
Came jasper pannels; then, anon, there burst
Forth creeping imagery of slighter trees,
And with the larger wove in small intricacies.
Approving all, she faded at self-will,
And shut the chamber up, close, hush'd and still,
Complete and ready for the revels rude,
When dreadful guests would come to spoil her solitude.

The day appear'd, and all the gossip rout.
O senseless Lycius! Madman! wherefore flout
The silent-blessing fate, warm cloister'd hours,
And show to common eyes these secret bowers?
The herd approach'd; each guest, with busy brain,
Arriving at the portal, gaz'd amain,
And enter'd marveling: for they knew the street,
Remember'd it from childhood all complete
Without a gap, yet ne'er before had seen
That royal porch, that high-built fair demesne;
So in they hurried all, maz'd, curious and keen:
Save one, who look'd thereon with eye severe,
And with calm-planted steps walk'd in austere;
'Twas Apollonius: something too be laugh'd,
As though some knotty problem, that had daft
His patient thought, had now begun to thaw,
And solve and melt:—'twas just as he foresaw.

He met within the murmurous vestibule
His young disciple. " 'Tis no common rule,
Lycius," said he, "for uninvited guest
To force himself upon you, and infest
With an unbidden presence the bright throng
Of younger friends; yet must I do this wrong,
And you forgive me," Lycius blush'd, and led
The old man through the inner doors broad-spread;
With reconciling words and courteous mein
Turning into sweet milk the sophist's spleen.

Of wealthy lustre was the banquet-room,
Fill'd with pervading brilliance and perfume:

Before each lucid pannel fuming stood
A censer fed with myrrh and spiced wood,
Each by a sacred tripod held aloft,
Whose slender feet wide-swerv'd upon the soft
Wool-woofed carpets: fifty wreaths of smoke
From fifty censers their light voyage took
To the high roof, still mimick'd as they rose
Along the mirror'd walls by twin-clouds odorous.
Twelve sphered tables, by silk seats insphered,
High as the level of a man's breast rear'd
On libbard's paws, upheld the heavy gold
Of cups and goblets, and the store thrice told
Of Ceres' horn, and, in huge vessels, wine
Come from the gloomy tun with merry shine.
Thus loaded with a feast the tables stood,
Each shrining in the midst the image of a God.

When in an antichamber every guest
Had felt the cold full sponge to pleasure press'd,
By minist'ring slaves, upon his hands and feet,
And fragrant oils with ceremony meet
Pour'd on his hair, they all mov'd to the feast
In white robes, and themselves in order placed
Around the silken couches, wondering
Whence all this mighty cost and blaze of wealth could
    spring.

Soft went the music the soft air along,
While fluent Greek a vowel'd undersong
Kept up among the guests, discoursing low
At first, for scarcely was the wine at flow;

But when the happy vintage touch'd their brains
Louder they talk, and louder come the strains
Of powerful instruments:—the gorgeous dyes,
The space, the splendour of the draperies,
The roof of awful richness, nectarous cheer,
Beautiful slaves, and Lamia's self, appear,
Now, when the wine has done its rosy deed,
And every soul from human trammels freed,
No more so strange; for merry wine, sweet wine,
Will make Elysian shades not too fair, too divine.
Soon was God Bacchus at meridian height;
Flush'd were their cheeks, and bright eyes double bright:
Garlands of every green, and every scent
From vales deflower'd, or forest-trees branch-rent,
In baskets of bright osier'd gold were brought
High as the handles heap'd, to suit the thought
Of every guest; that each, as he did please,
Might fancy-fit his brows, silk-pillow'd at his ease.

What wreath for Lamia? What for Lycius?
What for the sage, old Apollonius?
Upon her aching forehead be there hung
The leaves of willow and of adder's tongue;
And for the youth, quick, let us strip for him
The thyrsus, that his watching eyes may swim
Into forgetfulness; and, for the sage,
Let spear-grass and the spiteful thistle wage
War on his temples. Do not all charms fly
At the mere touch of cold philosophy?
There was an awful rainbow once in heaven:
We know her woof, her texture; she is given

In the dull catalogue of common things.
Philosophy will clip an Angel's wings,
Conquer all mysteries by rule and line,
Empty the haunted air, and gnomed mine—
Unweave a rainbow, as it erewhile made
The tender-person'd Lamia melt into a shade.

By her glad Lycius sitting, in chief place,
Scarce saw in all the room another face,
Till, checking his love trance, a cup he took
Full brimm'd, and opposite sent forth a look
'Cross the broad table, to beseech a glance
From his old teacher's wrinkled countenance,
And pledge him. The bald-head philosopher
Had fix'd his eye, without a twinkle or stir
Full on the alarmed beauty of the bride,
Brow-beating her fair form, and troubling her sweet pride.
Lycius then press'd her hand, with devout touch,
As pale it lay upon the rosy couch:
'Twas icy, and the cold ran through his veins;
Then sudden it grew hot, and all the pains
Of an unnatural heat shot to his heart.
"Lamia, what means this? Wherefore dost thou start?
Know'st thou that man?" Poor Lamia answer'd not.
He gaz'd into her eyes, and not a jot
Own'd they the lovelorn piteous appeal:
More, more he gaz'd: his human senses reel:
Some hungry spell that loveliness absorbs;
There was no recognition in those orbs.
"Lamia!" he cried—and no soft-toned reply.
The many heard, and the loud revelry

Grew hush; the stately music no more breathes;
The myrtle sicken'd in a thousand wreaths.
By faint degrees, voice, lute, and pleasure ceased;
A deadly silence step by step increased,
Until it seem'd a horrid presence there,
And not a man but felt the terror in his hair.
"Lamia!" he shriek'd; and nothing but the shriek
With its sad echo did the silence break.
"Begone, foul dream!" he cried, gazing again
In the bride's face, where now no azure vein
Wander'd on fair-spaced temples; no soft bloom
Misted the cheek; no passion to illume
The deep-recessed vision:—all was blight;
Lamia, no longer fair, there sat a deadly white.
"Shut, shut those juggling eyes, thou ruthless man!
Turn them aside, wretch! or the righteous ban
Of all the Gods, whose dreadful images
Here represent their shadowy presences,
May pierce them on the sudden with the thorn
Of painful blindness; leaving thee forlorn,
In trembling dotage to the feeblest fright
Of conscience, for their long offended might,
For all thine impious proud-heart sophistries,
Unlawful magic, and enticing lies.
Corinthians! look upon that grey-beard wretch!
Mark how, possess'd, his lashless eyelids stretch
Around his demon eyes! Corinthians, see!
My sweet bride withers at their potency."
"Fool!" said the sophist, in an under-tone
Gruff with contempt; which a death-nighing moan
From Lycius answer'd, as heart-struck and lost,
He sank supine beside the aching ghost.

"Fool! Fool!" repeated he, while his eyes still
Relented not, nor mov'd; "from every ill
Of life have I preserv'd thee to this day,
And shall I see thee made a serpent's prey?"
Then Lamia breath'd death breath; the sophist's eye,
Like a sharp spear, went through her utterly,
Keen, cruel, perceant, stinging: she, as well
As her weak hand could any meaning tell,
Motion'd him to be silent; vainly so,
He look'd and look'd again a level—No!
"A serpent!" echoed he; no sooner said,
Than with a frightful scream she vanished:
And Lycius' arms were empty of delight,
As were his limbs of life, from that same night.
On the high couch he lay!—his friends came round—
Supported him—no pulse, or breath they found,
And, in its marriage robe, the heavy body wound.

JOHN KEATS

ADONAIS

AN ELEGY ON THE DEATH
OF JOHN KEATS

'Αστὴρ πρὶν μὲν ἔλαμπες ἐνὶ ζωοῖσιν Ἐῷος·
νῦν δὲ θανὼν λάμπεις Ἕσπερος ἐν φθιμένοις.—PLATO.

I

I WEEP for Adonais—he is dead!
  O, weep for Adonais! though our tears
Thaw not the frost which binds so dear a head!
And thou, sad Hour, selected from all years
To mourn our loss, rouse thy obscure compeers,
And teach them thine own sorrow, say: "With me
Died Adonais; till the Future dares
Forget the Past, his fate and fame shall be
An echo and a light unto eternity!"

II

Where wert thou, mighty Mother, when he lay,
When thy Son lay, pierced by the shaft which flies
In darkness? where was lorn Urania
When Adonais died? With veilèd eyes,
'Mid listening Echoes, in her Paradise
She sate, while one, with soft enamoured breath,

[82]

Rekindled all the fading melodies,
With which, like flowers that mock the corse beneath,
He had adorned and hid the coming bulk of Death.

III

Oh, weep for Adonais—he is dead!
Wake, melancholy Mother, wake and weep!
Yet wherefore? Quench within their burning bed
Thy fiery tears, and let thy loud heart keep
Like his, a mute and uncomplaining sleep;
For he is gone, where all things wise and fair
Descend;—oh, dream not that the amorous Deep
Will yet restore him to the vital air;
Death feeds on his mute voice, and laughs at our despair.

IV

Most musical of mourners, weep again!
Lament anew, Urania!—He died,
Who was the Sire of an immortal strain,
Blind, old, and lonely, when his country's pride,
The priest, the slave, and the liberticide,
Trampled and mocked with many a lothèd rite
Of lust and blood; he went, unterrified,
Into the gulf of death; but his clear Sprite
Yet reigns o'er earth; the third among the sons of light.

V

Most musical of mourners, weep anew!
Not all to that bright station dared to climb;
And happier they their happiness who knew,
Whose tapers yet burn through that night of time

In which suns perished; others more sublime,
Struck by the envious wrath of man or god,
Have sunk, extinct in their refulgent prime;
And some yet live, treading the thorny road,
Which leads, through toil and hate, to Fame's serene
    abode.

VI

But now, thy youngest, dearest one, has perished—
The nursling of thy widowhood, who grew,
Like a pale flower by some sad maiden cherished,
And fed with true-love tears, instead of dew;
Most musical of mourners, weep anew!
Thy extreme hope, the loveliest and the last,
The bloom, whose petals nipped before they blew
Died on the promise of the fruit, is waste;
The broken lily lies—the storm is overpast.

VII

To that high Capital, where kingly Death
Keeps his pale court in beauty and decay,
He came; and bought, with price of purest breath,
A grave among the eternal.—Come away!
Haste, while the vault of blue Italian day
Is yet his fitting charnel-roof! while still
He lies, as if in dewy sleep he lay;
Awake him not! surely he takes his fill
Of deep and liquid rest, forgetful of all ill.

VIII

He will awake no more, oh, never more!—
Within the twilight chamber spreads apace

The shadow of white Death, and at the door
Invisible Corruption waits to trace
His extreme way to her dim dwelling-place;
The eternal Hunger sits, but pity and awe
Soothe her pale rage, nor dares she to deface
So fair a prey, till darkness, and the law
Of change, shall o'er his sleep the mortal curtain draw.

IX

Oh, weep for Adonais!—The quick Dreams,
The passion-wingèd Ministers of thought,
Who were his flocks, whom near the living streams
Of his young spirit he fed, and whom he taught
The love which was its music, wander not,—
Wander no more, from kindling brain to brain,
But droop there, whence they sprung; and mourn their
    lot
Round the cold heart, where, after their sweet pain,
They ne'er will gather strength, or find a home again.

X

And one with trembling hands clasps his cold head,
And fans him with her moonlight wings, and cries;
"Our love, our hope, our sorrow, is not dead;
See, on the silken fringe of his faint eyes,
Like dew upon a sleeping flower, there lies
A tear some Dream has loosened from his brain."
Lost Angel of a ruined Paradise!
She knew not 'twas her own; as with no stain
She faded, like a cloud which had outwept its rain.

XI

One from a lucid urn of starry dew
Washed his light limbs, as if embalming them;
Another clipped her profuse locks, and threw
The wreath upon him, like an anadem
Which frozen tears instead of pearls begem.
Another in her wilful grief would break
Her bow and wingèd reeds, as if to stem
A greater loss with one which was more weak;
And dull the barbèd fire against his frozen cheek.

XII

Another Splendor on his mouth alit,—
That mouth whence it was wont to draw the breath
Which gave it strength to pierce the guarded wit,
And pass into the panting heart beneath
With lightning and with music: the damp death
Quenched its caress upon his icy lips;
And, as a dying meteor stains a wreath
Of moonlight vapor, which the cold night clips,
It flushed through his pale limbs, and passed to its eclipse.

XIII

And others came,—Desires and Adorations,
Wingèd Persuasions and veiled Destinies,
Splendors, and Glooms, and glimmering Incarnations
Of hopes and fears, and twilight Phantasies;
And Sorrow, with her family of Sighs,
And Pleasure, blind with tears, led by the gleam
Of her own dying smile instead of eyes,
Came in slow pomp;—the moving pomp might seem
Like pageantry of mist on an autumnal stream.

XIV

All he had loved, and moulded into thought
From shape, and hue, and odor, and sweet sound,
Lamented Adonais. Morning sought
Her eastern watch tower, and her hair unbound,—
Wet with the tears which should adorn the ground,—
Dimmed the aërial eyes that kindle day:
Afar the melancholy thunder moaned,
Pale Ocean in unquiet slumber lay,
And the wild winds flew round, sobbing in their dismay.

XV

Lost Echo sits amid the voiceless mountains,
And feeds her grief with his remembered lay,
And will no more reply to winds or fountains,
Or amorous birds perched on the young green spray,
Or herdsman's horn, or bell at closing day;
Since she can mimic not his lips, more dear
Than those for whose disdain she pined away
Into a shadow of all sounds:—a drear
Murmur, between their songs, is all the woodmen hear.

XVI

Grief made the young Spring wild, and she threw down
Her kindling buds, as if she Autumn were,
Or they dead leaves; since her delight is flown,
For whom should she have waked the sullen year?
To Phoebus was not Hyacinth so dear
Nor to himself Narcissus, as to both
Thou, Adonais: wan they stand and sere
Amid the faint companions of their youth,
With dew all turned to tears; odour, to sighing ruth.

XVII

Thy spirit's sister, the lorn nightingale
Mourns not her mate with such melodious pain;
Not so the eagle, who like thee could scale
Heaven, and could nourish in the sun's domain
Her mighty youth with morning, doth complain,
Soaring and screaming round her empty nest,
As Albion wails for thee: the curse of Cain
Light on his head who pierced thy innocent breast,
And scared the angel soul that was its earthly guest!

XVIII

Ah, woe is me! Winter is come and gone,
But grief returns with the revolving year;
The airs and streams renew their joyous tone;
The ants, the bees, the swallows reappear;
Fresh leaves and flowers deck the dead Seasons' bier;
The amorous birds now pair in every brake,
And build their mossy homes in field and brere;
And the green lizard, and the golden snake,
Like unimprisoned flames, out of their trance awake.

XIX

Through wood and stream and field and hill and Ocean
A quickening life from the Earth's heart has burst
As it has ever done, with change and motion,
From the great morning of the world when first
God dawned on Chaos; in its stream immersed,
The lamps of Heaven flash with a softer light;
All baser things pant with life's sacred thirst;
Diffuse themselves; and spend in love's delight,
The beauty and the joy of their renewèd might.

XX

The leprous corpse, touched by this spirit tender,
Exhales itself in flowers of gentle breath;
Like incarnations of the stars, when splendour
Is changed to fragrance, they illumine death
And mock the merry worm that wakes beneath;
Nought we know, dies. Shall that alone which knows
Be as a sword consumed before the sheath
By sightless lightning?—the intense atom glows
A moment, then is quenched in a most cold repose.

XXI

Alas! that all we loved of him should be,
But for our grief, as if it had not been,
And grief itself be mortal! Woe is me!
Whence are we, and why are we? of what scene
The actors or spectators? Great and mean
Meet massed in death, who lends what life must
    burrow.
As long as skies are blue, and fields are green,
Evening must usher night, night urge the morrow,
Month follow month with woe, and year wake year to
    sorrow.

XXII

He will awake no more, oh, never more!
"Wake thou," cried Misery, "childless Mother, rise
Out of thy sleep, and slake, in thy heart's core,
A wound more fierce than his, with tears and sighs."
And all the Dreams that watched Urania's eyes,
And all the Echoes whom their sister's song

Had held in holy silence, cried: "Arise!"
Swift as a Thought by the snake Memory stung,
From her ambrosial rest the fading Splendour sprung.

XXIII

She rose like an autumnal Night, that springs
Out of the East, and follows wild and drear
The golden Day, which, on eternal wings,
Even as a ghost abandoning a bier,
Had left the Earth a corpse. Sorrow and fear
So struck, so roused, so rapped Urania;
So saddened round her like an atmosphere
Of stormy mist; so swept her on her way
Even to the mournful place where Adonais lay.

XXIV

Out of her secret Paradise she sped,
Through camps and cities rough with stone, and steel,
And human hearts, which to her aery tread
Yielding not, wounded the invisible
Palms of her tender feet where'er they fell:
And barbèd tongues, and thoughts more sharp than
    they,
Rent the soft Form they never could repel,
Whose sacred blood, like the young tears of May,
Paved with eternal flowers that undeserving way.

XXV

In the death-chamber for a moment Death,
Shamed by the presence of that living Might,
Blushed to annihilation, and the breath
Revisited those lips, and Life's pale light

Flashed through those limbs, so late her dear delight.
"Leave me not wild and drear and comfortless,
As silent lightning leaves the starless night!
Leave me not!" cried Urania: her distress
Roused Death: Death rose and smiled, and met her vain
    caress.

XXVI

"Stay yet awhile! speak to me once again;
Kiss me, so long but as a kiss may live;
And in my heartless breast and burning brain
That word, that kiss, shall all thoughts else survive,
With food of saddest memory kept alive,
Now thou art dead, as if it were a part
Of thee, my Adonais! I would give
All that I am to be as thou now art!
But I am chained to Time, and cannot thence depart!

XXVII

"O gentle child, beautiful as thou wert,
Why didst thou leave the trodden paths of men
Too soon, and with weak hands though mighty heart
Dare the unpastured dragon in his den?
Defenceless as thou wert, oh, where was then
Wisdom the mirrored shield, or scorn the spear?
Or hadst thou waited the full cycle, when
Thy spirit should have filled its crescent sphere,
The monsters of life's waste had fled from thee like deer.

XXVIII

"The herded wolves, bold only to pursue;
The obscene ravens, clamorous o'er the dead;

The vultures to the conqueror's banner true
Who feed where Desolation first has fed,
And whose wings rain contagion;—how they fled,
When, like Apollo, from his golden bow
The Pythian of the age one arrow sped
And smiled!—The spoilers tempt no second blow,
They fawn on the proud feet that spurn them lying low.

XXIX

"The sun comes forth, and many reptiles spawn;
He sets, and each ephemeral insect then
Is gathered into death without a dawn,
And the immortal stars awake again;
So is it in the world of living men:
A godlike mind soars forth, in its delight
Making earth bare and veiling heaven, and when
It sinks, the swarms that dimmed or shared its light
Leave to its kindred lamps the spirit's awful night."

XXX

Thus ceased she: and the mountain shepherds came,
Their garlands sere, their magic mantles rent;
The Pilgrim of Eternity, whose fame
Over his living head like Heaven is bent,
An early but enduring monument,
Came, veiling all the lightnings of his song
In sorrow; from her wilds Ierne sent
The sweetest lyrist of her saddest wrong,
And Love taught Grief to fall like music from his tongue.

XXXI

Midst others of less note, came one frail Form,
A phantom among men; companionless
As the last cloud of an expiring storm
Whose thunder is its knell; he, as I guess,
Had gazed on Nature's naked loveliness,
Actaeon-like, and now he fled astray
With feeble steps o'er the world's wilderness,
And his own thoughts, along that rugged way,
Pursued, like raging hounds, their father and their prey.

XXXII

A pardlike Spirit beautiful and swift—
A Love in desolation masked;—a Power
Girt round with weakness;—it can scarce uplift
The weight of the superincumbent hour;
It is a dying lamp, a falling shower,
A breaking billow;—even whilst we speak
Is it not broken? On the withering flower
The killing sun smiles brightly: on a cheek
The life can burn in blood, even while the heart may
    break.

XXXIII

His head was bound with pansies overblown,
And faded violets, white, and pied, and blue;
And a light spear topped with a cypress cone,
Round whose rude shaft dark ivy-tresses grew
Yet dripping with the forest's noonday dew,
Vibrated, as the ever-beating heart
Shook the weak hand that grasped it; of that crew
He came the last, neglected and apart;
A herd-abandoned deer struck by the hunter's dart.

XXXIV

All stood aloof, and at his partial moan
Smiled through their tears; well knew that gentle band
Who in another's fate now wept his own,
As in the accents of an unknown land
He sung new sorrow; sad Urania scanned
The Stranger's mien, and murmured: "Who are thou?"
He answered not, but with a sudden hand
Made bare his branded and ensanguined brow,
Which was like Cain's or Christ's—oh! that it should
    be so!

XXXV

What softer voice is hushed over the dead?
Athwart what brow is that dark mantle thrown?
What form leans sadly o'er the white death-bed,
In mockery of monumental stone,
The heavy heart heaving without a moan?
If it be He, who, gentlest of the wise,
Taught, soothed, loved, honoured the departed one,
Let me not vex, with inharmonious sighs,
The silence of that heart's accepted sacrifice.

XXXVI

Our Adonais has drunk poison—oh!
What deaf and viperous murderer could crown
Life's early cup with such a draught of woe?
The nameless worm would now itself disown:
It felt, yet could escape, the magic tone
Whose prelude held all envy, hate, and wrong,
But what was howling in one breast alone,
Silent with expectation of the song,
Whose master's hand is cold, whose silver lyre unstrung.

XXXVII

Live thou, whose infamy is not thy fame!
Live! fear no heavier chastisement from me,
Thou noteless blot on a remembered name!
But be thyself, and know thyself to be!
And ever at thy season be thou free
To spill the venom when thy fangs o'erflow;
Remorse and Self-contempt shall cling to thee;
Hot Shame shall burn upon thy secret brow,
And like a beaten hound tremble thou shalt—as now.

XXXVIII

Nor let us weep that our delight is fled
Far from these carrion kites that scream below;
He wakes or sleeps with the enduring dead;
Thou canst not soar where he is sitting now—
Dust to the dust! but the pure spirit shall flow
Back to the burning fountain whence it came,
A portion of the Eternal, which must glow
Through time and change, unquenchably the same,
Whilst thy cold embers choke the sordid hearth of shame.

XXXIX

Peace, peace! he is not dead, he doth not sleep—
He hath awakened from the dream of life—
'Tis we, who lost in stormy visions, keep
With phantoms an unprofitable strife,
And in mad trance, strike with our spirit's knife
Invulnerable nothings.—*We* decay
Like corpses in a charnel; fear and grief
Convulse us and consume us day by day,
And cold hopes swarm like worms within our living clay.

XL

He has outsoared the shadow of our night;
Envy and calumny and hate and pain,
And that unrest which men miscall delight,
Can touch him not and torture not again;
From the contagion of the world's slow stain
He is secure, and now can never mourn
A heart grown cold, a head grown gray in vain;
Nor, when the spirit's self has ceased to burn,
With sparkless ashes load an unlamented urn.

XLI

He lives, he wakes—'tis Death is dead, not he;
Mourn not for Adonais.—Thou young Dawn,
Turn all thy dew to splendour, for from thee
The spirit thou lamentest is not gone;
Ye caverns and ye forests, cease to moan!
Cease, ye faint flowers and fountains, and thou Air,
Which like a mourning veil thy scarf hadst thrown
O'er the abandoned Earth, now leave it bare
Even to the joyous stars which smile on its despair!

XLII

He is made one with Nature: there is heard
His voice in all her music, from the moan
Of thunder, to the song of night's sweet bird;
He is a presence to be felt and known
In darkness and in light, from herb and stone,
Spreading itself where'er that Power may move
Which has withdrawn his being to its own;
Which wields the world with never-wearied love,
Sustains it from beneath, and kindles it above.

XLIII

He is a portion of the loveliness
Which once he made more lovely: he doth bear
His part, while the one Spirit's plastic stress
Sweeps through the dull dense world, compelling there,
All new successions to the forms they wear;
Torturing th' unwilling dross that checks its flight
To its own likeness, as each mass may bear;
And bursting in its beauty and its might
From trees and beasts and men into the Heaven's light.

XLIV

The splendours of the firmament of time
May be eclipsed, but are extinguished not;
Like stars to their appointed height they climb,
And death is a low mist which cannot blot
The brightness it may veil. When lofty thought
Lifts a young heart above its mortal lair,
And love and life contend in it, for what
Shall be its earthly doom, the dead live there
And move like winds of light on dark and stormy air.

XLV

The inheritors of unfulfilled renown
Rose from their thrones, built beyond mortal thought,
Far in the Unapparent. Chatterton
Rose pale,—his solemn agony had not
Yet faded from him; Sidney, as he fought
And as he fell and as he lived and loved
Sublimely mild, a Spirit without spot,
Arose; and Lucan, by his death approved:
Oblivion as they rose shrank like a thing reproved.

XLVI

And many more, whose names on Earth are dark,
But whose transmitted effluence cannot die
So long as fire outlives the parent spark,
Rose, robed in dazzling immortality.
"Thou art become as one of us," they cry,
"It was for thee yon kingless sphere has long
Swung blind in unascended majesty,
Silent alone amid an Heaven of Song.
Assume thy wingèd throne, thou Vesper of our throng!"

XLVII

Who mourns for Adonais? Oh, come forth,
Fond wretch! and know thyself and him aright.
Clasp with thy panting soul the pendulous Earth;
As from a centre, dart thy spirit's light
Beyond all worlds, until its spacious might
Satiate the void circumference: then shrink
Even to a point within our day and night;
And keep thy heart light lest it make thee sink
When hope has kindled hope, and lured thee to the brink.

XLVIII

Or go to Rome, which is the sepulchre,
Oh, not of him, but of our joy: 'tis nought
That ages, empires, and religions there
Lie buried in the ravage they have wrought;
For such as he can lend,—they borrow not
Glory from those who made the world their prey;
And he is gathered to the kings of thought
Who waged contention with their time's decay,
And of the past are all that cannot pass away.

XLIX

Go thou to Rome,—at once the Paradise,
The grave, the city, and the wilderness;
And where its wrecks like shattered mountains rise,
And flowering weeds, and fragrant copses dress
The bones of Desolation's nakedness
Pass, till the spirit of the spot shall lead
Thy footsteps to a slope of green access
Where, like an infant's smile, over the dead
A light of laughing flowers along the grass is spread;

L

And gray walls moulder round, on which dull Time
Feeds, like slow fire upon a hoary brand;
And one keen pyramid with wedge sublime,
Pavilioning the dust of him who planned
This refuge for his memory, doth stand
Like flame transformed to marble; and beneath,
A field is spread, on which a newer band
Have pitched in Heaven's smile their camp of death,
Welcoming him we lose with scarce extinguished breath.

LI

Here pause: these graves are all too young as yet
To have outgrown the sorrow which consigned
Its charge to each; and if the seal is set,
Here, on one fountain of a mourning mind,
Break it not thou! too surely shalt thou find
Thine own well full, if thou returnest home,
Of tears and gall. From the world's bitter wind
Seek shelter in the shadow of the tomb.
What Adonais is, why fear we to become?

LII

The One remains, the many change and pass;
Heaven's light forever shines, Earth's shadows fly;
Life, like a dome of many-coloured glass,
Stains the white radiance of Eternity,
Until Death tramples it to fragments.—Die,
If thou wouldst be with that which thou dost seek!
Follow where all is fled!—Rome's azure sky,
Flowers, ruins, statues, music, words, are weak
The glory they transfuse with fitting truth to speak.

LIII

Why linger, why turn back, why shrink, my Heart?
Thy hopes are gone before: from all things here
They have departed; thou shouldst now depart!
A light is passed from the revolving year,
And man, and woman; and what still is dear
Attracts to crush, repels to make thee wither.
The soft sky smiles,—the low wind whispers near:
'Tis Adonais calls! oh, hasten thither,
No more let Life divide what Death can join together.

LIV

That Light whose smile kindles the Universe,
That Beauty in which all things work and move,
That Benediction which the eclipsing Curse
Of birth can quench not, that sustaining Love
Which through the web of being blindly wove
By man and beast and earth and air and sea,
Burns bright or dim, as each are mirrors of
The fire for which all thirst; now beams on me,
Consuming the last clouds of cold mortality.

LV

The breath whose might I have invoked in song
Descends on me; my spirit's bark is driven,
Far from the shore, far from the trembling throng
Whose sails were never to the tempest given;
The massy earth and spherèd skies are riven!
I am borne darkly, fearfully, afar;
Whilst, burning through the inmost veil of Heaven,
The soul of Adonais, like a star,
Beacons from the abode where the Eternal are.

PERCY BYSSHE SHELLEY

HYMN TO INTELLECTUAL BEAUTY

I

THE awful shadow of some unseen Power
   Floats though unseen among us,—visiting
  This various world with as inconstant wing
As summer winds that creep from flower to flower,—
Like moonbeams that behind some piny mountain
    shower,
    It visits with inconstant glance
    Each human heart and countenance;
Like hues and harmonies of evening,—
    Like clouds in starlight widely spread,—
    Like memory of music fled,—
    Like aught that for its grace may be
Dear, and yet dearer for its mystery.

II

Spirit of BEAUTY, that dost consecrate
  With thine own hues all thou dost shine upon
  Of human thought or form,—where art thou gone?
Why dost thou pass away and leave our state,
This dim vast vale of tears, vacant and desolate?
    Ask why the sunlight not for ever
    Weaves rainbows o'er yon mountain-river,

Why aught should fail and fade that once is shown,
　　Why fear and dream and death and birth
　　Cast on the daylight of this earth
　　Such gloom,—why man has such a scope
For love and hate, despondency and hope?

III

No voice from some sublimer world hath ever
　　To sage or poet these responses given—
　　Therefore the names of Demon, Ghost, and Heaven,
Remain the records of their vain endeavour,
Frail spells—whose uttered charm might not avail to
　　　　sever,
　　　From all we hear and all we see,
　　　Doubt, chance, and mutability.
Thy light alone—like mist o'er mountains driven,
　　Or music by the night-wind sent
　　Through strings of some still instrument,
　　Or moonlight on a midnight stream,
Gives grace and truth to life's unquiet dream.

IV

Love, Hope, and Self-esteem, like clouds depart
　　And come, for some uncertain moments lent.
　　Man were immortal, and omnipotent,
Didst thou, unknown and awful as thou art,
Keep with thy glorious train firm state within his heart.
　　　Thou messenger of sympathies,
　　　That wax and wane in lovers' eyes—
Thou—that to human thought art nourishment,
　　　Like darkness to a dying flame!
　　　Depart not as thy shadow came,

Depart not—lest the grave should be,
Like life and fear, a dark reality.

V

While yet a boy I sought for ghosts, and sped
   Through many a listening chamber, cave and ruin,
   And starlight wood, with fearful steps pursuing
Hopes of high talk with the departed dead.
I called on poisonous names with which our youth is fed;
     I was not heard—I saw them not—
     When musing deeply on the lot
Of life, at that sweet time when winds are wooing
     All vital things that wake to bring
     News of birds and blossoming,—
     Sudden, thy shadow fell on me;
I shrieked, and clasped my hands in ecstasy!

VI

I vowed that I would dedicate my powers
   To thee and thine—have I not kept the vow?
   With beating heart and streaming eyes, even now
I call the phantoms of a thousand hours
Each from his voiceless grave: they have in visioned
     bowers
     Of studious zeal or love's delight
     Outwatched with me the envious night—
They know that never joy illumed my brow
     Unlinked with hope that thou wouldst free
     This world from its dark slavery,
     That thou—O awful LOVELINESS,
Wouldst give whate'er these words cannot express.

[104]

VII

The day becomes more solemn and serene
  When noon is past—there is a harmony
  In autumn, and a lustre in its sky,
Which through the summer is not heard or seen,
As if it could not be, as if it had not been!
      Thus let thy power, which like the truth
      Of nature on my passive youth
    Descended, to my onward life supply
      Its calm—to one who worships thee,
      And every form containing thee,
      Whom, SPIRIT fair, thy spells did bind
To fear himself, and love all human kind.

                    PERCY BYSSHE SHELLEY

THE WORLD'S GREAT AGE
BEGINS ANEW

Final Chorus from *Hellas*

THE world's great age begins anew,
   The golden years return,
The earth doth like a snake renew
   Her winter weeds outworn:
Heaven smiles, and faiths and empires gleam,
Like wrecks of a dissolving dream.

A brighter Hellas rears its mountains
   From waves serener far;
A new Peneus rolls his fountains
   Against the morning star.
Where fairer Tempes bloom, there sleep
Young Cyclads on a sunnier deep.

A loftier Argo cleaves the main,
   Fraught with a later prize;
Another Orpheus sings again,
   And loves, and weeps, and dies.
A new Ulysses leaves once more
Calypso for his native shore.

Oh, write no more the tale of Troy,
    If earth Death's scroll must be!
Nor mix with Laian rage the joy
    Which dawns upon the free:
Although a subtler Sphinx renew
Riddles of death Thebes never knew.

Another Athens shall arise,
    And to remoter time
Bequeath, like sunset to the skies,
    The splendour of its prime;
And leave, if nought so bright may live,
All earth can take or Heaven can give.

Saturn and Love their long repose
    Shall burst, more bright and good
Than all who fell, than One who rose,
    Than many unsubdued:
Not gold, not blood, their altar dowers,
But votive tears and symbol flowers.

Oh, cease! must hate and death return?
    Cease! must men kill and die?
Cease! drain not to its dregs the urn
    Of bitter prophecy.
The world is weary of the past,
Oh, might it die or rest at last!

                  PERCY BYSSHE SHELLEY

TO HELEN

Helen, thy beauty is to me
  Like those Nicéan barks of yore,
That gently, o'er a perfumed sea,
  The weary, way-worn wanderer bore
  To his own native shore.

On desperate seas long wont to roam,
  Thy hyacinth hair, thy classic face,
Thy Naiad airs have brought me home
  To the glory that was Greece,
  And the grandeur that was Rome.

Lo! in yon brilliant window-niche
  How statue-like I see thee stand,
The agate lamp within thy hand!
  Ah, Psyche, from the regions which
  Are Holy-Land!

EDGAR ALLAN POE

A MUSICAL INSTRUMENT

I

WHAT was he doing, the great god Pan,
    Down in the reeds by the river?
Spreading ruin and scattering ban,
Splashing and paddling with hoofs of a goat,
And breaking the golden lilies afloat
    With the dragon-fly on the river.

II

He tore out a reed, the great god Pan,
    From the deep cool bed of the river;
The limpid water turbidly ran,
And the broken lilies a-dying lay,
And the dragon-fly had fled away,
    Ere he brought it out of the river.

III

High on the shore sat the great god Pan
    While turbidly flowed the river;
And hacked and hewed as a great god can,
With his hard bleak steel at the patient reed,
Till there was not a sign of the leaf indeed
    To prove it fresh from the river.

IV

He cut it short, did the great god Pan,
  (How tall it stood in the river!)
Then drew the pith, like the heart of a man,
Steadily from the outside ring,
And notched the poor dry empty thing
  In holes, as he sat by the river.

V

"This is the way," laughed the great god Pan
  (Laughed while he sat by the river),
"The only way, since gods began
To make sweet music, they could succeed."
Then, dropping his mouth to a hole in the reed,
  He blew in power by the river.

VI

Sweet, sweet, sweet, O Pan!
  Piercing sweet by the river!
Blinding sweet, O great god Pan!
The sun on the hill forgot to die,
And the lilies revived, and the dragon-fly
  Came back to dream on the river.

VII

Yet half a beast is the great god Pan,
  To laugh as he sits by the river,
Making a poet out of a man:
The true gods sigh for the cost and pain,—
For the reed which grows nevermore again
  As a reed with the reeds in the river.

ELIZABETH BARRETT BROWNING

IPHIGENIA
AND AGAMEMNON

IPHIGENIA, when she heard her doom
    At Aulis, and when all beside the King
Had gone away, took his right hand, and said,
"O father! I am young and very happy.
I do not think the pious Calchas heard
Distinctly what the Goddess spake. Old-age
Obscures the senses. If my nurse, who knew
My voice so well, sometimes misunderstood
While I was resting on her knee both arms
And hitting it to make her mind my words,
And looking in her face, and she in mine,
Might he not also hear one word amiss,
Spoken from so far off, even from Olympus?"
The father placed his cheek upon her head,
And tears dropt down it, but the king of men
Replied not. Then the maiden spake once more.
"O father! sayst thou nothing? Hear'st thou not
Me, whom thou ever hast, until this hour,
Listened to fondly, and awakened me
To hear my voice amid the voice of birds,
When it was inarticulate as theirs,
And the down deadened it within the nest?"
He moved her gently from him, silent still,

And this, and this alone, brought tears from her,
Although she saw fate nearer: then with sighs,
"I thought to have laid down my hair before
Benignant Artemis, and not have dimmed
Her polisht altar with my virgin blood;
I thought to have selected the white flowers
To please the Nymphs, and to have asked of each
By name, and with no sorrowful regret,
Whether, since both my parents willed the change,
I might at Hymen's feet bend my clipt brow;
And (after those who mind us girls the most)
Adore our own Athena, that she would
Regard me mildly with her azure eyes.
But, father! to see you no more, and see
Your love, O father! go ere I am gone." . . .
Gently he moved her off, and drew her back,
Bending his lofty head far over hers,
And the dark depths of nature heaved and burst.
He turned away; not far, but silent still.
She now first shuddered; for in him, so nigh,
So long a silence seemed the approach of death,
And like it. Once again she raised her voice.
"O father! if the ships are now detained,
And all your vows move not the Gods above,
When the knife strikes me there will be one prayer
The less to them: and purer can there be
Any, or more fervent than the daughter's prayer
For her dear father's safety and success?"
A groan that shook him shook not his resolve.
An aged man now entered, and without
One word, stept slowly on, and took the wrist

Of the pale maiden. She looked up, and saw
The fillet of the priest and calm cold eyes.
Then turned she where her parent stood, and cried
"O father! grieve no more: the ships can sail."

WALTER SAVAGE LANDOR

HELEN AND IPHIGENIA

From *A Dream of Fair Women*

At length I saw a lady within call,
    Stiller than chisell'd marble, standing there;
A daughter of the gods, divinely tall,
    And most divinely fair.

Her loveliness with shame and with surprise
    Froze my swift speech: she turning on my face
The star-like sorrows of immortal eyes,
    Spoke slowly in her place.

"I had great beauty: ask thou not my name:
    No one can be more wise than destiny.
Many drew swords and died. Where'er I came
    I brought calamity."

"No marvel, sovereign lady: in fair field
    Myself for such a face had boldly died,"
I answer'd free; and turning I appeal'd
    To one that stood beside.

But she, with sick and scornful looks averse,
    To her full height her stately stature draws;

"My youth," she said, "was blasted with a curse:
    This woman was the cause.

"I was cut off from hope in that sad place,
    Which men call'd Aulis in those iron years:
My father held his hand upon his face;
    I, blinded with my tears,

"Still strove to speak: my voice was thick with sighs
    As in a dream. Dimly I could descry
The stern black-bearded kings with wolfish eyes,
    Waiting to see me die.

"The high masts flicker'd as they lay afloat;
    The crowds, the temples, waver'd, and the shore;
The bright death quiver'd at the victim's throat;
    Touch'd; and I knew no more."

Whereto the other with a downward brow:
    "I would the white cold heavy-plunging foam,
Whirl'd by the wind, had roll'd me deep below,
    Then when I left my home."

                              ALFRED, LORD TENNYSON

TITHONUS

THE woods decay, the woods decay and fall,
  The vapours weep their burthen to the ground,
Man comes and tills the field and lies beneath,
And after many a summer dies the swan.
Me only cruel immortality
Consumes: I wither slowly in thine arms,
Here at the quiet limit of the world,
A white-hair'd shadow roaming like a dream
The ever-silent spaces of the East,
Far-folded mists, and gleaming halls of morn.

  Alas! for this gray shadow, once a man—
So glorious in his beauty and thy choice,
Who madest him thy chosen, that he seem'd
To his great heart none other than a God!
I ask'd thee, "Give me immortality."
Then didst thou grant mine asking with a smile,
Like wealthy men who care not how they give.
But thy strong Hours indignant work'd their wills,
And beat me down and marr'd and wasted me,
And tho' they could not end me, left me maim'd
To dwell in presence of immortal youth,
Immortal age beside immortal youth,
And all I was, in ashes. Can thy love,

Thy beauty, make amends, tho' even now,
Close over us, the silver star, thy guide,
Shines in those tremulous eyes that fill with tears
To hear me? Let me go: take back thy gift:
Why should a man desire in any way
To vary from the kindly race of men,
Or pass beyond the goal of ordinance
Where all should pause, as is most meet for all?

A soft air fans the cloud apart; there comes
A glimpse of that dark world where I was born.
Once more the old mysterious glimmer steals
From thy pure brows, and from thy shoulders pure,
And bosom beating with a heart renew'd.
Thy cheek begins to redden thro' the gloom,
Thy sweet eyes brighten slowly close to mine,
Ere yet they blind the stars, and the wild team
Which love thee, yearning for thy yoke, arise,
And shake the darkness from their loosen'd manes,
And beat the twilight into flakes of fire.

Lo! ever thus thou growest beautiful
In silence, then before thine answer given
Departest, and thy tears are on my cheek.

Why wilt thou ever scare me with thy tears,
And make me tremble lest a saying learnt,
In days far-off, on that dark earth, be true?
"The Gods themselves cannot recall their gifts."

Ay me! ay me! with what another heart
In days far-off, and with what other eyes

I used to watch—if I be he that watch'd—
The lucid outline forming round thee; saw
The dim curls kindle into sunny rings;
Changed with thy mystic change, and felt my blood
Glow with the glow that slowly crimson'd all
Thy presence and thy portals, while I lay,
Mouth, forehead, eyelids, growing dewy-warm
With kisses balmier than half-opening buds
Of April, and I could hear the lips that kiss'd
Whispering I knew not what of wild and sweet,
Like that strange song I heard Apollo sing,
While Ilion like a mist rose into towers.

Yet hold me not for ever in thine East:
How can my nature longer mix with thine?
Coldly thy rosy shadows bathe me, cold
Are all thy lights, and cold my wrinkled feet
Upon thy glimmering thresholds, when the steam
Floats up from those dim fields about the homes
Of happy men that have the power to die,
And grassy barrows of the happier dead.
Release me, and restore me to the ground;
Thou seëst all things, thou wilt see my grave:
Thou wilt renew thy beauty morn by morn;
I earth in earth forget these empty courts,
And thee returning on thy silver wheels.

ALFRED, LORD TENNYSON

OENONE

THERE lies a vale in Ida, lovelier
    Than all the valleys of Ionian hills.
The swimming vapour slopes athwart the glen,
Puts forth an arm, and creeps from pine to pine,
And loiters, slowly drawn. On either hand
The lawns and meadow-ledges midway down
Hang rich in flowers, and far below them roars
The long brook falling thro' the clov'n ravine
In cataract after cataract to the sea.
Behind the valley topmost Gargarus
Stands up and takes the morning: but in front
The gorges, opening wide apart, reveal
Troas and Ilion's column'd citadel,
The crown of Troas.

                    Hither came at noon
Mournful Oenone, wandering forlorn
Of Paris, once her playmate on the hills.
Her cheek had lost the rose, and round her neck
Floated her hair or seem'd to float in rest.
She, leaning on a fragment twined with vine,
Sang to the stillness, till the mountain-shade
Sloped downward to her seat from the upper cliff.

"O mother Ida, many-fountain'd Ida,
Dear mother Ida, harken ere I die.
For now the noonday quiet holds the hill:
The grasshopper is silent in the grass:
The lizard, with his shadow on the stone,
Rests like a shadow, and the cicala sleeps.
The purple flower droops: the golden bee
Is lily-cradled: I alone awake.
My eyes are full of tears, my heart of love,
My heart is breaking, and my eyes are dim,
And I am all aweary of my life.

"O mother Ida, many-fountain'd Ida,
Dear mother Ida, harken ere I die.
Hear me O Earth, hear me O Hills, O Caves
That house the cold crown'd snake! O mountain brooks,
I am the daughter of a River-God,
Hear me, for I will speak, and build up all
My sorrow with my song, as yonder walls
Rose slowly to a music slowly breathed,
A cloud that gather'd shape: for it may be
That, while I speak of it, a little while
My heart may wander from its deeper woe.

"O mother Ida, many-fountain'd Ida,
Dear mother Ida, harken ere I die.
I waited underneath the dawning hills,
Aloft the mountain lawn was dewy-dark,
And dewy-dark aloft the mountain pine:
Beautiful Paris, evil-hearted Paris,
Leading a jet-black goat white-horn'd, white-hooved,
Came up from reedy Simois all alone.

"O mother Ida, harken ere I die.
Far-off the torrent call'd me from the cleft:
Far up the solitary morning smote
The streaks of virgin snow. With down-dropt eyes
I sat alone: white-breasted like a star
Fronting the dawn he moved; a leopard skin
Droop'd from his shoulder, but his sunny hair
Cluster'd about his temples like a God's:
And his cheek brighten'd as the foam-bow brightens
When the wind blows the foam, and all my heart
Went forth to embrace him coming ere he came.

"Dear mother Ida, harken ere I die.
He smiled, and opening out his milk-white palm
Disclosed a fruit of pure Hesperian gold,
That smelt ambrosially, and while I look'd
And listen'd, the full-flowing river of speech
Came down upon my heart.

        " 'My own Oenone,
Beautiful-brow'd Oenone, my own soul,
Behold this fruit, whose gleaming rind ingrav'n
"For the most fair," would seem to award it thine,
As lovelier than whatever Oread haunt
The knolls of Ida, loveliest in all grace
Of movement, and the charm of married brows.'

"Dear mother Ida, harken ere I die.
He prest the blossom of his lips to mine,
And added 'This was cast upon the board,
When all the full-faced presence of the Gods
Ranged in the halls of Peleus; whereupon
Rose feud, with question unto whom 'twere due:

[121]

But light-foot Iris brought it yester-eve,
Delivering, that to me, by common voice
Elected umpire, Herè comes to-day,
Pallas and Aphroditè, claiming each
This meed of fairest. Thou, within the cave
Behind yon whispering tuft of oldest pine,
Mayst well behold them unbeheld, unheard
Hear all, and see thy Paris judge of Gods.'

"Dear mother Ida, harken ere I die.
It was the deep midnoon: one silvery cloud
Had lost his way between the piny sides
Of this long glen. Then to the bower they came,
Naked they came to that smooth-swarded bower,
And at their feet the crocus brake like fire,
Violet, amaracus, and asphodel,
Lotos and lilies: and a wind arose,
And overhead the wandering ivy and vine,
This way and that, in many a wild festoon
Ran riot, garlanding the gnarled boughs
With bunch and berry and flower thro' and thro'.

"O mother Ida, harken ere I die.
On the tree-tops a crested peacock lit,
And o'er him flow'd a golden cloud, and lean'd
Upon him, slowly dropping fragrant dew.
Then first I heard the voice of her, to whom
Coming thro' Heaven, like a light that grows
Larger and clearer, with one mind the Gods
Rise up for reverence. She to Paris made
Proffer of royal power, ample rule
Unquestion'd, overflowing revenue

[122]

Wherewith to embellish state, 'from many a vale
And river-sunder'd champaign clothed with corn,
Or labour'd mine undrainable of ore.
Honour,' she said, 'and homage, tax and toll,
From many an inland town and haven large,
Mast-throng'd beneath her shadowing citadel
In glassy bays among her tallest towers.'

"O mother Ida, harken ere I die.
Still she spake on and still she spake of power,
'Which in all action is the end of all;
Power fitted to the season; wisdom-bred
And throned of wisdom—from all neighbour crowns
Alliance and allegiance, till thy hand
Fail from the sceptre-staff. Such boon from me,
From me, Heaven's Queen, Paris, to thee king-born,
A shepherd all thy life but yet king-born,
Should come most welcome, seeing men, in power
Only, are likest gods, who have attain'd
Rest in a happy place and quiet seats
Above the thunder, with undying bliss
In knowledge of their own supremacy.'

"Dear mother Ida, harken ere I die.
She ceased, and Paris held the costly fruit
Out at arm's-length, so much the thought of power
Flatter'd his spirit; but Pallas where she stood
Somewhat apart, her clear and bared limbs
O'erthwarted with the brazen-headed spear
Upon her pearly shoulder leaning cold,
The while, above, her full and earnest eye
Over her snow-cold breast and angry cheek
Kept watch, waiting decision, made reply.

" 'Self-reverence, self-knowledge, self-control,
These three alone lead life to sovereign power.
Yet not for power (power of herself
Would come uncall'd for) but to live by law,
Acting the law we live by without fear;
And, because right is right, to follow right
Were wisdom in the scorn of consequence.'

"Dear mother Ida, harken ere I die.
Again she said: 'I woo thee not with gifts.
Sequel of guerdon could not alter me
To fairer. Judge thou me by what I am,
So shalt thou find me fairest.
               Yet, indeed,
If gazing on divinity disrobed
Thy mortal eyes are frail to judge of fair,
Unbias'd by self-profit, oh! rest thee sure
That I shall love thee well and cleave to thee,
So that my vigour, wedded to thy blood,
Shall strike within thy pulses, like a God's,
To push thee forward thro' a life of shocks,
Dangers, and deed, until endurance grow
Sinew'd with action, and the full-grown will,
Circled thro' all experiences, pure law
Commeasure perfect freedom.'
              "Here she ceas'd,
And Paris ponder'd, and I cried, 'O Paris,
Give it to Pallas!' but he heard me not,
Or hearing would not hear me, woe is me!

"O mother Ida, many-fountain'd Ida,
Dear mother Ida, harken ere I die.

[124]

Idalian Aphroditè beautiful,
Fresh as the foam, new-bathed in Paphian wells,
With rosy slender fingers backward drew
From her warm brows and bosom her deep hair
Ambrosial, golden round her lucid throat
And shoulder: from the violets her light foot
Shone rosy-white, and o'er her rounded form
Between the shadows of the vine-bunches
Floated the glowing sunlights, as she moved.

"Dear mother Ida, harken ere I die.
She with a subtle smile in her mild eyes,
The herald of her triumph, drawing nigh
Half-whisper'd in his ear, 'I promise thee
The fairest and most loving wife in Greece,'
She spoke and laugh'd: I shut my sight for fear:
But when I look'd, Paris had raised his arm,
And I beheld great Herè's angry eyes,
As she withdrew into the golden cloud,
And I was left alone within the bower;
And from that time to this I am alone,
And I shall be alone until I die.

"Yet, mother Ida, harken ere I die.
Fairest—why fairest wife? am I not fair?
My love hath told me so a thousand times.
Methinks I must be fair, for yesterday,
When I past by, a wild and wanton pard,
Eyed like the evening star, with playful tail
Crouch'd fawning in the weed. Most loving is she?
Ah me, my mountain shepherd, that my arms
Were wound about thee, and my hot lips prest

Close, close to thine in that quick-falling dew
Of fruitful kisses, thick as Autumn rains
Flash in the pools of whirling Simois.

   "O mother, hear me yet before I die.
They came, they cut away my tallest pines,
My tall dark pines, that plumed the craggy ledge
High over the blue gorge, and all between
The snowy peak and snow-white cataract
Foster'd the callow eaglet—from beneath
Whose thick mysterious boughs in the dark morn
The panther's roar came muffled, while I sat
Low in the valley. Never, never more
Shall lone Oenone see the morning mist
Sweep thro' them; never see them overlaid
With narrow moon-lit slips of silver cloud,
Between the loud stream and the trembling stars.

   "O mother, hear me yet before I die.
I wish that somewhere in the ruin'd folds,
Among the fragments tumbled from the glens,
Or the dry thickets, I could meet with her,
The Abominable, that uninvited came
Into the fair Peleïan banquet-hall,
And cast the golden fruit upon the board,
And bred this change; that I might speak my mind,
And tell her to her face how much I hate
Her presence, hated both of Gods and men.

   "O mother, hear me yet before I die.
Hath he not sworn his love a thousand times,
In this green valley, under this green hill,

[126]

Ev'n on this hand, and sitting on this stone?
Seal'd it with kisses? water'd it with tears?
O happy tears, and how unlike to these!
O happy Heaven, how canst thou see my face?
O happy earth, how canst thou bear my weight?
O death, death, death, thou ever-floating cloud,
There are enough unhappy on this earth,
Pass by the happy souls, that love to live:
I pray thee, pass before my light of life,
And shadow all my soul, that I may die.
Thou weightest heavy on the heart within,
Weigh heavy on my eyelids: let me die.

    "O mother, hear me yet before I die.
I will not die alone, for fiery thoughts
Do shape themselves within me, more and more,
Whereof I catch the issue, as I hear
Dead sounds at night come from the inmost hills,
Like footsteps upon wool.   I dimly see
My far-off doubtful purpose, as a mother
Conjectures of the features of her child
Ere it is born: her child!—a shudder comes
Across me: never child be born of me,
Unblest, to vex me with his father's eyes!

    "O mother, hear me yet before I die.
Hear me, O earth.   I will not die alone,
Lest their shrill happy laughter come to me
Walking the cold and starless road of Death
Uncomforted, leaving my ancient love
With the Greek woman.   I will rise and go
Down into Troy, and ere the stars come forth

Talk with the wild Cassandra, for she says
A fire dances before her, and a sound
Rings ever in her ears of armed men.
What this may be I know not, but I know
That, wheresoe'er I am by night and day,
All earth and air seem only burning fire."

ALFRED, LORD TENNYSON

THE LOTOS-EATERS

"COURAGE!" he said, and pointed toward the land,
  "This mounting wave will roll us shoreward soon."
In the afternon they came unto a land
In which it seemed always afternoon.
All round the coast the languid air did swoon,
Breathing like one that hath a weary dream.
Full-faced above the valley stood the moon;
And like a downward smoke, the slender stream
Along the cliff to fall and pause and fall did seem.

A land of streams! some, like a downward smoke,
Slow-dropping veils of thinnest lawn, did go;
And some thro' wavering lights and shadows broke,
Rolling a slumbrous sheet of foam below.
They saw the gleaming river seaward flow
From the inner land: far off, three mountain-tops,
Three silent pinnacles of aged snow,
Stood sunset-flush'd: and, dew'd with showery drops,
Up-clomb the shadowy pine above the woven copse.

The charmed sunset linger'd low adown
In the red West: thro' mountain clefts the dale
Was seen far inland, and the yellow down
Border'd with palm, and many a winding vale

And meadow, set with slender galingale;
A land where all things always seem'd the same!
And round about the keel with faces pale,
Dark faces pale against that rosy flame,
The mild-eyed melancholy Lotos-eaters came.

Branches they bore of that enchanted stem,
Laden with flower and fruit, whereof they gave
To each, but whoso did receive of them,
And taste, to him the gushing of the wave
Far far away did seem to mourn and rave
On alien shores; and if his fellow spake,
His voice was thin, as voices from the grave;
And deep-asleep he seem'd, yet all awake,
And music in his ears his beating heart did make.

They sat them down upon the yellow sand,
Between the sun and moon upon the shore;
And sweet it was to dream of Fatherland,
Of child, and wife, and slave; but evermore
Most weary seem'd the sea, weary the oar,
Weary the wandering fields of barren foam.
Then some one said, "We will return no more";
And all at once they sang, "Our island home
Is far beyond the wave; we will no longer roam."

CHORIC SONG

I

There is sweet music here that softer falls
Than petals from blown roses on the grass,

Or night-dews on still waters between walls
Of shadowy granite, in a gleaming pass;
Music that gentlier on the spirit lies,
Than tir'd eyelids upon tir'd eyes;
Music that brings sweet sleep down from the blissful skies.
Here are cool mosses deep,
And thro' the moss the ivies creep,
And in the stream the long-leaved flowers weep,
And from the craggy ledge the poppy hangs in sleep.

II

Why are we weigh'd upon with heaviness,
And utterly consumed with sharp distress,
While all things else have rest from weariness?
All things have rest: why should we toil alone,
We only toil, who are the first of things,
And make perpetual moan,
Still from one sorrow to another thrown:
Nor ever fold our wings,
And cease from wanderings,
Nor steep our brows in slumber's holy balm;
Nor harken what the inner spirit sings,
"There is no joy but calm!"
Why should we only toil, the roof and crown of things?

III

Lo! in the middle of the wood,
The folded leaf is woo'd from out the bud
With winds upon the branch, and there
Grows green and broad, and takes no care,
Sun-steep'd at noon, and in the moon
Nightly dew-fed; and turning yellow

Falls, and floats adown the air.
Lo! sweeten'd with the summer light,
The full-juiced apple, waxing over-mellow,
Drops in a silent autumn night.
All its allotted length of days,
The flower ripens in its place,
Ripens and fades, and falls, and hath no toil,
Fast-rooted in the fruitful soil.

IV

Hateful is the dark-blue sky,
Vaulted o'er the dark-blue sea.
Death is the end of life; ah, why
Should life all labour be?
Let us alone. Time driveth onward fast,
And in a little while our lips are dumb.
Let us alone. What is it that will last?
All things are taken from us, and become
Portions and parcels of the dreadful Past.
Let us alone. What pleasure can we have
To war with evil? Is there any peace
In ever climbing up the climbing wave?
All things have rest, and ripen toward the grave
In silence; ripen, fall and cease:
Give us long rest or death, dark death, or dreamful **ease**.

V

How sweet it were, hearing the downward stream,
With half-shut eyes ever to seem
Falling asleep in a half-dream!
To dream and dream, like yonder amber light,
Which will not leave the myrrh-bush on the height;

To hear each other's whisper'd speech;
Eating the Lotos day by day,
To watch the crisping ripples on the beach,
And tender curving lines of creamy spray;
To lend our hearts and spirits wholly
To the influence of mild-minded melancholy;
To muse and brood and live again in memory,
With those old faces of our infancy
Heap'd over with a mound of grass,
Two handfuls of white dust, shut in an urn of brass!

VI

Dear is the memory of our wedded lives,
And dear the last embraces of our wives
And their warm tears: but all hath suffer'd change:
For surely now our household hearths are cold.
Our sons inherit us: our looks are strange:
And we should come like ghosts to trouble joy.
Or else the island princes over-bold
Have eat our substance, and the minstrel sings
Before them of the ten-years' war in Troy,
And our great deeds, as half-forgotten things.
Is there confusion in the little isle?
Let what is broken so remain.
The Gods are hard to reconcile:
'Tis hard to settle order once again.
There *is* confusion worse than death,
Trouble on trouble, pain on pain,
Long labour unto aged breath,
Sore tasks to hearts worn out with many wars
And eyes grown dim with gazing on the pilot-stars.

VII

But, propt on beds of armaranth and moly,
How sweet (while warm airs lull us, blowing lowly)
With half-dropt eyelids still,
Beneath a heaven dark and holy,
To watch the long bright river drawing slowly
His waters from the purple hill—
To hear the dewy echoes calling
From cave to cave thro' the thick-twined vine—
To watch the emerald-colour'd water falling
Thro' many a wov'n acanthus-wreath divine!
Only to hear and see the far-off sparkling brine,
Only to hear were sweet, stretch'd out beneath the pine.

VIII

The Lotos blooms below the barren peak:
The Lotos blows by every winding creek:
All day the wind breathes low with mellower tone:
Thro' every hollow cave and alley lone
Round and round the spicy downs the yellow Lotos-dust
    is blown.
We have had enough of action, and of motion we,
Roll'd to starboard, roll'd to larboard, when the surge was
    seething free,
Where the wallowing monster spouted his foam-fountains
    in the sea.
Let us swear an oath, and keep it with an equal mind,
In the hollow Lotos-land to live and lie reclined
On the hills like Gods together, careless of mankind.
For they lie beside their nectar, and the bolts are hurl'd
Far below them in the valleys, and the clouds are lightly
    curl'd

Round their golden houses, girdled with the gleaming
  world:
Where they smile in secret, looking over wasted lands,
Blight and famine, plague and earthquake, roaring deeps
  and fiery sands,
Clanging fights, and flaming towns, and sinking ships,
  and praying hands.
But they smile, they find a music centred in a doleful song
Steaming up, a lamentation and an ancient tale of wrong,
Like a tale of little meaning tho' the words are strong;
Chanted from an ill-used race of men that cleave the soil,
Sow the seed, and reap the harvest with enduring toil,
Storing yearly little dues of wheat, and wine and oil;
Till they perish and they suffer—some, 'tis whisper'd—
  down in hell
Suffer endless anguish, others in Elysian valleys dwell,
Resting weary limbs at last on beds of asphodel.
Surely, surely, slumber is more sweet than toil, the shore
Than labour in the deep mid-ocean, wind and wave and
  oar;
Oh rest ye, brother mariners, we will not wander more.

ALFRED, LORD TENNYSON

ULYSSES

IT LITTLE profits that an idle king,
By this still hearth, among these barren crags,
Matched with an aged wife, I mete and dole
Unequal laws unto a savage race,
That hoard, and sleep, and feed, and know not me.
I cannot rest from travel. I will drink
Life to the lees. All times I have enjoyed
Greatly, have suffered greatly, both with those
That loved me, and alone; on shore, and when
Through scudding drifts the rainy Hyades
Vexed the dim sea. I am become a name;
For always roaming with a hungry heart
Much have I seen and known; cities of men,
And manners, climates, councils, governments,
Myself not least, but honoured of them all,—
And drunk delight of battle with my peers,
Far on the ringing plains of windy Troy.
I am a part of all that I have met;
Yet all experience is an arch where-through
Gleams that untravelled world whose margin fades
Forever and forever when I move.
How dull it is to pause, to make an end,
To rust unburnished, not to shine in use!
As though to breathe were life! Life piled on life

Were all too little, and of one to me
Little remains; but every hour is saved
From that eternal silence, something more,
A bringer of new things; and vile it were
For some three suns to store and hoard myself,
And this gray spirit yearning in desire
To follow knowledge like a sinking star,
Beyond the utmost bound of human thought.

   This is my son, mine own Telemachus,
To whom I leave the sceptre and the isle—
Well-loved of me, discerning to fulfil
This labour, by slow prudence to make mild
A rugged people, and through soft degrees
Subdue them to the useful and the good.
Most blameless is he, centred in the sphere
Of common duties, decent not to fail
In offices of tenderness, and pay
Meet adoration to my household gods,
When I am gone. He works his work, I mine.

   There lies the port; the vessel puffs her sail;
There gloom the dark, broad seas. My mariners,
Souls that have toiled, and wrought, and thought with
      me,—
That ever with a frolic welcome took
The thunder and the sunshine, and opposed
Free hearts, free foreheads—you and I are old;
Old age hath yet his honour and his toil;
Death closes all. But something ere the end,
Some work of noble note, may yet be done,
Not unbecoming men that strove with gods.
The lights begin to twinkle from the rocks;
The long day wanes; the slow moon climbs; the deep

Moans round with many voices. Come, my friends,
'Tis not too late to seek a newer world.
Push off, and sitting well in order smite
The sounding furrows; for my purpose holds
To sail beyond the sunset, and the baths
Of all the western stars, until I die.
It may be that the gulfs will wash us down.
It may be we shall touch the Happy Isles,
And see the great Achilles, whom we knew.
Though much is taken, much abides; and though
We are not now that strength which in old days
Moved earth and heaven, that which we are, we are;
   One equal temper of heroic hearts,
Made weak by time and fate, but strong in will
To strive, to seek, to find, and not to yield.

ALFRED, LORD TENNYSON

PHILOMELA

Hark! ah, the Nightingale!
    The tawny-throated!
Hark! from that moonlit cedar what a burst!
What triumph! hark—what pain!

O Wanderer from a Grecian shore,
Still, after many years, in distant lands,
Still nourishing in thy bewilder'd brain
That wild, unquench'd, deep-sunken, old-world pain—
Say, will it never heal?
And can this fragrant lawn
With its cool trees, and night,
And the sweet tranquil Thames,
And moonshine, and the dew,
To thy rack'd heart and brain
Afford no balm?
Dost thou to-night behold
Here, through the moonlight on this English grass,
The unfriendly palace in the Thracian wild?
Dost thou again peruse
With hot cheeks and sear'd eyes
The too clear web, and thy dumb Sister's shame?
Dost thou once more assay
Thy flight, and feel come over thee,

Poor Fugitive, the feathery change
Once more, and once more seem to make resound
With love and hate, triumph and agony,
Lone Daulis, and the high Cephissian vale?
Listen, Eugenia—
How thick the bursts come crowding through the leaves!
Again—thou hearest!
Eternal Passion!
Eternal Pain!

MATTHEW ARNOLD

PALLADIUM

SET where the upper streams of Simoïs flow
  Was the Palladium, high 'mid rock and wood;
And Hector was in Ilium, far below,
And fought, and saw it not—but there it stood!

It stood, and sun and moonshine rained their light
On the pure columns of its glen-built hall,
Backward and forward rolled the waves of fight
Round Troy—but while this stood, Troy could not fall.

So, in its lovely moonlight, lives the soul.
Mountains surround it and sweet virgin air;
Cold plashing, past it, crystal waters roll;
We visit it by moments, ah, too rare!

We shall renew the battle in the plain
Tomorrow; red with blood will Xanthus be;
Hector and Ajax will be there again,
Helen will come upon the wall to see.

Then we shall rust in shade, or shine in strife,
And fluctuate 'twixt blind hopes and blind despairs,
And fancy that we put forth all our life,
And never know how with the soul it fares.

Still doth the soul, from its lone fastness high,
Upon our life a ruling effluence send.
And when it fails, fight as we will, we die;
And while it lasts, we cannot wholly end.

MATTHEW ARNOLD

TO A FRIEND

Who prop, thou ask'st, in these bad days, my mind?—
He much, the old man, who, clearest-souled of men,
Saw The Wide Prospect, and the Asian Fen,
And Tmolus hill, and Smyrna bay, though blind.
Much he, whose friendship I not long since won,
That halting slave, who in Nicopolis
Taught Arrian, when Vespasian's brutal son
Cleared Rome of what most shamed him. But be his
My special thanks, whose even-balanced soul,
From first youth tested up to extreme old age,
Business could not make dull, nor passion wild;
Who saw life steadily, and saw it whole;
The mellow glory of the Attic stage,
Singer of sweet Colonus, and its child.

MATTHEW ARNOLD

DOVER BEACH

THE SEA is calm tonight,
   The tide is full, the moon lies fair
Upon the Straits—on the French coast the light
Gleams and is gone; the cliffs of England stand,
Glimmering and vast, out in the tranquil bay.
Come to the window; sweet is the night-air!
Only, from the long line of spray
Where the sea meets the moon-blanched land,
Listen! you hear the grating roar
Of pebbles which the waves draw back, and fling,
At their return, up the high strand,
Begin, and cease, and then again begin,
With tremulous cadence slow, and bring
The eternal note of sadness in.

Sophocles long ago
Heard it on the Aegean, and it brought
Into his mind the turbid ebb and flow
Of human misery; we
Find also in the sound a thought,
Hearing it by this distant northern sea.

The Sea of Faith
Was once, too, at the full, and round earth's shore

Lay like the folds of a bright girdle furled,
But now I only hear
Its melancholy, long, withdrawing roar,
Retreating, to the breath
Of the night-wind, down the vast edges drear
And naked shingles of the world.

Ah, love, let us be true
To one another! for the world, which seems
To lie before us like a land of dreams,
So various, so beautiful, so new,
Hath really neither joy, nor love, nor light,
Nor certitude, nor peace, nor help for pain;
And we are here as on a darkling plain
Swept with confused alarms of struggle and flight,
Where ignorant armies clash by night.

MATTHEW ARNOLD

ANTIGONE

THE BURIED voice bespake Antigone.

"O Sister! couldst thou know, as thou wilt know,
The bliss above, the reverence below,
Enkindled by thy sacrifice for me;
Thou wouldst at once with holy ecstasy
Give thy warm limbs into the yearning earth.
Sleep, Sister! for Elysium's dawning birth,—
And faith will fill thee with what is to be!
Sleep, for the Gods are watching over thee!
Thy dream will steer thee to perform their will,
As silently their influence they instil.
O Sister! in the sweetness of thy prime,
Thy hand has plucked the bitter flower of death
But this will dower thee with Elysian breath,
That fade into a never-fading clime.
Dear to the Gods are those that do like thee
A solemn duty! for the tyranny
Of kings is feeble to the soul that dares
Defy them to fulfil its sacred cares:
And weak against a mighty will are men.
O, Torch between two brothers! in whose gleam
Our slaughtered House doth shine as one again.
Tho' severed by the sword; now may thy dream

Kindle desire in thee for us, and thou,
Forgetting not thy lover and his vow,
Leaving no human memory forgot,
Shalt cross, not unattended, the dark stream
Which runs by thee in sleep and ripples not.
The large stars glitter thro' the anxious night,
And the deep sky broods low to look at thee:
The air is hush'd and dark o'er land and sea,
And all is waiting for the morrow light:
So do thy kindred spirits wait for thee.
O Sister! soft as the downward rill,
Will those first daybeams from the distant hill
Fall on the smoothness of thy placid brow,
Like this calm sweetness breathing thro' me now:
And when the fated sounds shall wake thine eyes,
Wilt thou, confiding in the supreme will,
In all thy maiden steadfastness arise,
Firm to obey and earnest to fulfil;
Remembering this night thou didst not sleep,
And this same brooding sky beheld thee creep,
Defiant of unnatural decree,
To where I lay upon the outcast land;
Before the iron gates upon the plain;
A wretched, graveless ghost, whose wailing chill
Came to thy darkened door imploring thee;
Yearning for burial like my brother slain;—
And all was dared for love and piety!
This thought will nerve again thy virgin hand
To serve its purpose and its destiny."

She woke, they led her forth and all was still.

GEORGE MEREDITH

[147]

THE GARDEN OF
PROSERPINE

Here, where the world is quiet;
   Here, where all trouble seems
Dead winds' and spent waves' riot
   In doubtful dreams of dreams:
I watch the green field growing
For reaping folk and sowing,
For harvest-time and mowing,
   A sleepy world of streams.

I am tired of tears and laughter,
   And men that laugh and weep;
Of what may come hereafter
   For men that sow to reap:
I am weary of days and hours,
Blown buds of barren flowers,
Desires and dreams and powers
   And everything but sleep.

Here life has death for neighbor;
   And far from eye or ear
Wan waves and wet winds labor,
   Weak ships and spirits steer;

[148]

They drive adrift, and whither
They wot not who make thither.—
But no such winds blow hither,
   And no such things grow here;

No growth of moor or coppice,
   No heather-flower or vine:
But bloomless buds of poppies,
   Green grapes of Proserpine,—
Pale beds of blowing rushes,
Where no leaf blooms or blushes
Save this whereout she crushes
   For dead men deadly wine.

Pale, without name or number,
   In fruitless fields of corn,
They bow themselves and slumber
   All night till light is born;
And like a soul belated,
In hell and heaven unmated,
By cloud and mist abated
   Comes out of darkness morn.

Though one were strong as seven,
   He too with death shall dwell,
Nor wake with wings in heaven,
   Nor weep for pains in hell;
Though one were fair as roses,
His beauty clouds and closes;
And well though love reposes,
   In the end it is not well.

Pale, beyond porch and portal,
    Crowned with calm leaves, she stands
Who gathers all things mortal
    With cold immortal hands:
Her languid lips are sweeter
Than Love's, who fears to greet her,
To men that mix and meet her
    From many times and lands.

She waits for each and other,
    She waits for all men born;
Forgets the earth her mother,
    The life of fruits and corn;
And spring and seed and swallow
Take wing for her and follow
Where summer song rings hollow
    And flowers are put to scorn.

There go the loves that wither,
    The old loves with wearier wings;
And all dead years draw thither,
    And all disastrous things;
Dead dreams of days forsaken,
Blind buds that snows have shaken,
Wild leaves that winds have taken,
    Red strays of ruined springs.

We are not sure of sorrow,
    And joy was never sure;
Today will die tomorrow;
    Time stoops to no man's lure;

[150]

And Love, grown faint and fretful,
With lips but half regretful
Sighs, and with eyes forgetful
   Weeps that no loves endure.

From too much love of living,
   From hope and fear, set free,
We thank with brief thanksgiving
   Whatever gods may be,
That no life lives for ever;
That dead men rise up never;
That even the weariest river
   Winds somewhere safe to sea.

Then star nor sun shall waken,
   Nor any change of light;
Nor sound of waters shaken,
   Nor any sound or sight;
Nor wintry leaves nor vernal,
Nor days, nor things diurnal:
Only the sleep eternal
   In an eternal night.

ALGERNON CHARLES SWINBURNE

CLEON

"As certain also of your own poets have said."

CLEON the poet (from the the sprinkled isles,
   Lily on lily, that o'erlace the sea,
And laugh their pride when the light wave lisps Greece)—
To Protos in his Tyranny: much health!

They give thy letter to me, even now:
I read and seem as if I heard thee speak.
The master of thy galley still unlades
Gift after gift; they block my court at last
And pile themselves along its portico
Royal with sunset, like a thought of thee:
And one white she-slave from the group dispersed
Of black and white slaves (like the chequer-work
Pavement, at once my nation's work and gift,
Now covered with this settle-down of doves),
One lyric woman, in her crocus vest
Woven of sea-wools, with her two white hands
Commends to me the strainer and the cup
Thy lip hath bettered ere it blesses mine.

Well-counselled, king, in thy munificence!
For so shall men remark, in such an act
Of love for him whose song gives life its joy,

Thy recognition of the use of life;
Nor call thy spirit barely adequate
To help on life in straight ways, broad enough
For vulgar souls, by ruling and the rest.
Thou, in the daily building of thy tower,—
Whether in fierce and sudden spasms of toil,
Or through dim lulls of unapparent growth,
Or when the general work 'mid good acclaim
Climbed with the eye to cheer the architect,—
Didst ne'er engage in work for mere work's sake—
Hadst ever in thy heart the luring hope
Of some eventual rest a-top of it,
Whence, all the tumult of the building hushed,
Thou first of men mightst look out to the East:
The vulgar saw thy tower, thou sawest the sun.
For this, I promise on thy festival
To pour libation, looking o'er the sea,
Making this slave narrate thy fortunes, speak
Thy great words, and describe thy royal face—
Wishing thee wholly where Zeus lives the most,
Within the eventual element of calm.

  Thy letter's first requirement meets me here.
It is as thou hast heard: in one short life
I, Cleon, have effected all those things
Thou wonderingly dost enumerate.
That epos on thy hundred plates of gold
Is mine,—and also mine the little chant,
So sure to rise from every fishing-bark
When, lights at prow, the seamen haul their net.
The image of the sun-god on the phare,
Men turn from the sun's self to see, is mine;

The Pœcile, o'er-storied its whole length,
As thou didst hear, with painting, is mine too.
I know the true proportions of a man
And woman also, not observed before;
And I have written three books on the soul,
Proving absurd all written hitherto,
And putting us to ignorance again.
For music,—why, I have combined the moods,
Inventing one. In brief, all arts are mine;
Thus much the people know and recognise,
Throughout our seventeen islands. Marvel not.
We of these latter days, with greater mind
Than our forerunners, since more composite,
Look not so great, beside their simple way,
To a judge who only sees one way at once,
One mind-point and no other at a time,—
Compares the small part of a man of us
With some whole man of the heroic age,
Great in his way—not ours, nor meant for ours.
And ours is greater, had we skill to know:
For, what we call this life of men on earth,
This sequence of the soul's achievements here
Being, as I find much reason to conceive,
Intended to be viewed eventually
As a great whole, not analysed to parts,
But each part having reference to all,—
How shall a certain part, pronounced complete,
Endure effacement by another part?
Was the thing done?—then, what's to do again?
See, in the chequered pavement opposite,
Suppose the artist made a perfect rhomb,
And next a lozenge, then a trapezoid—

He did not overlay them, superimpose
The new upon the old and blot it out,
But laid them on a level in his work,
Making at last a picture; there it lies.
So, first the perfect separate forms were made,
The portions of mankind; and after, so,
Occurred the combination of the same.
For where had been a progress, otherwise?
Mankind, made up of all the single men,—
In such a synthesis the labour ends.
Now mark me! those divine men of old time
Have reached, thou sayest well, each at one point
The outside verge that rounds our faculty;
And where they reached, who can do more than reach?
It takes but little water just to touch
At some one point the inside of a sphere,
And, as we turn the sphere, touch all the rest
In due succession: but the finer air
Which not so palpably nor obviously,
Though no less universally, can touch
The whole circumference of that emptied sphere,
Fills it more fully than the water did;
Holds thrice the weight of water in itself
Resolved into a subtler element.
And yet the vulgar call the sphere first full
Up to the visible height—and after, void;
Not knowing air's more hidden properties.
And thus our soul, misknown, cries out to Zeus
To vindicate his purpose in our life:
Why stay we on the earth unless to grow?
Long since, I imaged, wrote the fiction out,
That he or other god descended here

And, once for all, showed simultaneously
What, in its nature, never can be shown,
Piecemeal or in succession;—showed, I say,
The worth both absolute and relative
Of all his children from the birth of time,
His instruments for all appointed work.
I now go on to image,—might we hear
The judgment which should give the due to each,
Show where the labour lay and where the ease,
And prove Zeus' self, the latent everywhere!
This is a dream:—but no dream, let us hope,
That years and days, the summers and the springs,
Follow each other with unwaning powers.
The grapes which dye thy wine are richer far,
Through culture, than the wild wealth of the rock;
The suave plum than the savage-tasted drupe;
The pastured honey-bee drops choicer sweet;
The flowers turn double, and the leaves turn flowers;
That young and tender crescent-moon, thy slave,
Sleeping above her robe as buoyed by clouds,
Refines upon the women of my youth.
What, and the soul alone deteriorates?
I have not chanted verse like Homer, no—
Nor swept string like Terpander, no—nor carved
And painted men like Phidias and his friend:
I am not great as they are, point by point.
But I have entered into sympathy
With these four, running these into one soul,
Who, separate, ignored each other's art.
Say, is it nothing that I know them all?
The wild flower was the larger; I have dashed
Rose-blood upon its petals, prick'd its cup's

Honey with wine, and driven its seed to fruit,
And show a better flower if not so large:
I stand myself. Refer this to the gods
Whose gift alone it is! which, shall I dare
(All pride apart) upon the absurd pretext
That such a gift by chance lay in my hand,
Discourse of lightly or depreciate?
It might have fallen to another's hand: what then?
I pass too surely: let at least truth stay!

And next, of what thou followest on to ask.
This being with me as I declare, O king,
My works, in all these varicoloured kinds,
So done by me, accepted so by men—
Thou askest, if (my soul thus in men's hearts)
I must not be accounted to attain
The very crown and proper end of life?
Inquiring thence how, now life closeth up,
I face death with success in my right hand:
Whether I fear death less than dost thyself
The fortunate of men? "For" (writest thou)
"Thou leavest much behind, while I leave nought.
Thy life stays in the poems men shall sing,
The pictures men shall study; while my life,
Complete and whole now in its power and joy,
Dies altogether with my brain and arm,
Is lost indeed; since, what survives myself?
The brazen statue to o'erlook my grave,
Set on the promontory which I named.
And that—some supple courtier of my heir
Shall use its robed and sceptred arm, perhaps,

To fix the rope to, which best drags it down.
I go then: triumph thou, who dost not go!"

Nay, thou art worthy of hearing my whole mind.
Is this apparent, when thou turn'st to muse
Upon the scheme of earth and man in chief,
That admiration grows as knowledge grows?
That imperfection means perfection hid,
Reserved in part, to grace the after-time?
If, in the morning of philosophy,
Ere aught had been recorded, nay perceived,
Thou, with the light now in thee, couldst have looked
On all earth's tenantry, from worm to bird,
Ere man, her last, appeared upon the stage—
Thou wouldst have seen them perfect, and deduced
The perfectness of others yet unseen.
Conceding which,—had Zeus then questioned thee
"Shall I go on a step, improve on this,
Do more for visible creatures than is done?"
Thou wouldst have answered, "Ay, by making each
Grow conscious in himself—by that alone.
All's perfect else: the shell sucks fast the rock,
The fish strikes through the sea, the snake both swims
And slides, forth range the beasts, the birds take flight,
Till life's mechanics can no further go—
And all this joy in natural life is put
Like fire from off thy finger into each,
So exquisitely perfect is the same.
But 'tis pure fire, and they mere matter are;
It has them, not they it: and so I choose
For man, thy last premeditated work
(If I might add a glory to the scheme)

[158]

That a third thing should stand apart from both,
A quality arise within the soul,
Which, intro-active, made to supervise
And feel the force it has, may view itself,
And so be happy." Man might live at first
The animal life: but is there nothing more?
In due time, let him critically learn
How he lives; and, the more he gets to know
Of his own life's adaptabilities,
The more joy-giving will his life become.
Thus man, who hath this quality, is best.

But thou, king, hadst more reasonably said:
"Let progress end at once,—man make no step
Beyond the natural man, the better beast,
Using his senses, not the sense of sense."
In man there's failure, only since he left
The lower and inconscious forms of life.
We called it an advance, the rendering plain
Man's spirit might grow conscious of man's life,
And, by new lore so added to the old,
Take each step higher over the brute's head.
This grew the only life, the pleasure-house,
Watch-tower and treasure-fortress of the soul,
Which whole surrounding flats of natural life
Seemed only fit to yield subsistence to;
A tower that crowns a country. But alas!
The soul now climbs it just to perish there!
For thence we have discovered ('tis no dream—
We know this, which we had not else perceived)
That there 's a world of capability
For joy, spread round about us, meant for us,

Inviting us; and still the soul craves all,
And still the flesh replies, "Take no jot more
Than ere thou clombst the tower to look abroad!
Nay, so much less, as that fatigue has brought
Deduction to it." We struggle—fain to enlarge
Our bounded physical recipiency,
Increase our power, supply fresh oil to life,
Repair the waste of age and sickness. No,
It skills not: life 's inadequate to joy,
As the soul sees joy, tempting life to take.
They praise a fountain in my garden here
Wherein a Naiad sends the water-bow
Thin from her tube; she smiles to see it rise.
What if I told her, it is just a thread
From that great river which the hills shut up,
And mock her with my leave to take the same?
The artificer has given her one small tube
Past power to widen or exchange—what boots
To know she might spout oceans if she could?
She cannot lift beyond her first thin thread,
And so a man can use but a man's joy
While he sees God's. Is it for Zeus to boast,
"See, man, how happy I live, and despair—
That I may be still happier—for thy use!"
If this were so, we could not thank our Lord,
As hearts beat on to doing: 'tis not so—
Malice it is not. Is it carelessness?
Still, no. If care—where is the sign, I ask—
And get no answer: and agree in sum,
O king, with thy profound discouragement,
Who seest the wider but to sigh the more.
Most progress is most failure! thou sayest well.

[160]

The last point now:—thou dost except a case—
Holding joy not impossible to one
With artist-gifts—to such a man as I—
Who leave behind me living works indeed;
For, such a poem, such a painting lives.
What? dost thou verily trip upon a word,
Confound the accurate view of what joy is
 (Caught somewhat clearer by my eyes than thine)
With feeling joy? confound the knowing how
And showing how to live (my faculty)
With actually living?—Otherwise
Where is the artist's vantage o'er the king?
Because in my great epos I display
How divers men young, strong, fair, wise, can act—
Is this as though I acted? if I paint,
Carve the young Phœbus, am I therefore young?
Methinks I'm older that I bowed myself
The many years of pain that taught me art!
Indeed, to know is something, and to prove
How all this beauty might be enjoyed, is more:
But, knowing nought, to enjoy is something too.
Yon rower with the moulded muscles there,
Lowering the sail, is nearer it than I.
I can write love-odes—thy fair slave 's an ode.
I get to sing of love, when grown too grey
For being beloved: she turns to that young man,
The muscles all a-ripple on his back.
I know the joy of kingship: well—thou art king!

  "But," sayest thou— (and I marvel, I repeat,
To find thee tripping on a mere word) "what
Thou writest, paintest, stays: that does not die:

Sappho survives, because we sing her songs,
And Æschylus, because we read his plays!"
Why, if they live still, let them come and take
Thy slave in my despite, drink from thy cup,
Speak in my place. Thou diest while I survive?
Say rather that my fate is deadlier still,
In this, that every day my sense of joy
Grows more acute, my soul (intensified
By power and insight) more enlarged, more keen;
While every day my hairs fall more and more,
My hand shakes, and the heavy years increase—
The horror quickening still from year to year,
The consummation coming past escape
When I shall know most, and yet least enjoy—
When all my works wherein I prove my worth,
Being present still to mock me in men's mouths,
Alive still, in the praise of such as thou,
I, I the feeling, thinking, acting man,
The man who loved his life so over-much,
Sleep in my urn. It is so horrible,
I dare at times imagine to my need
Some future state revealed to us by Zeus,
Unlimited in capability
For joy, as this is in desire for joy,
—To seek which, the joy-hunger forces us:
That, stung by straitness of our life, made strait
On purpose to make prized the life at large—
Freed by the throbbing impulse we call death,
We burst there as the worm into the fly,
Who, while a worm still, wants his wings. But no!
Zeus has not yet revealed it; and alas,
He must have done so, were it possible!

Live long and happy, and in that thought die:
Glad for what was! Farewell. And for the rest,
I cannot tell thy messenger aright
Where to deliver what he bears of thine
To one called Paulus; we have heard his fame
Indeed, if Christus be not one with him—
I know not, nor am troubled much to know.
Thou canst not think a mere barbarian Jew,
As Paulus proves to be, one circumcised,
Hath access to a secret shut from us?
Thou wrongest our philosophy, O king,
In stooping to inquire of such an one,
As if his answer could impose at all!
He writeth, doth he? well, and he may write.
Oh, the Jew findeth scholars! certain slaves
Who touched on this same isle, preached him and Christ;
And (as I gathered from a bystander)
Their doctrine could be held by no sane man.

ROBERT BROWNING

BIBLICAL AND MEDIEVAL THEMES

MUTABILITIE

I

WHEN I bethinke me on that speech while-ere,
      Of *Mutability,* and well it way:
Me seemes, that though she all unworthy were
Of the Heav'ns Rule; yet very sooth to say,
In all things else she beares the greatest sway.
Which makes me loath this state of life so tickle,
And love of things so vaine to cast away;
      Whose flowring pride, so fading and so fickle,
Short *Time* shall soon cut down with his consuming sickle.

II

Then gin I thinke on that which Nature sayd,
      Of that same time when no more *Change* shall be,
But stedfast rest of all things firmely stayd
Upon the pillours of Eternity,
That is contrayr to *Mutabilitie:*
For, all that moveth, doth in *Change* delight:
But thence-forth all shall rest eternally
      With Him that is the God of Sabbaoth hight:
O that great Sabbaoth God, graunt me that Sabaoths
      sight.

EDMUND SPENSER

WHEN IN THE CHRONICLE
OF WASTED TIME

WHEN in the chronicle of wasted time
   I see descriptions of the fairest wights,
And beauty making beautiful old rime
In praise of ladies dead and lovely knights,
Then, in the blazon of sweet beauty's best,
Of hand, of foot, of lip, of eye, of brow,
I see their antique pen would have expressed
Even such a beauty as you master now.
So all their praises are but prophecies
Of this our time, all you prefiguring;
And, for they looked but with divining eyes,
They had not skill enough your worth to sing;
   For we, which now behold these present days,
   Have eyes to wonder, but lack tongues to praise.

WILLIAM SHAKESPEARE

THOU HAST MADE ME

Thou hast made me, and shall thy work decay?
    Repair me now, for now mine end doth haste,
I run to death, and death meets me as fast,
And all my pleasures are like yesterday;
I dare not move my dim eyes any way,
Despair behind, and death before doth cast
Such terror, and my feeble flesh doth waste
By sin in it, which it t'wards hell doth weigh;
Only thou art above, and when towards thee
By thy leave I can look, I rise again;
But our old subtle foe so tempteth me,
That not one hour my self I can sustain;
Thy Grace may wing me to prevent his art,
And thou like Adamant draw mine iron heart.

JOHN DONNE

AT THE ROUND EARTH'S IMAGIN'D CORNERS

At the round earth's imagin'd corners, blow
Your trumpets, Angels, and arise, arise
From death, you numberless infinities
Of souls, and to your scattered bodies go,
All whom the flood did, and fire shall o'erthrow,
All whom war, dearth, age, agues, tyrannies,
Despair, law, chance, hath slain, and you whose eyes,
Shall behold God, and never taste death's woe.
But let them sleep, Lord, and me mourn a space,
For, if above all these, my sins abound,
'Tis late to ask abundance of thy grace,
When we are there; here on this lowly ground,
Teach me how to repent; for that's as good
As if thou hadst seal'd my pardon, with thy blood.

JOHN DONNE

DEATH, BE NOT PROUD

DEATH be not proud, though some have called thee
    Mighty and dreadful, for, thou art not so,
For, those, whom thou think'st, thou dost overthrow,
Die not, poor death, nor yet canst thou kill me.
From rest and sleep, which but thy pictures be,
Much pleasure, then from thee, much more must flow,
And soonest our best men with thee do go,
Rest of their bones, and souls delivery.
Thou art slave to Fate, Chance, kings, and desperate men,
And dost with poison, war, and sickness dwell,
And poppy or charms can make us sleep as well,
And better then thy stroke; why swell'st thou then;
One short sleep past, we wake eternally,
And death shall be no more; death, thou shalt die.

                                        JOHN DONNE

BATTER MY HEART, THREE PERSON'D GOD

BATTER my heart, three person'd God; for, you
As yet but knock, breathe, shine, and seek to mend,
That I may rise, and stand, o'erthrow me, and bend
Your force, to break, blow, burn and make me new.
I, like an usurpt town, to another due,
Labour to admit you, but Oh, to no end,
Reason your viceroy in me, me should defend,
But is captiv'd, and proves weak or untrue.
Yet dearly I love you, and would be loved fain,
But am betroth'd unto your enemy:
Divorce me, untie, or break that knot again;
Take me to you, imprison me, for I
Except you enthrall me, never shall be free,
Nor ever chaste, except you ravish me.

                                        JOHN DONNE

A HYMN TO GOD THE FATHER

Wilt thou forgive that sin, where I begun,
   Which is my sin, though it were done before?
Wilt thou forgive those sins through which I run
   And do run still, though still I do deplore?
      When thou hast done, thou hast not done,
            For I have more.

Wilt thou forgive that sin, by which I'have won
   Others to sin, and made my sin their door?
Wilt thou forgive that sin which I did shun
   A year or two, but wallowed in a score?
      When thou hast done, thou hast not done,
            For I have more.

I have a sin of fear that when I have spun
   My last thread, I shall perish on the shore;
Swear by thyself that at my Death, thy Son
   Shall shine as he shines now, and heretofore;
      And having done that, thou hast done,
            I fear no more.

JOHN DONNE

JORDAN

Who says that fictions only and false hair
    Become a verse? Is there in truth no beauty?
Is all good structure in a winding stair?
May no lines pass, except they do their duty
    Not to a true, but painted chair?

Is it no verse, except enchanted groves
And sudden arbors shadow course-spun lines?
Must purling streams refresh a lover's loves?
Must all be veil'd, while he that reads, divines,
    Catching the sense at two removes?

Shepherds are honest people; let them sing:
Riddle who list, for me, and pull for Prime:
I envy no man's nightingale or spring;
Nor let them punish me with loss of rhyme,
    Who plainly say, *My God, My King.*

GEORGE HERBERT

THE COLLAR

I STRUCK the board, and cried, No more.
                              I will abroad.
What? shall I ever sigh and pine?
My lines and life are free; free as the road,
     Loose as the wind, as large as store.
              Shall I be still in suit?
     Have I no harvest but a thorn
     To let me blood, and not restore
What I have lost with cordial fruit?
                              Sure there was wine
     Before my sighs did dry it: there was corn
     Before my tears did drown it.
     Is the year only lost to me?
          Have I no bays to crown it?
No flowers, no garlands gay? all blasted?
                              All wasted?
     Not so, my heart: but there is fruit,
                    And thou hast hands.
     Recover all thy sigh-blown age
On double pleasures: leave thy cold dispute
Of what is fit, and not; forsake thy cage,
                    Thy rope of sands,

Which petty thoughts have made, and made to thee
    Good cable, to enforce and draw,
                    And be thy law,
    While thou didst wink and wouldst not see.
                Away; take heed:
                I will abroad.
Call in thy death's head there: tie up thy fears.
                He that forbears
        To suit and serve his need,
                Deserves his load.
But as I rav'd and grew more fierce and wild
                At every word,
Methought I heard one calling, *Child:*
    And I replied, *My Lord.*

                            GEORGE HERBERT

THE PULLEY

WHEN God at first made man,
    Having a glass of blessings standing by,
"Let us," said He, "pour on him all we can;
Let the world's riches, which dispersèd lie,
    Contract into a span."

    So strength first made a way,
Then beauty flowed, then wisdom, honour, pleasure;
    When almost all was out, God made a stay,
Perceiving that, alone of all His treasure,
    Rest in the bottom lay.

    "For if I should," said He,
"Bestow this jewel also on My creature,
    He would adore My gifts instead of Me,
And rest in Nature, not the God of Nature:
    So both should losers be.

    "Yet let him keep the rest,
But keep them with repining restlessness;
    Let him be rich and weary, that at least,
If goodness lead him not, yet weariness
    May toss him to My breast."

                                    GEORGE HERBERT

AARON

Holiness on the head,
　Light and perfections on the breast,
Harmonious bells below, raising the dead
　To lead them unto life and rest.
　　Thus are true Aarons drest.

Profaneness in my head,
　Defects and darkness in my breast,
A noise of passions ringing me for dead
　Unto a place where is no rest.
　　Poor priest thus am I drest.

Only another head
　I have, another heart and breast,
Another music, making live not dead,
　Without whom I could have no rest:
　　In him I am well drest.

Christ is my only head,
　My alone only heart and breast,
My only music, striking me ev'n dead;
　That to the old man I may rest,
　　And be in him new drest.

So holy in my head,
   Perfect and light in my dear breast,
My doctrine tun'd by Christ, (who is not dead,
   But lives in me while I do rest)
      Come people; Aaron's drest.

GEORGE HERBERT

EASTER WINGS

Lord, who createdst man in wealth and store,
   Though foolishly he lost the same,
    Decaying more and more,
      Till he became
        Most poor:
        With thee
      O let me rise
    As larks, harmoniously,
  And sing this day thy victories:
Then shall the fall further the flight in me.

My tender age in sorrow did begin:
   And still with sicknesses and shame
    Thou did so punish sin,
      That I became
        Most thin.
        With thee
      Let me combine,
    And feel this day thy victory:
  For, if I imp my wing on thine,
Affliction shall advance the flight in me.

GEORGE HERBERT

DISCIPLINE

THROW away thy rod.
  Thow away thy wrath:
      O my God,
Take the gentle path.

For my heart's desire
Unto thine is bent:
      I aspire
To a full consent.

Not a word or look
I affect to own,
      But by book,
And thy book alone.

Though I fail, I weep:
Though I halt in pace,
      Yet I creep
To the throne of grace.

Then let wrath remove;
Love will do the deed:
      For with love
Stony hearts will bleed.

Love is swift of foot;
Love's a man of war,
        And can shoot,
And can hit from far.

Who can scrape his bow?
That which wrought on thee,
        Brought thee low,
Needs must work on me.

Throw away thy rod;
Though man frailties hath,
        Thou art God:
Throw away thy wrath.

GEORGE HERBERT

VIRTUE

Sweet day, so cool, so calm, so bright,
The bridal of the earth and sky:
The dew shall weep thy fall tonight;
       For thou must die.

Sweet rose, whose hue angry and brave
Bids the rash gazer wipe his eye:
Thy root is ever in its grave,
       And thou must die.

Sweet spring, full of sweet days and roses,
A box where sweets compacted lie;
My music shows ye have your closes,
       And all must die.

Only a sweet and virtuous soul,
Like season'd timber, never gives;
But though the whole world turn to coal,
       Then chiefly lives.

GEORGE HERBERT

LOVE

Love bade me welcome: yet my soul drew back,
        Guilty of dust and sin.
But quick-ey'd Love, observing me grow slack
        From my first entrance in,
Drew nearer to me, sweetly questioning,
        If I lack'd any thing.

A guest, I answer'd, worthy to be here:
        Love said, you shall be he.
I the unkind, ungrateful? Ah my dear,
        I cannot look on thee.
Love took my hand, and smiling did reply,
        Who made the eyes but I?

Truth Lord, but I have marr'd them: let my shame
        Go where it doth deserve.
And know you not, says Love, who bore the blame?
        My dear, then I will serve.
You must sit down, says Love, and taste my meat:
        So I did sit and eat.

GEORGE HERBERT

THE RETREAT

Happy those early days! when I
    Shin'd in my Angel-infancy.
Before I understood this place
Appointed for my second race,
Or taught my soul to fancy ought
But a white, Celestial thought,
When yet I had not walkt above
A mile, or two, from my first love,
And looking back (at that short space,)
Could see a glimpse of his bright-face;
When on some *gilded Cloud,* or *flower*
My gazing soul would dwell an hour,
And in those weaker glories spy
Some shadows of eternity;
Before I taught my tongue to wound
My Conscience with a sinful sound,
Or had the black art to dispense
A sev'ral sin to ev'ry sense,
But felt through all this fleshy dress
Bright *shoots* of everlastingness.
    O how I long to travel back
And tread again that ancient track!
That I might once more reach that plain,
Where first I left my glorious train,

From whence th' Enlightened spirit sees
That shady City of Palm trees;
But (ah!) my soul with too much stay
Is drunk, and staggers in the way.
Some men a forward motion love,
But I by backward steps would move,
And when this dust falls to the urn
In that state I came return.

HENRY VAUGHAN

MAN

Weighing the steadfastness and state
    Of some mean things which here below reside,
Where birds like watchful clocks the noiseless date
    And intercourse of times divide,
Where bees at night get home and hive, and flowers
        Early, as well as late,
Rise with the sun, and set in the same bowers;

I would (said I) my God would give
The staidness of these things to man! for these
To his divine appointments ever cleave,
    And no new business breaks their peace;
The birds nor sow, nor reap, yet sup and dine,
        The flowers without clothes live,
Yet *Solomon* was never drest so fine.

Man hath still either toys, or care,
He hath no root, nor to one place is tied,
But ever restless and irregular
    About this earth doth run and ride,
He knows he hath a home, but scarce knows where,
        He says it is so far
That he hath quite forgot how to go there.

He knocks at all doors, strays and roams,
Nay hath not so much wit as some stones have
Which in the darkest nights point to their homes,
    By some hid sense their maker gave;
Man is the shuttle, to whose winding quest
        And passage through these looms
God order'd motion, but ordain'd no rest.

HENRY VAUGHAN

THE WORLD

I saw Eternity the other night,
   Like a great Ring of pure and endless light,
      All calm, as it was bright;
And round beneath it, Time, in hours, days, years,
      Driven by the spheres,
Like a vast shadow moved, in which the world
      And all her train were hurled.
The doting lover in his quaintest strain
      Did there complain;
Near him, his lute, his fancy, and his flights,
      Wit's four delights;
With gloves, and knots the silly snares of pleasure,
      Yet his dear treasure,
All scattered lay, while he his eyes did pour
      Upon a flower.

The darksome statesman, hung with weights and woe,
Like a thick midnight-fog, moved there so slow,
      He did nor stay, nor go;
Condemning thoughts (like sad eclipses) scowl
      Upon his soul,
And clouds of crying witnesses without
      Pursued him with one shout.

Yet digged the mole, and lest his ways be found,
    Worked under ground,
Where he did clutch his prey. But one did see
    That policy;
Churches and altars fed him; perjuries
    Were gnats and flies;
It rained about him blood and tears; but he
    Drank them as free.

The fearful miser on a heap of rust
Sat pining all his life there, did scarce trust
    His own hands with the dust,
Yet would not place one piece above, but lives
    In fear of thieves.
Thousands there were as frantic as himself,
    And hugged each one his pelf;
The downright epicure placed heaven in sense,
    And scorned pretence;
While others, slipt into a wide excess,
    Said little less;
The weaker sort slight, trivial wares enslave,
    Who think them brave,
And poor, despisèd Truth sat counting by
    Their victory.

Yet some, who all this while did weep and sing,
And sing and weep, soared up into the Ring;
    But most would use no wing.
O fools, said I, thus to prefer dark night
    Before true light!
To live in grots and caves, and hate the day
    Because it shows the way,

The way, which from this dead and dark abode
    Leads up to God,
A way where you might tread the sun, and be
    More bright than he!
But, as I did their madness so discuss,
    One whispered thus,
"This Ring the Bridegroom did for none provide,
    But for his bride."

HENRY VAUGHAN

THE WATERFALL

WITH what deep murmurs through times silent stealth
   Doth thy transparent, cool and watery wealth
         Here flowing fall,
         And chide, and call,
As if his liquid, loose retinue stayed
Lingering, and were of this steep place afraid,
         The common pass
         Where, clear as glass,
         All must descend
         Not to an end:
But quickened by this deep and rocky grave,
Rise to a longer course more bright and brave.

         Dear stream! dark bank, where often I
         Have sate, and pleas'd my pensive eye,
         Why, since each drop of thy quick store
         Runs thither, whence it flow'd before,
         Should poor souls fear a shade or night,
         Who came (sure) from a sea of light?
         Or since those drops are all sent back
         So sure to thee, that none doth lack,
         Why should frail flesh doubt any more
         That what God takes, he'll not restore?

O useful Element and clear!
My sacred wash and cleanser here,
My first consigner unto those
Fountains of life, where the Lamb goes!
What sublime truths, and wholesome themes,
Lodge in thy mystical, deep streams!
Such as dull man can never find
Unless that Spirit lead his mind,
Which first upon thy face did move,
And hatch'd all with his quickening love.
As this loud brook's incessant fall
In streaming rings restagnates all,
Which reach by course the bank, and then
Are no more seen, just so pass men.
O my invisible estate,
My glorious liberty, still late!
Thou art the Channel my soul seeks,
Not this with Cataracts and Creeks.

HENRY VAUGHAN

ON HIS BLINDNESS

WHEN I consider how my light is spent
    Ere half my days, in this dark world and wide,
  And that one talent which is death to hide,
  Lodged with me useless, though my soul more bent
To serve therewith my Maker, and present
  My true account, lest He returning chide;
  "Doth God exact day-labour, light denied?"
  I fondly ask: but Patience, to prevent
That murmur, soon replies: "God doth not need
  Either man's work, or His own gifts; who best
  Bear His mild yoke, they serve Him best: His state
Is kingly; thousands at His bidding speed,
  And post o'er land and ocean without rest;
  They also serve who only stand and wait."

JOHN MILTON

TO THE LORD GENERAL
CROMWELL

CROMWELL, our chief of men, who through a cloud
    Not of war only, but detractions rude,
  Guided by faith and matchless fortitude,
  To peace and truth thy glorious way hast ploughed,
And on the neck of crownèd Fortune proud
  Hast reared God's trophies, and His work pursued,
  While Darwen stream with blood of Scots imbrued,
  And Dunbar field resounds thy praises loud,
And Worcester's laureat wreath. Yet much remains
  To conquer still; peace hath her victories
  No less renowned than war: new foes arise,
Threatening to bind our souls with secular chains:
  Help us to save free conscience from the paw
  Of hireling wolves, whose gospel is their maw.

JOHN MILTON

ON THE LATE MASSACRE
IN PIEDMONT

A VENGE, O Lord, thy slaughtered saints, whose bones
  Lie scattered on the Alpine mountains cold;
 Even them who kept thy truth so pure of old,
 When all our fathers worshipped stocks and stones,
Forget not: in thy book record their groans
 Who were thy sheep, and in their ancient fold
 Slain by the bloody Piedmontese, that rolled
 Mother with infant down the rocks. Their moans
The vales redoubled to the hills, and they
 To Heav'n. Their martyred blood and ashes sow
 O'er all th' Italian fields, where still doth sway
The triple tyrant; that from these may grow
 A hundred fold, who, having learned thy way,
 Early may fly the Babylonian woe.

          JOHN MILTON

ON THE MORNING
OF CHRIST'S NATIVITY

I

THIS is the month, and this the happy morn,
Wherein the Son of heav'n's eternal king,
Of wedded Maid, and Virgin Mother born,
Our great redemption from above did bring;
For so the holy sages once did sing,
That He our deadly forfeit should release,
And with His Father work us a perpetual peace.

II

That glorious form, that light unsufferable,
And that far-beaming blaze of majesty,
Wherewith He wont at heav'n's high council-table
To sit the midst of Trinal Unity,
He laid aside; and here with us to be,
Forsook the courts of everlasting day,
And chose with us a darksome house of mortal clay.

III

Say, heav'nly Muse, shall not thy sacred vein
Afford a present to the Infant God?
Hast thou no verse, no hymn, or solemn strain,

To welcome Him to this His new abode,
Now while the heav'n by the sun's team untrod,
 Hath took no print of the approaching light,
And all the spangled host keep watch in squadrons
  bright?

IV

See how from far upon the eastern road
The star-led wizards haste with odours sweet:
O, run; prevent them with thy humble ode,
And lay it lowly at His blessèd feet;
Have thou the honour first thy Lord to greet,
 And join thy voice unto the Angel quire,
From out His secret altar touched with hallowed fire.

THE HYMN

I

IT was the winter wild,
While the heaven-born child
 All meanly wrapt in the rude manger lies;
Nature in awe to Him
Had dofft her gaudy trim,
 With her great Master so to sympathize:
It was no season then for her
To wanton with the sun, her lusty paramour.

II

Only with speeches fair
She woos the gentle air
 To hide her guilty front with innocent snow,
And on her naked shame,

Pollute with sinful blame;
    The saintly veil of maiden white to throw,
Confounded that her Maker's eyes
Should look so near upon her foul deformities.

III

But He her fears to cease,
Sent down the meek-eyed Peace;
    She, crowned with olive green, came softly sliding
Down through the turning sphere
His ready harbinger,
    With turtle wing the amorous clouds dividing;
And waving wide her myrtle wand,
She strikes a universal peace through sea and land.

IV

Nor war, or battle's sound
Was heard the world around:
    The idle spear and shield were high up hung,
The hookèd chariot stood
Unstained with hostile blood,
    The trumpet spake not to the armèd throng,
And kings sat still with awful eye,
As if they surely knew their sov'reign Lord was by.

V

But peaceful was the night,
Wherein the Prince of light
    His reign of peace upon the earth began:
The winds with wonder whist

Smoothly the waters kist,
   Whispering new joys to the mild ocean,
Who now hath quite forgot to rave,
While birds of calm sit brooding on the charmèd wave.

VI

The stars with deep amaze
Stand fixed in steadfast gaze,
   Bending one way their precious influence,
And will not take their flight,
For all the morning light,
   Or Lucifer that often warned them thence;
But in their glimmering orbs did glow,
Until their Lord Himself bespake, and bid them go.

VII

And though the shady gloom
Had given day her room,
   The sun himself withheld his wonted speed,
And hid his head for shame,
As his inferior flame
   The new enlightened world no more should need;
He saw a greater sun appear
Than his bright throne, or burning axletree could bear.

VIII

The shepherds on the lawn,
Or ere the point of dawn,
   Sat simply chatting in a rustic row;
Full little thought they then

That the mighty Pan
  Was kindly come to live with them below;
Perhaps their loves, or else their sheep,
Was all that did their silly thoughts so busy keep.

IX

When such music sweet
Their hearts and ears did greet,
  As never was by mortal finger strook,
Divinely-warbled voice
Answering the stringèd noise,
  As all their souls in blissful rapture took:
The air such pleasure loth to lose,
With thousand echoes still prolongs each heavenly close.

X

Nature that heard such sound,
Beneath the hollow round
  Of Cynthia's seat, the airy region thrilling,
Now was almost won
To think her part was done,
  And that her reign had here its last fulfilling;
She knew such harmony alone
Could hold all heaven and earth in happier union.

XI

At last surrounds their sight
A globe of circular light,
  That with long beams the shamefaced night arrayed;
The helmèd Cherubim,

And sworded Seraphim,
   Are seen in glittering ranks with wings displayed,
Harping in loud and solemn quire,
With unexpressive notes to Heaven's new-born Heir.

XII

Such music (as 'tis said)
Before was never made,
   But when of old the sons of morning sung,
While the Creator great
His constellations set,
   And the well-balanced world on hinges hung,
And cast the dark foundations deep,
And bid the welt'ring waves their oozy channel keep.

XIII

Ring out, ye crystal spheres,
Once bless our human ears,
   If ye have power to touch our senses so;
And let your silver chime
Move in melodious time,
   And let the base of heav'n's deep organ blow;
And with your ninefold harmony
Make up full concert to th' angelic symphony.

XIV

For if such holy song
Inwrap our fancy long,
   Time will run back, and fetch the age of gold,
And speckled Vanity

Will sicken soon and die,
  And leprous Sin will melt from earthly mould;
And Hell itself will pass away,
And leave her dolorous mansions to the peering day.

XV

Yea Truth and Justice then
Will down return to men,
  Orbed in a rainbow; and, like glories wearing,
Mercy will sit between,
Throned in celestial sheen,
  With radiant feet the tissued clouds down steering:
And heav'n, as at some festival,
Will open wide the gates of her high palace hall.

XVI

But wisest Fate says No,
This must not yet be so,
  The Babe yet lies in smiling infancy,
That on the bitter cross
Must redeem our loss;
  So both Himself and us to glorify;
Yet first to those ychained in sleep,
The wakeful trump of doom must thunder through the
    deep;

XVII

With such a horrid clang
As on mount Sinai rang,
  While the red fire, and smouldering clouds out brake:
The agèd earth aghast,

With terror of that blast,
   Shall from the surface to the centre shake;
When at the world's last session,
The dreadful Judge in middle air shall spread His throne.

XVIII

And then at last our bliss
Full and perfect is,
   But now begins; for from this happy day
The old Dragon under ground
In straiter limits bound,
   Not half so far casts his usurpèd sway,
And wroth to see his kingdom fail,
Swinges the scaly horror of his folded tail.

XIX

The oracles are dumb,
No voice or hideous hum
   Runs through the archèd roof in words deceiving.
Apollo from his shrine
Can no more divine,
   With hollow shriek the steep of Delphos leaving.
No nightly trance, or breathèd spell
Inspires the pale-eyed priest from the prophetic cell.

XX

The lonely mountains o'er,
And the resounding shore,
   A voice of weeping heard and loud lament;
From haunted spring, and dale

Edged with poplar pale,
   The parting genius is with sighing sent;
With flower-inwoven tresses torn
The Nymphs in twilight shade of tangled thickets mourn.

XXI

In consecrated earth,
And on the holy hearth,
   The Lars, and Lemures moan with midnight plaint;
In urns, and altars round,
A drear and dying sound
   Affrights the Flamens at their service quaint;
And the chill marble seems to sweat,
While each peculiar Power foregoes his wonted seat.

XXII

Peor and Baälim
Forsake their temples dim,
   With that twice-battered God of Palestine;
And moonèd Ashtaroth,
Heav'n's queen and mother both,
   Now sits not girt with tapers' holy shine;
The Lybic Hammon shrinks his horn,
In vain the Tyrian maids their wounded Thammuz
   mourn,

XXIII

And sullen Moloch, fled,
Hath left in shadows dread
   His burning idol all of blackest hue;
In vain with cymbals' ring

They call the grisly king,
  In dismal dance about the furnace blue;
The brutish gods of Nile as fast,
Isis and Orus, and the dog Anubis haste.

XXIV

Nor is Osiris seen
In Memphian grove or green,
  Trampling the unshowered grass with lowings loud:
Nor can he be at rest
Within his sacred chest,
  Nought but profoundest hell can be his shroud;
In vain with timbrelled anthems dark
The sable-stoled sorcerers bear his worshipped ark.

XXV

He feels from Juda's land
The dreaded Infant's hand,
  The rays of Bethlehem blind his dusky eyn;
Nor all the gods beside,
Longer dare abide,
  Not Typhon huge ending in snaky twine:
Our Babe, to show His Godhead true,
Can in His swaddling bands control the damnèd crew.

XXVI

So, when the sun in bed,
Curtained with cloudy red,
  Pillows his chin upon an orient wave,
The flocking shadows pale

Troop to th' infernal jail,
  Each fettered ghost slips to his several grave;
And the yellow-skirted Fayes
Fly after the night-steeds, leaving their moon-loved maze.

XXVII

But see the Virgin blest
Hath laid her Babe to rest,
  Time is our tedious song should here have ending:
Heav'n's youngest teemèd star
Hath fixed her polished car,
  Her sleeping Lord with handmaid lamp attending;
And all about the courtly stable
Bright harnessed Angels sit in order serviceable.

JOHN MILTON

A SONG FOR ST. CECILIA'S DAY

NOVEMBER 22, 1687

FROM harmony, from heavenly harmony
    This universal frame began;
  When Nature underneath a heap
    Of jarring atoms lay,
    And could not heave her head,
The tuneful voice was heard from high,
    Arise, ye more than dead.

Then cold and hot and moist and dry
  In order to their stations leap,
    And Music's power obey.
From harmony, from heavenly harmony
    This universal frame began;
    From harmony to harmony
Through all the compass of the notes it ran,
The diapason closing full in Man.

What passion cannot Music raise and quell?
    When Jubal struck the chorded shell,
  His listening brethren stood around,
    And, wondering, on their faces fell
  To worship that celestial sound.

[208]

Less than a god they thought there could not dwell
    Within the hollow of that shell,
    That spoke so sweetly, and so well.
What passion cannot Music raise and quell?

    The trumpet's loud clangor
        Excites us to arms
    With shrill notes of anger
        And mortal alarms.
    The double, double, double beat
        Of the thundering drum
        Cries, hark! the foes come;
Charge, charge, 'tis too late to retreat!
        The soft complaining flute
        In dying notes discovers
        The woes of hopeless lovers,
Whose dirge is whispered by the warbling lute.

    Sharp violins proclaim
Their jealous pangs and desperation,
Fury, frantic indignation,
Depth of pains and height of passion,
        For the fair, disdainful dame.

But, oh! what art can teach,
What human voice can reach
        The sacred organ's praise?
    Notes inspiring holy love,
Notes that wing their heavenly ways
        To mend the choirs above.

Orpheus could lead the savage race,
And trees unrooted left their place,
    Sequacious of the lyre;
But bright Cecilia raised the wonder higher;
When to her organ vocal breath was given,
An angel heard, and straight appeared,
    Mistaking earth for heaven.

GRAND CHORUS

As from the power of sacred lays
    The spheres began to move,
And sung the great Creator's praise
    To all the blest above;
So when the last and dreadful hour
This crumbling pageant shall devour,
The trumpet shall be heard on high,
The dead shall live, the living die,
And Music shall untune the sky.

JOHN DRYDEN

THE LAMB

LITTLE Lamb, who made thee?
    Dost thou know who made thee?
Gave thee life and bid thee feed
By the stream and o'er the mead;
Gave thee clothing of delight,
Softest clothing, woolly, bright;
Gave thee such a tender voice,
Making all the vales rejoice?
    Little Lamb, who made thee?
    Dost thou know who made thee?

    Little Lamb, I'll tell thee;
    Little Lamb, I'll tell thee:
He is callèd by thy name,
For he calls himself a Lamb.
He is meek, and he is mild;
He became a little child.
I a child, and thou a lamb,
We are callèd by his name.
    Little Lamb, God bless thee!
    Little Lamb, God bless thee!

WILLIAM BLAKE

THE TIGER

Tiger! tiger! burning bright
   In the forests of the night,
What immortal hand or eye
Could frame thy fearful symmetry?

In what distant deeps or skies
Burned the fire of thine eyes?
On what wings dare he aspire?
What the hand dare seize the fire?

And what shoulder, and what art,
Could twist the sinews of thy heart?
And when thy heart began to beat,
What dread hand? and what dread feet?

What the hammer? what the chain?
In what furnace was thy brain?
What the anvil? what dread grasp
Dare its deadly terrors clasp?

When the stars threw down their spears,
And watered heaven with their tears,
Did he smile his work to see?
Did he who made the Lamb make thee?

WILLIAM BLAKE

Tiger! tiger! burning bright
In the forests of the night,
What immortal hand or eye
Dare frame thy fearful symmetry?

WILLIAM BLAKE

THE DIVINE IMAGE

To Mercy, Pity, Peace, and Love
   All pray in their distress;
And to these virtues of delight
Return their thankfulness.

For Mercy, Pity, Peace, and Love
Is God, our Father dear,
And Mercy, Pity, Peace, and Love
Is man, His child and care.

For Mercy has a human heart,
Pity a human face,
And Love, the human form divine,
And Peace, the human dress.

Then every man, of every clime,
That prays in his distress,
Prays to the human form divine,
Love, Mercy, Pity, Peace.

And all must love the human form,
In heathen, Turk, or Jew;
Where Mercy, Love, and Pity dwell
There God is dwelling too.

WILLIAM BLAKE

THE DESTRUCTION OF SENNACHERIB

THE ASSYRIAN came down like the wolf on the fold,
    And his cohorts were gleaming in purple and gold;
And the sheen of their spears was like stars on the sea,
When the blue wave rolls nightly on deep Galilee.

Like the leaves of the forest when Summer is green,
That host with their banners at sunset were seen:
Like the leaves of the forest when Autumn hath blown,
That host on the morrow lay wither'd and strown.

For the Angel of Death spread his wings on the blast,
And breathed in the face of the foe as he pass'd;
And the eyes of the sleepers wax'd deadly and chill,
And their hearts but once heaved, and for ever grew still!

And there lay the steed with his nostril all wide,
But through it there roll'd not the breath of his pride;
And the foam of his gasping lay white on the turf,
And cold as the spray of the rock-beating surf.

And there lay the rider distorted and pale,
With the dew on his brow, and the rust on his mail:
And the tents were all silent, the banner alone,
The lances unlifted, the trumpet unblown.

And the widows of Ashur are loud in their wail,
And the idols are broke in the temple of Baal;
And the might of the Gentile, unsmote by the sword,
Hath melted like snow in the glance of the Lord!

GEORGE GORDON, LORD BYRON

SONNET I, DIVINA COMMEDIA

O FT have I seen at some cathedral door
　　A laborer, pausing in the dust and heat,
　Lay down his burden, and with reverent feet
Enter, and cross himself, and on the floor
Kneel to repeat his paternoster o'er;
　　Far off the noises of the world retreat;
　　The loud vociferations of the street
Become an undistinguishable roar.

So, as I enter here from day to day,
　And leave my burden at this minster gate,
Kneeling in prayer, and not ashamed to pray,
　The tumult of the time disconsolate
To inarticulate murmurs dies away,
　While the eternal ages watch and wait.

HENRY WADSWORTH LONGFELLOW

THE EVE OF ST. AGNES

I

St. Agnes' Eve—Ah, bitter chill it was!
The owl, for all his feathers, was a-cold;
The hare limp'd trembling through the frozen grass,
And silent was the flock in woolly fold:
Numb were the Beadsman's fingers, while he told
His rosary, and while his frosted breath,
Like pious incense from a censer old,
Seem'd taking flight for heaven, without a death,
Past the sweet Virgin's picture, while his prayer he saith.

II

His prayer he saith, this patient, holy man;
Then takes his lamp, and riseth from his knees,
And back returneth, meagre, barefoot, wan,
Along the chapel aisle by slow degrees:
The sculptur'd dead, on each side, seem to freeze,
Emprison'd in black, purgatorial rails:
Knights, ladies, praying in dumb orat'ries,
He passeth by; and his weak spirit fails
To think how they may ache in icy hoods and mails.

III

Northward he turneth through a little door,
And scarce three steps, ere Music's golden tongue
Flatter'd to tears this aged man and poor;
But no—already had his deathbell rung:
The joys of all his life were said and sung:
His was harsh penance on St. Agnes' Eve:
Another way he went, and soon among
Rough ashes sat he for his soul's reprieve,
And all night kept awake, for sinners' sake to grieve.

IV

That ancient Beadsman heard the prelude soft;
And so it chanc'd, for many a door was wide,
From hurry to and fro. Soon, up aloft,
The silver, snarling trumpets 'gan to chide:
The level chambers, ready with their pride,
Were glowing to receive a thousand guests:
The carved angels, ever eager-eyed,
Star'd, where upon their heads the cornice rests,
With hair blown back, and wings put cross-wise on their
    breasts.

V

At length burst in the argent revelry,
With plume, tiara, and all rich array,
Numerous as shadows haunting faerily
The brain, new stuff'd, in youth, with triumphs gay
Of old romance. These let us wish away,
And turn, sole-thoughted, to one Lady there,
Whose heart had brooded, all that wintry day,
On love, and wing'd St. Agnes' saintly care,
As she had heard old dames full many times declare.

VI

They told her how, upon St. Agnes' Eve,
Young virgins might have visions of delight,
And soft adorings from their loves receive
Upon the honey'd middle of the night,
If ceremonies due they did aright;
As, supperless to bed they must retire,
And couch supine their beauties, lilly white;
Nor look behind, nor sideways, but require
Of Heaven with upward eyes for all that they desire.

VII

Full of this whim was thoughtful Madeline:
The music, yearning like a God in pain,
She scarcely heard: her maiden eyes divine,
Fix'd on the floor, saw many a sweeping train
Pass by—she heeded not at all: in vain
Came many a tiptoe, amorous cavalier,
And back retir'd; not cool'd by high disdain,
But she saw not: her heart was otherwhere:
She sigh'd for Agnes' dreams, the sweetest of the year.

VIII

She danc'd along with vague, regardless eyes,
Anxious her lips, her breathing quick and short:
The hallow'd hour was near at hand: she sighs
Amid the timbrels, and the throng'd resort
Of whispers in anger, or in sport;
'Mid looks of love, defiance, hate, and scorn,
Hoodwink'd with faery fancy; all amort,
Save to St. Agnes and her lambs unshorn,
And all the bliss to be before to-morrow morn.

IX

So, purposing each moment to retire,
She linger'd still. Meantime, across the moors,
Had come young Porphyro, with heart on fire
For Madeline. Beside the portal doors,
Buttress'd from moonlight, stands he, and implores
All saints to give him sight of Madeline,
But for one moment in the tedious hours,
That he might gaze and worship all unseen;
Perchance speak, kneel, touch, kiss—in sooth such things
    have been.

X

He ventures in: let no buzz'd whisper tell:
All eyes be muffled, or a hundred swords
Will storm his heart, Love's fev'rous citadel:
For him, those chambers held barbarian hordes,
Hyena foemen, and hot-blooded lords,
Whose very dogs would execrations howl
Against his lineage: not one breast affords
Him any mercy, in that mansion foul,
Save one old beldame, weak in body and in soul.

XI

Ah, happy chance! the aged creature came,
Shuffling along with ivory-headed wand,
To where he stood, hid from the torch's flame,
Behind a broad hall-pillar, far beyond
The sound of merriment and chorus bland:
He startled her; but soon she knew his face,
And grasped his fingers in her palsied hand,
Saying, "Mercy, Porphyro! hie thee from this place:
They are all here to-night, the whole blood-thirsty race!

XII

"Get hence! get hence! there's dwarfish Hildebrand;
He had a fever late, and in the fit
He cursed thee and thine, both house and land:
Then there's that old Lord Maurice, not a whit
More tame for his gray hairs—Alas me! flit!
Flit like a ghost away."—"Ah, Gossip dear,
We're safe enough; here in this arm-chair sit,
And tell me how"—"Good Saints! not here, not here;
Follow me, child, or else these stones will be thy bier."

XIII

He follow'd through a lowly arched way,
Brushing the cobwebs with his lofty plume,
And as she mutter'd "Well-a—well-a-day!"
He found him in a little moonlight room,
Pale, lattic'd, chill, and silent as a tomb.
"Now tell me where is Madeline," said he,
"O tell me, Angela, by the holy loom
Which none but secret sisterhood may see,
When they St. Agnes' wool are weaving piously."

XIV

"St. Agnes! Ah! it is St. Agnes' Eve—
Yet men will murder upon holy days:
Thou must hold water in a witch's sieve,
And be liege-lord of all the Elves and Fays,
To venture so: it fills me with amaze
To see thee, Porphyro!—St. Agnes' Eve!
God's help! my lady fair the conjuror plays
This very night: good angels her deceive!
But let me laugh awhile, I've mickle time to grieve."

[222]

XV

Feebly she laugheth in the languid moon,
While Porphyro upon her face doth look,
Like puzzled urchin on an aged crone
Who keepeth clos'd a wond'rous riddle-book,
As spectacled she sits in chimney nook.
But soon his eyes grew brilliant, when she told
His lady's purpose; and he scarce could brook
Tears, at the thought of those enchantments cold,
And Madeline asleep in lap of legends old.

XVI

Sudden a thought came like a full-blown rose,
Flushing his brow, and in his pained heart
Made purple riot: then doth he propose
A stratagem, that makes the beldame start:
"A cruel man and impious thou art:
Sweet lady, let her pray, and sleep, and dream
Alone with her good angels, far apart
From wicked men like thee. Go, go!—I deem
Thou canst not surely be the same that thou didst seem."

XVII

"I will not harm her, by all saints I swear,"
Quoth Porphyro: "O may I ne'er find grace
When my weak voice shall whisper its last prayer,
If one of her soft ringlets I displace,
Or look with ruffian passion in her face:
Good Angela, believe me by these tears;
Or I will, even in a moment's space,
Awake, with horrid shout, my foemen's ears,
And beard them, though they be more fang'd than wolves
    and bears."

XVIII

"Ah! why wilt thou affright a feeble soul?
A poor, weak, palsy-stricken, churchyard thing,
Whose passing-bell may ere the midnight toll;
Whose prayers for thee, each morn and evening,
Were never miss'd."—Thus plaining, doth she bring
A gentler speech from burning Porphyro;
So woful, and of such deep sorrowing,
That Angela gives promise she will do
Whatever he shall wish, betide her weal or woe.

XIX

Which was, to lead him, in close secrecy,
Even to Madeline's chamber, and there hide
Him in a closet, of such privacy
That he might see her beauty unespied,
And win perhaps that night a peerless bride,
While legion'd faeries pac'd the coverlet,
And pale enchantment held her sleepy-eyed.
Never on such a night have lovers met,
Since Merlin paid his Demon all the monstrous debt.

XX

"It shall be as thou wishest," said the Dame:
"All cates and dainties shall be stored there
Quickly on this feast-night: by the tambour frame
Her own lute thou wilt see: no time to spare,
For I am slow and feeble, and scarce dare
On such a catering trust my dizzy head.
Wait here, my child, with patience; kneel in prayer
The while: Ah! thou must needs the lady wed,
Or may I never leave my grave among the dead."

XXI

So saying, she hobbled off with busy fear.
The lover's endless minutes slowly pass'd;
The dame return'd, and whisper'd in his ear
To follow her; with aged eyes aghast
From fright of dim espial. Safe at last,
Through many a dusky gallery, they gain
The maiden's chamber, silken, hush'd, and chaste;
Where Porphyro took covert, pleas'd amain.
His poor guide hurried back with agues in her brain.

XXII

Her falt'ring hand upon the balustrade,
Old Angela was feeling for the stair,
When Madeline, St. Agnes' charmed maid,
Rose, like a mission'd spirit, unaware:
With silver taper's light, and pious care,
She turn'd, and down the aged gossip led
To a safe level matting. Now prepare,
Young Porphyro, for gazing on that bed;
She comes, she comes again, like ring-dove fray'd and fled.

XXIII

Out went the taper as she hurried in;
Its little smoke, in pallid moonshine, died:
She clos'd the door, she panted, all akin
To spirits of the air, and visions wide:
No uttered syllable, or, woe betide!
But to her heart, her heart was voluble,
Paining with eloquence her balmy side;
As though a tongueless nightingale should swell
Her throat in vain, and die, heart-stifled, in her dell.

XXIV

A casement high and triple-arch'd there was,
All garlanded with carven imag'ries
Of fruits, and flowers, and bunches of knot-grass,
And diamonded with panes of quaint device,
Innumerable of stains and splendid dyes,
As are the tiger-moth's deep-damask'd wings;
And in the midst, 'mong thousand heraldries,
And twilight saints, and dim emblazonings,
A shielded scutcheon blush'd with blood of queens and
    kings.

XXV

Full on this casement shone the wintry moon,
And threw warm gules on Madeline's fair breast,
As down she knelt for heaven's grace and boon;
Rose-bloom fell on her hands, together prest,
And on her silver cross soft amethyst,
And on her hair a glory, like a saint:
She seem'd a splendid angel, newly drest,
Save wings, for heaven:—Porphyro grew faint:
She knelt, so pure a thing, so free from mortal taint.

XXVI

Anon his heart revives: her vespers done,
Of all its wreathed pearls her hair she frees;
Unclasps her warmed jewels one by one;
Loosens her fragrant boddice; by degrees
Her rich attire creeps rustling to her knees:
Half-hidden, like a mermaid in sea-weed,
Pensive awhile she dreams awake, and sees,
In fancy, fair St. Agnes in her bed,
But dares not look behind, or all the charm is fled.

XXVII

Soon, trembling in her soft and chilly nest,
In sort of wakeful swoon, perplex'd she lay,
Until the poppied warmth of sleep oppress'd
Her soothed limbs, and soul fatigued away;
Flown, like a thought, until the morrow-day;
Blissfully haven'd both from joy and pain;
Clasp'd like a missal where swart Paynims pray;
Blinded alike from sunshine and from rain,
As though a rose should shut, and be a bud again.

XXVIII

Stol'n to this paradise, and so entranced,
Porphyro gazed upon her empty dress,
And listen'd to her breathing, if it chanced
To wake into a slumberous tenderness;
Which when he heard, that minute did he bless,
And breath'd himself: then from the closet crept,
Noiseless as fear in a wide wilderness,
And over the hush'd carpet, silent, stept,
And 'tween the curtains peep'd, where, lo!—how fast she
    slept.

XXIX

Then by the bed-side, where the faded moon
Made a dim, silver twilight, soft he set
A table, and, half anguish'd, threw thereon
A cloth of woven crimson, gold, and jet:—
O for some drowsy Morphean amulet!
The boisterous, midnight, festive clarion,
The kettle-drum, and far-heard clarinet,
Affray his ears, though but in dying tone:—
The hall door shuts again, and all the noise is gone.

XXX

And still she slept an azure-lidded sleep,
In blanched linen, smooth, and lavender'd,
While he from forth the closet brought a heap
Of candied apple, quince, and plum, and gourd;
With jellies soother than the creamy curd,
And lucent syrops, tinct with cinnamon;
Manna and dates, in argosy transferr'd
From Fez; and spiced dainties, every one,
From silken Samarcand to cedar'd Lebanon.

XXXI

These delicates he heap'd with glowing hand
On golden dishes and in baskets bright
Of wreathed silver: sumptuous they stand
In the retired quiet of the night,
Filling the chilly room with perfume light.—
"And now, my love, my seraph fair, awake!
Thou art my heaven, and I thine eremite:
Open thine eyes, for meek St. Agnes' sake,
Or I shall drowse beside thee, so my soul doth ache."

XXXII

Thus whispering, his warm, unnerved arm
Sank in her pillow. Shaded was her dream
By the dusk curtains:—'twas a midnight charm
Impossible to melt as iced stream:
The lustrous salvers in the moonlight gleam;
Broad golden fringe upon the carpet lies:
It seem'd he never, never could redeem
From such a stedfast spell his lady's eyes;
So mus'd awhile, entoil'd in woofed phantasies.

XXXIII

Awakening up, he took her hollow lute,—
Tumultuous,—and, in chords that tenderest be,
He play'd an ancient ditty, long since mute,
In Provence call'd, "La belle dame sans mercy:"
Close to her ear touching the melody;—
Wherewith disturb'd, she utter'd a soft moan:
He ceased—she panted quick—and suddenly
Her blue affrayed eyes wide open shone:
Upon his knees he sank, pale as smooth-sculptured stone.

XXXIV

Her eyes were open, but she still beheld,
Now wide awake, the vision of her sleep:
There was a painful change, that nigh expell'd
The blisses of her dream so pure and deep
At which fair Madeline began to weep,
And moan forth witless words with many a sigh;
While still her gaze on Porphyro would keep;
Who knelt, with joined hands and piteous eye,
Fearing to move or speak, she look'd so dreamingly.

XXXV

"Ah, Porphyro!" said she, "but even now
Thy voice was at sweet tremble in mine ear,
Made tuneable with every sweetest vow;
And those sad eyes were spiritual and clear:
How chang'd thou art! how pallid, chill, and drear!
Give me that voice again, my Porphyro,
Those looks immortal, those complainings dear!
Oh, leave me not in this eternal woe,
For if thou diest, my Love, I know not where to go."

XXXVI

Beyond a mortal man impassion'd far
At these voluptuous accents, he arose,
Ethereal, flush'd, and like a throbbing star
Seen mid the sapphire heaven's deep repose;
Into her dream he melted, as the rose
Blendeth its odour with the violet,—
Solution sweet: meantime the frost-wind blows
Like Love's alarum pattering the sharp sleet
Against the window-panes; St. Agnes' moon hath set.

XXXVII

'Tis dark: quick pattereth the flaw-blown sleet:
"This is no dream, my bride, my Madeline!"
'Tis dark: the iced gusts still rave and beat:
"No dream, alas! alas! and woe is mine!
Porphyro will leave me here to fade and pine.—
Cruel! what traitor could thee hither bring?
I curse not, for my heart is lost in thine,
Though thou forsakest a deceived thing;—
A dove forlorn and lost with sick unpruned wing."

XXXVIII

"My Madeline! sweet dreamer! lovely bride!
Say, may I be for aye thy vassal blest?
Thy beauty's shield, heart-shap'd and vermeil dyed?
Ah, silver shrine, here will I take my rest
After so many hours of toil and quest,
A famish'd pilgrim,—sav'd by miracle.
Though I have found, I will not rob thy nest
Saving of thy sweet self; if thou think'st well
To trust, fair Madeline, to no rude infidel.

[230]

XXXIX

"Hark! 'tis an elfin-storm from faery land,
Of haggard seeming, but a boon indeed:
Arise—arise! the morning is at hand;—
The bloated wassaillers will never heed:—
Let us away, my love, with happy speed;
There are no ears to hear, or eyes to see,—
Drown'd all in Rhenish and the sleepy mead:
Awake! arise! my love, and fearless be,
For o'er the southern moors I have a home for thee."

XL

She hurried at his words, beset with fears,
For there were sleeping dragons all around,
At glaring watch, perhaps, with ready spears—
Down the wide stairs a darkling way they found.—
In all the house was heard no human sound.
A chain-droop'd lamp was flickering by each door;
The arras, rich with horseman, hawk, and hound,
Flutter'd in the besieging wind's uproar;
And the long carpets rose along the gusty floor.

XLI

They glide, like phantoms, into the wide hall;
Like phantoms, to the iron porch, they glide;
Where lay the Porter, in uneasy sprawl,
With a huge empty flagon by his side:
The wakeful bloodhound rose, and shook his hide,
But his sagacious eye an inmate owns:
By one, and one, the bolts full easy slide;—
The chains lie silent on the footworn stones;—
The key turns, and the door upon its hinges groans.

XLII

And they are gone: aye, ages long ago
These lovers fled away into the storm.
That night the Baron dreamt of many a woe,
And all his warrior-guests, with shade and form
Of witch, and demon, and large coffin-worm,
Were long be-nightmar'd. Angela the old
Died palsy-twitch'd, with meagre face deform;
The Beadsman, after thousand aves told,
For aye unsought-for slept among his ashes cold.

JOHN KEATS

MORTE D'ARTHUR

So ALL day long the noise of battle roll'd
    Among the mountains by the winter sea,
Until King Arthur's table, man by man,
Had fallen in Lyonnesse about their lord,
King Arthur; then, because his wound was deep,
The bold Sir Bedivere uplifted him,
Sir Bedivere, the last of all his knights,
And bore him to a chapel nigh the field,
A broken chancel with a broken cross,
That stood on a dark strait of barren land.
On one side lay the ocean, and on one
Lay a great water, and the moon was full.
    Then spake King Arthur to Sir Bedivere:
"The sequel of to-day unsolders all
The goodliest fellowship of famous knights
Whereof this world holds record. Such a sleep
They sleep—the men I loved. I think that we
Shall never more, at any future time,
Delight our souls with talk of knightly deeds,
Walking about the gardens and the halls
Of Camelot, as in the days that were.
I perish by this people which I made,—
Tho' Merlin sware that I should come again
To rule once more—but let what will be, be,

I am so deeply smitten thro' the helm
That without help I cannot last till morn.
Thou therefore take my brand Excalibur,
Which was my pride; for thou rememberest how
In those old days, one summer noon, an arm
Rose up from out the bosom of the lake,
Clothed in white samite, mystic, wonderful,
Holding the sword—and how I row'd across
And took it, and have worn it, like a king;
And, wheresoever I am sung or told
In aftertime, this also shall be known.
But now delay not; take Excalibur,
And fling him far into the middle mere;
Watch what thou seest, and lightly bring me word."
   To him replied the bold Sir Bedivere:
"It is not meet, Sir King, to leave thee thus,
Aidless, alone, and smitten thro' the helm.
A little thing may harm a wounded man.
Yet I thy hest will all perform at full,
Watch what I see, and lightly bring thee word."
   So saying, from the ruin'd shrine he stept
And in the moon athwart the place of tombs,
Where lay the mighty bones of ancient men,
Old knights, and over them the sea-wind sang
Shrill, chill, with flakes of foam. He, stepping down
By zigzag paths and juts of pointed rock,
Came on the shining levels of the lake.
   There drew he forth the brand Excalibur,
And o'er him, drawing it, the winter moon,
Brightening the skirts of a long cloud, ran forth
And sparkled keen with frost against the hilt;
For all the haft twinkled with diamond sparks,

[234]

Myriads of topaz-lights, and jacinth-work
Of subtlest jewelry. He gazed so long
That both his eyes were dazzled, as he stood,
This way and that dividing the swift mind,
In act to throw; but at the last it seem'd
Better to leave Excalibur conceal'd
There in the many-knotted water-flags,
That whistled stiff and dry about the marge.
So strode he back slow to the wounded king.
　　Then spake King Arthur to Sir Bedivere:
"Hast thou perform'd my mission which I gave?
What is it thou hast seen, or what hast heard?"
　　And answer made the bold Sir Bedivere:
"I heard the ripple washing in the reeds,
And the wild water lapping on the crag."
　　To whom replied King Arthur, faint and pale:
"Thou hast betray'd thy nature and thy name,
Not rendering true answer, as beseem'd
Thy fealty, nor like a noble knight;
For surer sign had follow'd, either hand,
Or voice, or else a motion of the mere.
This is a shameful thing for men to lie.
Yet now, I charge thee, quickly go again
As thou art lief and dear, and do the thing
I bade thee, watch, and lightly bring me word."
　　Then went Sir Bedivere the second time
Across the ridge, and paced beside the mere,
Counting the dewy pebbles, fix'd in thought;
But when he saw the wonder of the hilt,
How curiously and strangely chased, he smote
His palms together, and he cried aloud:
　　"And if indeed I cast the brand away,

Surely a precious thing, one worthy note,
Should thus be lost forever from the earth,
Which might have pleased the eyes of many men.
What good should follow this, if this were done?
What harm, undone? deep harm to disobey,
Seeing obedience is the bond of rule.
Were it well to obey then, if a king demand
An act unprofitable, against himself?
The king is sick, and knows not what he does.
What record, or what relic of my lord
Should be to aftertime, but empty breath
And rumours of a doubt? but were this kept,
Stored in some treasure-house of mighty kings,
Some one might show it at a joust of arms,
Saying, 'King Arthur's sword, Excalibur,
Wrought by the lonely maiden of the lake;
Nine years she wrought it, sitting in the deeps
Upon the hidden bases of the hills.'
So might some old man speak in the aftertime
To all the people, winning reverence;
But now much honour and much fame were lost."

     So spake he, clouded with his own conceit,
And hid Excalibur the second time,
And so strode back slow to the wounded king.

     Then spoke King Arthur, breathing heavily:
"What is it thou hast seen, or what hast heard?"

     And answer made the bold Sir Bedivere:
"I heard the water lapping on the crag,
And the long ripple washing in the reeds."

     To whom replied King Arthur, much in wrath:
"Ah, miserable and unkind, untrue,
Unknightly, traitor-hearted! Woe is me!

[236]

Authority forgets a dying king,
Laid widow'd of the power in his eye
That bow'd the will. I see thee what thou art,
For thou, the latest-left of all my knights,
In whom should meet the offices of all,
Thou wouldst betray me for the precious hilt;
Either from lust of gold, or like a girl
Valuing the giddy pleasure of the eyes.
Yet, for a man may fail in duty twice,
And the third time may prosper, get thee hence;
But, if thou spare to fling Excalibur,
I will arise and slay thee with my hands."
    Then quickly rose Sir Bedivere, and ran,
And, leaping down the ridges lightly, plunged
Among the bulrush-beds, and clutch'd the sword,
And strongly wheel'd and threw it. The great brand
Made lightnings in the splendor of the moon,
And flashing round and round, and whirl'd in an arch
Shot like a streamer of the northern morn,
Seen where the moving isles of winter shock
By night, with noises of the northern sea.
So flash'd and fell the brand Excalibur;
But ere he dipt the surface, rose an arm
Cloth'd in white samite, mystic, wonderful,
And caught him by the hilt, and brandish'd him
Three times, and drew him under in the mere.
And lightly went the other to the king.
    Then spoke King Arthur, drawing thicker breath:
"Now see I by thine eyes that this is done.
Speak out; what is it thou hast heard, or seen?"
    And answer made the bold Sir Bedivere:
"Sir King, I closed mine eyelids, lest the gems

Should blind my purpose, for I never saw,
Nor shall see, here or elsewhere, till I die,
Not tho' I live three lives of mortal men,
So great a miracle as yonder hilt.
Then with both hands I flung him, wheeling him;
But when I look'd again, behold an arm,
Clothed in white samite, mystic, wonderful,
That caught him by the hilt, and brandish'd him
Three times, and drew him under in the mere."
    And answer made King Arthur, breathing hard:
"My end draws nigh; 'tis time that I were gone.
Make broad thy shoulders to receive my weight,
And bear me to the margin; yet I fear
My wound hath taken cold, and I shall die."
    So saying, from the pavement he half rose,
Slowly, with pain, reclining on his arm,
And looking wistfully with wide blue eyes
As in a picture. Him Sir Bedivere
Remorsefully regarded thro' his tears,
And would have spoken, but he found not words,
Then took with care, and kneeling on one knee,
O'er both his shoulders drew the languid hands,
And rising bore him thro' the place of tombs.
    But, as he walk'd, King Arthur panted hard,
Like one that feels a nightmare on his bed
When all the house is mute. So sigh'd the king,
Muttering and murmuring at his ear, "Quick, quick!
I fear it is too late, and I shall die."
But the other swiftly strode from ridge to ridge,
Clothed with his breath, and looking, as he walk'd,
Larger than human on the frozen hills.
He heard the deep behind him, and a cry

Before. His own thought drove him like a goad.
Dry clash'd his harness in the icy caves
And barren chasms, and all to left and right
The bare black cliff clang'd round him, as he based
His feet on juts of slippery crag that rang
Sharp-smitten with the dint of armed heels—
And on a sudden, lo! the level lake,
And the long glories of the winter moon.

Then saw they how there hove a dusky barge,
Dark as a funeral scarf from stem to stern,
Beneath them; and descending they were ware
That all the decks were dense with stately forms
Black-stoled, black-hooded, like a dream—by these
Three queens with crowns of gold—and from them rose
A cry that shiver'd to the tingling stars,
And, as it were one voice, an agony
Of lamentation, like a wind that shrills
All night in a waste land, where no one comes,
Or hath come, since the making of the world.

Then murmur'd Arthur, "Place me in the barge,"
And to the barge they came. There those three queens
Put forth their hands, and took the king, and wept.
But she that rose the tallest of them all
And fairest laid his head upon her lap
And loosed the shatter'd casque, and chafed his hands,
And call'd him by his name, complaining loud,
And dropping bitter tears against his brow
Striped with dark blood; for all his face was white
And colourless, and like the wither'd moon
Smote by the fresh beam of the springing east;
And all his greaves and cuisses dash'd with drops
Of onset; and the light and lustrous curls—

[239]

That made his forehead like a rising sun
High from the dais-throne—were parch'd with dust;
Or, clotted into points and hanging loose,
Mix'd with the knightly growth that fringed his lips.
So like a shatter'd column lay the king;
Not like that Arthur who, with lance in rest,
From spur to plume a star of tournament,
Shot thro' the lists of Camelot, and charged
Before the eyes of ladies and of kings.

Then loudly cried the bold Sir Bedivere:
"Ah! my Lord Arthur, whither shall I go?
Where shall I hide my forehead and my eyes?
For now I see the true old times are dead,
When every morning brought a noble chance,
And every chance brought out a noble knight.
Such times have been not since the light that led
The holy Elders with the gift of myrrh.
But now the whole ROUND TABLE is dissolved
Which was an image of the mighty world;
And I, the last, go forth companionless,
And the days darken round me, and the years,
Among new men, strange faces, other minds."

And slowly answer'd Arthur from the barge:
"The old order changeth, yielding place to new,
And God fulfills himself in many ways,
Lest one good custom should corrupt the world.
Comfort thyself; what comfort is in me?
I have lived my life, and that which I have done
May He within himself make pure! but thou,
If thou shouldst never see my face again,
Pray for my soul. More things are wrought by prayer
Than this world dreams of. Wherefore, let thy voice

Rise like a fountain for me night and day.
For what are men better than sheep or goats
That nourish a blind life within the brain,
If, knowing God, they lift not hands of prayer
Both for themselves and those who call them friend?
For so the whole round earth is every way
Bound by gold chains about the feet of God.
But now farewell. I am going a long way
With these thou seest—if indeed I go—
For all my mind is clouded with a doubt—
To the island-valley of Avilion;
Where falls not hail, or rain, or any snow,
Nor ever wind blows loudly, but it lies
Deep-meadow'd, happy, fair with orchard lawns
And bowery hollows crown'd with summer sea,
Where I will heal me of my grievous wound."
   So said he, and the barge with oar and sail
Moved from the brink, like some full-breasted swan
That, fluting a wild carol ere her death,
Ruffles her pure cold plume, and takes the flood
With swarthy webs. Long stood Sir Bedivere
Revolving many memories, till the hull
Look'd one black dot against the verge of dawn,
And on the mere the wailing died away.

ALFRED, LORD TENNYSON

SAUL

I

SAID Abner, "At last thou art come! Ere I tell, ere thou
    speak,
Kiss my cheek, wish me well!" Then I wished it, and did
    kiss his cheek.
And he, "Since the King, O my friend, for thy counte-
    nance sent,
Neither drunken nor eaten have we; nor until from his
    tent
Thou return with the joyful assurance the King liveth
    yet,
Shall our lip with the honey be bright, with the water
    be wet.
For out of the black mid-tent's silence, a space of three
    days,
Not a sound hath escaped to thy servants, of prayer nor of
    praise,
To betoken that Saul and the Spirit have ended their
    strife,
And that, faint in his triumph, the monarch sinks back
    upon life.

II

"Yet now my heart leaps, O beloved! God's child with his
    dew

On thy gracious gold hair, and those lilies still living and
    blue

Just broken to twine round thy harp-strings, as if no wild
    heat

Were now raging to torture the desert!"

III

                        Then I, as was meet,

Knelt down to the God of my fathers, and rose on my feet,

And ran o'er the sand burnt to powder. The tent was
    unlooped;

I pulled up the spear that obstructed, and under I
    stooped;

Hands and knees on the slippery grass-patch, all withered
    and gone,

That extends to the second enclosure, I groped my way on

Till I felt where the foldskirts fly open. Then once more
    I prayed,

And opened the foldskirts and entered, and was not afraid

But spoke, "Here is David, thy servant!" And no voice
    replied.

At the first I saw nought but the blackness; but soon I
    descried

A something more black than the blackness—the vast,
    the upright

Main prop which sustains the pavilion: and slow into
    sight

Grew a figure against it, gigantic and blackest of all.
Then a sunbeam, that burst thro' the tent-roof, showed
    Saul.

IV

He stood as erect as that tent-prop, both arms stretched
    out wide
On the great cross-support in the centre, that goes to
    each side;
He relaxed not a muscle, but hung there as, caught in
    his pangs
And waiting his change, the king-serpent all heavily
    hangs,
Far away from his kind, in the pine, till deliverance come
With the spring-time,—so agonised Saul, drear and stark,
    blind and dumb.

V

Then I tuned my harp,—took off the lilies we twine
    round its chords
Lest they snap 'neath the stress of the noontide—those
    sunbeams like swords!
And I first played the tune all our sheep know, as, one
    after one,
So docile they come to the pen-door till folding be done.
They are white and untorn by the bushes, for lo, they
    have fed
Where the long grasses stifle the water within the stream's
    bed;
And now one after one seeks its lodging, as star follows
    star
Into eve and the blue far above us,—so blue and so far!

VI

—Then the tune for which quails on the cornland will
    each leave his mate
To fly after the player; then, what makes the crickets elate
Till for boldness they fight one another; and then, what
    has weight
To set the quick jerboa a-musing outside his sand-house—
There are none such as he for a wonder, half bird and
    half mouse!
God made all the creatures and gave them our love and
    our fear,—
To give sign, we and they are his children, one family
    here.

VII

Then I played the help-tune of our reapers, their wine-
    song, when hand
Grasps at hand, eye lights eye in good friendship, and
    great hearts expand
And grow one in the sense of this world's life.—And then,
    the last song
When the dead man is praised on his journey: "Bear,
    bear him along,
With his few faults shut up like dead flowerets! Are balm
    seeds not here
To console us? The land has none left such as he on the
    bier.
Oh, would we might keep thee, my brother!"—And then,
    the glad chaunt
Of the marriage: first go the young maidens; next, she
    whom we vaunt

As the beauty, the pride of our dwelling.—And then, the
    great march
Wherein man runs to man to assist him, and buttress an
    arch
Naught can break: who shall harm them, our friends?—
    Then, the chorus intoned—
As the Levites go up to the altar in glory enthroned.
But I stopped here: for here in the darkness Saul groaned.

VIII

And I paused, held my breath in such silence, and listened
    apart:
And the tent shook, for mighty Saul shuddered; and
    sparkles 'gan dart
From the jewels that woke in his turban, at once with a
    start,—
All its lordly male-sapphires, and rubies courageous at
    heart.
So the head: but the body still moved not, still hung there
    erect.
And I bent once again to my playing, pursued it un-
    checked,
As I sang:—

IX

    "Oh, our manhood's prime vigor!
    No spirit feels waste,
Not a muscle is stopped in its playing nor sinew unbraced.
Oh, the wild joys of living! the leaping from rock up to
    rock;
The strong rending of boughs from the fir-tree; the cool
    silver shock

Of the plunge in a pool's living water; the hunt of the
    bear;

And the sultriness showing the lion is couched in his lair.

And the meal,—the rich dates yellowed over with gold
    dust divine,

And the locust-flesh steeped in the pitcher, the full
    draught of wine;

And the sleep in the dried river-channel, where bulrushes
    tell

That the water was wont to go warbling so softly and
    well.

How good is man's life, the mere living! how fit to employ

All the heart and the soul and the senses forever in joy!—

Hast thou loved the white locks of thy father, whose sword
    thou didst guard

When he trusted thee forth with the armies, for glorious
    reward?

Didst thou see the thin hands of thy mother, held up as
    men sung

The low song of the nearly-departed; and hear her faint
    tongue

Joining in, while it could, to the witness, 'Let one more
    attest:

I have lived, seen God's hand through a lifetime, and all
    was for best?'

Then they sung through their tears in strong triumph,
    not much, but the rest.—

And thy brothers, the help and the contest, the working
    whence grew

Such result as, from seething grape-bundles, the spirit
    strained true;

And the friends of thy boyhood,—that boyhood of wonder
    and hope,
Present promise, and wealth of the future beyond the
    eye's scope:
Till lo, thou art grown to a monarch; a people is thine;
And all gifts, which the world offers singly, on one head
    combine!
On one head, all the beauty and strength; love and rage
    (like the throe
That, a-work in the rock, helps its labor and lets the
    gold go);
High ambition and deeds which surpass it, fame crowning
    them;—all
Brought to blaze on the head of one creature,—King
    Saul!"

x

And lo, with that leap of my spirit,—heart, hand, harp
    and voice,
Each lifting Saul's name out of sorrow, each bidding
    rejoice
Saul's fame in the light it was made for—as when, dare
    I say,
The Lord's army, in rapture of service, strains through
    its array,
And upsoareth the cherubim-chariot—"Saul!" cried I,
    and stopped,
And waited the thing that should follow. Then Saul,
    who hung propped
By the tent's cross-support in the centre, was struck by
    his name.

Have ye seen when Spring's arrowy summons goes right
  to the aim,

And some mountain,—the last to withstand her, that held
  (he alone,

While the vale laughed in freedom and flowers) on a
  broad bust of stone

A year's snow bound about for a breastplate,—leaves
  grasp of the sheet?

Fold on fold all at once it crowds thunderously down to
  his feet:

And there fronts you, stark, black, but alive yet, your
  mountain of old,

With his rents, the successive bequeathings of ages un-
  told,—

Yea, each harm got in fighting your battles, each furrow
  and scar

Of his head thrust 'twixt you and the tempest,—all hail,
  there they are!

—Now again to be softened with verdure, again hold
  the nest

Of the dove, tempt the goat and its young to the green
  on his crest

For their food in the ardors of summer.—One long shudder thrilled

All the tent till the very air tingled; then sank and was
  stilled

At the King's self left standing before me, released and
  aware.

What was gone, what remained? All to traverse 'twixt
  hope and despair;

Death was past, life not come: so he waited. Awhile his
  right hand

Held the brow,—helped the eyes left too vacant forthwith
    to remand
To their place what new objects should enter: 'twas Saul
    as before.
I looked up and dared gaze at those eyes; nor was hurt
    any more
Than by slow pallid sunsets in autumn ye watch from
    the shore,
At their sad level gaze o'er the ocean—a sun's slow decline
Over hills which, resolved in stern silence, o'erlap and
    entwine
Base with base, to knit strength more intensely: so, arm
    folded arm
O'er the chest whose slow heavings subsided.

XI

                    What spell or what charm,
(For, awhile there was trouble within me) what next
    should I urge
To sustain him where song had restored him?—Song
    filled to the verge
His cup with the wine of this life, pressing all that it
    yields
Of mere fruitage, the strength and the beauty! Beyond,
    on what fields,
Glean a vintage more potent and perfect to brighten the
    eye
And bring blood to the lip, and commend them the cup
    they put by?
He saith, "It is good"; still he drinks not: he lets me
    praise life,
Gives assent, yet would die for his own part.

XII

Then fancies grew rife
Which had come long ago on the pastures, when round
me the sheep
Fed in silence—above, the one eagle wheeled slow as in
sleep;
And I lay in my hollow and mused on the world that
might lie
'Neath his ken, though I saw but the strip 'twixt the hill
and the sky:
And I laughed—"Since my days are ordained to be passed
with my flocks,
Let me people at least, with my fancies, the plains and
the rocks,
Dream the life I am never to mix with, and image the
show
Of mankind as they live in those fashions I hardly shall
know!
Schemes of life, its best rules and right uses, the courage
that gains,
And the prudence that keeps what men strive for." And
now these old trains
Of vague thought came again; I grew surer; so, once more
the string
Of my harp made response to my spirit, as thus—

XIII

"Yea, my King,"
I began—"thou dost well in rejecting mere comforts that
spring
From the mere mortal life held in common by man and
by brute:

In our flesh grows the branch of this life, in our soul it
   bears fruit.

Thou hast marked the slow rise of the tree,—how its
   stem trembled first

Till it passed the kid's lip, the stag's antler; then safely
   outburst

The fan-branches all round; and thou mindest when
   these too, in turn

Broke a-bloom and the palm-tree seemed perfect: yet
   more was to learn,

E'en the good that comes in with the palm-fruit. Our
   dates shall we slight,

When their juice brings a cure for all sorrow? or care for
   the plight

Of the palm's self whose slow growth produced them?
   Not so! stem and branch

Shall decay, nor be known in their place, while the palm-
   wine shall staunch

Every wound of man's spirit in winter. I pour thee such
   wine.

Leave the flesh to the fate it was fit for! the spirit be
   thine!

By the spirit, when age shall o'ercome thee, thou still
   shalt enjoy

More indeed, than at first when inconscious, the life of
   a boy.

Crush that life, and behold its wine running! Each deed
   thou hast done

Dies, revives, goes to work in the world; until e'en as the
   sun

Looking down on the earth, though clouds spoil him,
   though tempests efface,

Can find nothing his own deed produced not, must every-
    where trace

The results of his past summer-prime,—so, each ray of
    thy will,

Every flash of thy passion and prowess, long over, shall
    thrill

Thy whole people, the countless, with ardour, till they
    too give forth

A like cheer to their sons, who in turn, fill the South and
    the North

With the radiance thy deed was the germ of. Carouse in
    the past!

But the license of age has its limit; thou diest at last:

As the lion when age dims his eyeball, the rose at her
    height

So with man—so his power and his beauty for ever take
    flight.

No! Again a long draught of my soul-wine! Look forth
    o'er the years!

Thou hast done now with eyes for the actual; begin with
    the seer's!

Is Saul dead? In the depth of the vale make his tomb—
    bid arise

A grey mountain of marble heaped four-square, till, built
    to the skies,

Let it mark where the great First King slumbers: whose
    fame would ye know?

Up above see the rock's naked face, where the record
    shall go

In great characters cut by the scribe,—Such was Saul,
    so he did;

With the sages directing the work, by the populace chid,—

For not half, they'll affirm, is comprised there! Which
    fault to amend,

In the grove with his kind grows the cedar, whereon they
    shall spend

(See, in tablets 'tis level before them) their praise, and
    record

With the gold of the graver, Saul's story,—statesman's
    great word

Side by side with the poet's sweet comment. The river's
    a-wave

With smooth paper-reeds grazing each other when
    prophet-winds rave:

So the pen gives unborn generations their due and their
    part

In thy being! Then, first of the mighty, thank God that
    thou art!"

XIV

And behold while I sang . . . but O Thou who didst
    grant me that day,

And before it not seldom hast granted thy help to essay,

Carry on and complete an adventure,—my shield and
    my sword

In that act where my soul was thy servant, thy word was
    my word,—

Still be with me, who then at the summit of human
    endeavour

And scaling the highest, man's thought could, gazed hope-
    less as ever

On the new stretch of heaven above me—till, mighty to
    save,

Just one lift of thy hand cleared that distance—God's
    throne from man's grave!

Let me tell out my tale to its ending—my voice to my
heart
Which can scarce dare believe in what marvels last night
I took part,
As this morning I gather the fragments, alone with my
sheep,
And still fear lest the terrible glory evanish like sleep!
For I wake in the grey dewy covert, while Hebron up-
heaves
The dawn struggling with night on his shoulder, and
Kidron retrieves
Slow the damage of yesterday's sunshine.

xv

I say then,—my song
While I sang thus, assuring the monarch, and ever more
strong
Made a proffer of good to console him—he slowly resumed
His old motions and habitudes kingly. The right-hand
replumed
His black locks to their wonted composure, adjusted the
swathes
Of his turban, and see—the huge sweat that his counte-
nance bathes,
He wipes off with the robe; and he girds now his loins as
of yore,
And feels slow for the armlets of price, with the clasp set
before.
He is Saul, ye remember in glory,—ere error had bent
The broad brow from the daily communion; and still,
though much spent

Be the life and the bearing that front you, the same,
    God did choose,

To receive what a man may waste, desecrate, never quite
    lose.

So sank he along by the tent-prop till, stayed by the pile

Of his armour and war-cloak and garments, he leaned
    there awhile,

And sat out my singing,—one arm round the tent-prop,
    to raise

His bent head, and the other hung slack—till I touched
    on the praise

I foresaw from all men in all time, to the man patient
    there;

And thus ended, the harp falling forward. Then first I
    was 'ware

That he sat, as I say, with my head just above his vast
    knees

Which were thrust out on each side around me, like oak-
    roots which please

To encircle a lamb when it slumbers. I looked up to know

If the best I could do had brought solace: he spoke not,
    but slow

Lifted up the hand slack at his side, till he laid it with
    care

Soft and grave, but in mild settled will, on my brow:
    thro' my hair

The large fingers were pushed, and he bent back my head,
    with kind power—

All my face back, intent to peruse it, as men do a flower.

Thus held he me there with his great eyes that scru-
    tinised mine—

And oh, all my heart how it loved him! but where was
    the sign?
I yearned,—"Could I help thee, my father, inventing
    a bliss,
I would add, to that life of the past, both the future, and
    this:
I would give thee new life altogether, as good, ages hence,
As this moment,—had love but the warrant, love's heart
    to dispense!"

XVI

Then the truth came upon me. No harp more—no song
    more! Outbroke:—

XVII

"I have gone the whole round of creation: I saw and I
    spoke.
I, a work of God's hand for that purpose, received in my
    brain,
And pronounced on, the rest of his handwork,—returned
    him again
His creation's approval or censure; I spoke as I saw.
I report, as a man may of God's work: all's love, yet all's
    law.
Now I lay down the judgeship he lent me. Each faculty
    tasked
To perceive him, has gained an abyss, where a dewdrop
    was asked.
Have I knowledge? confounded it shrivels at Wisdom laid
    bare.
Have I forethought? how purblind, how blank to the
    Infinite Care!
Do I task any faculty highest, to image success?

I but open my eyes,—and perfection, no more and no less,
In the kind I imagined, full-fronts me: and God is seen
    God
In the star, in the stone, in the flesh, in the soul, and
    the clod.
And thus looking within and around me, I ever renew
(With that stoop of the soul which, in bending, upraises
    it too)
The submission of man's nothing-perfect to God's all-
    complete,
As, by each new obeisance in spirit, I climb to his feet.
    —Yet with all this abounding experience, this deity
        known,
I shall dare to discover some province, some gift of my
    own!
There's a faculty pleasant to exercise, hard to hoodwink,
I am fain to keep still in abeyance (I laugh as I think)
Lest, insisting to claim and parade in it, wot ye, I worst
E'en the Giver in one gift:—behold, I could love if I
    durst!
But I sink the pretension, as fearing a man may o'ertake
God's own speed in the one way of love: I abstain for
    love's sake!
—What, my soul? see thus far and no farther? when
    doors, great and small,
Nine-and-ninety flew ope at our touch, should the hun-
    dredth appal?
In the least things have faith, yet distrust in the greatest
    of all?
Do I find love so full in my nature, God's ultimate gift,
That I doubt his own love can compete with it? Here, the
    parts shift?

Here, the creature surpass the Creator,—the end, what
    Began?
Would I fain, in my impotent yearning, do all for this
    man,
And dare doubt He alone shall not help him, who yet
    alone can?
Would it ever have entered my mind,—the bare will,
    much less power,—
To bestow on this Saul what I sang of, the marvellous
    dower
Of the life he was gifted and filled with? to make such a
    soul,
Such a body, and then such an earth for insphering the
    whole?
  —And doth it not enter my mind (as my warm tears
    attest),
These good things being given, to go on, and give one
    more, the best?
Ay, to save, and redeem and restore him, maintain at the
    height
This perfection,—succeed with life's dayspring death's
    minute of night?
Interpose at the difficult minute, snatch Saul the mistake,
Saul the failure, the ruin he seems now—and bid him
    awake
From the dream, the probation, the prelude, to find him-
    self set
Clear and safe in new light and new life,—a new har-
    mony yet
To be run, and continued, and ended—who knows?—
    or endure!

The man taught enough by life's dream, of the rest to
    make sure:
By the pain-throb, triumphantly winning intensified bliss;
And the next world's reward and repose, by the struggles
    in this.

XVIII

"I believe it! 'Tis thou, God, that givest, 'tis I who receive:
In the first is the last, in thy will is my power to believe.
All's one gift: thou canst grant it, moreover, as prompt
    to my prayer
As I breathe out this breath, as I open these arms to the
    air.
From thy will stream the worlds, life and nature, thy
    dread Sabaoth:
I will?—the mere atoms despise me! Why am I not loth
To look that, even that, in the face too? Why is it I dare
Think but lightly of such impuissance? What stops my
    despair?
This:—'tis not what man Does which exalts him, but
    what man Would do!
See the King—I would help him but cannot, the wishes
    fall through.
Could I wrestle to raise him from sorrow, grow poor to
    enrich,—
To fill up his life, starve my own out,—I would; knowing
    which,
I know that my service is perfect. Oh, speak through me
    now!
Would I suffer for him that I love? So wouldst thou—
    so wilt thou!
So shall crown thee the topmost, ineffablest, uttermost
    crown—

And thy love fill infinitude wholly, nor leave, up nor
    down,
One spot for the creature to stand in! It is by no breath,
Turn of eye, wave of hand, that salvation joins issue with
    death!
As thy Love is discovered almighty, almighty be proved
Thy power, that exists with and for it, of being Beloved!
He who did most, shall bear most: the strongest shall
    stand the most weak.
'Tis the weakness in strength, that I cry for! my flesh,
    that I seek
In the Godhead! I seek and I find it. O Saul, it shall be
A Face like my face that receives thee; a Man like to me,
Thou shalt love and be loved by, for ever: a Hand like
    this hand
Shall throw open the gates of new life to thee! See the
    Christ stand!"

XIX

I know not too well how I found my way home in the
    night.
There were witnesses, cohorts about me, to left and to
    right,
Angels, powers, the unuttered, unseen, the alive, the
    aware:
I repressed, I got through them as hardly, as strugglingly
    there,
As a runner beset by the populace famished for news—
Life or death. The whole earth was awakened, hell loosed
    with her crews;
And the stars of night beat with emotion, and tingled and
    shot

Out in fire the strong pain of pent knowledge: but I
    fainted not,
For the Hand still impelled me at once and supported,
    suppressed
All the tumult, and quenched it with quiet, and holy
    behest,
Till the rapture was shut in itself, and the earth sank
    to rest.
Anon at the dawn, all that trouble had withered from
    earth—
Not so much, but I saw it die out in the day's tender
    birth;
In the gathered intensity brought to the grey of the hills;
In the shuddering forests' held breath; in the sudden
    wind-thrills;
In the startled wild beasts that bore off, each with eye
    sidling still
Though averted with wonder and dread; in the birds stiff
    and chill
That rose heavily, as I approached them, made stupid
    with awe!
E'en the serpent that slid away silent,—he felt the new
    Law.
The same stared in the white humid faces upturned by
    the flowers;
The same worked in the heart of the cedar, and moved
    the vine-bowers:
And the little brooks witnessing murmured, persistent
    and low,
With their obstinate, all but hushed voices—"E'en so,
    it is so!"

ROBERT BROWNING

SOLILOQUY OF THE SPANISH CLOISTER

Gr-r-r—there go, my heart's abhorrence!
  Water your damned flower-pots, do!
If hate killed men, Brother Lawrence,
  God's blood, would not mine kill you!
What? your myrtle-bush wants trimming?
  Oh, that rose has prior claims—
Needs its leaden vase filled brimming?
  Hell dry you up with its flames!

At the meal we sit together:
  Salve tibi! I must hear
Wise talk of the kind of weather,
  Sort of season, time of year:
*Not a plenteous cork-crop: scarcely
  Dare we hope oak-galls, I doubt:*
What's the Latin name for "parsley"?
  What's the Greek name for Swine's Snout?

Whew! We'll have our platter burnished,
  Laid with care on our own shelf!
With a fire-new spoon we've furnished,
  And a goblet for ourself,

Rinsed like something sacrificial
    Ere 'tis fit to touch our chaps—
Marked with L for our initial!
    (He-he! There his lily snaps!)

Saint, forsooth! While brown Dolores
    Squats outside the Convent bank
With Sanchicha, telling stories,
    Steeping tresses in the tank,
Blue-black, lustrous, thick like horsehairs,
    —Can't I see his dead eye glow,
Bright as 'twere a Barbary corsair's?
    (That is, if he'd let it show!)

When he finishes refection,
    Knife and fork he never lays
Cross-wise, to my recollection,
    As do I, in Jesu's praise.
I the Trinity illustrate,
    Drinking watered orange-pulp—
In three sips the Arian frustrate;
    While he drains his at one gulp.

Oh, those melons! If he's able
    We're to have a feast! so nice!
One goes to the Abbot's table,
    All of us get each a slice.
How go on your flowers? None double?
    Not one fruit-sort can you spy?
Strange!—And I, too, at such trouble,
    Keep them close-nipped on the sly!

ROBERT BROWNING

There's a great text in Galatians,
  Once you trip on it, entails
Twenty-nine distinct damnations,
  One sure, if another fails:
If I trip him just a-dying,
  Sure of heaven as sure can be,
Spin him round and send him flying
  Off to hell, a Manichee?

Or, my scrofulous French novel
  On gray paper with blunt type!
Simply glance at it, you grovel
  Hand and foot in Belial's gripe:
If I double down its pages
  At the woeful sixteenth print,
When he gathers his greengages,
  Ope a sieve and slip it in't?

Or, there's Satan!—one might venture
  Pledge one's soul to him, yet leave
Such a flaw in the indenture
  As he'd miss till, past retrieve,
Blasted lay that rose-acacia
  We're so proud of! *Hy, Zy, Hine* . . .
'St, there's Vespers! *Plena gratiâ,*
  Ave, Virgo! Gr-r-r—you swine!

ROBERT BROWNING

THE BURDEN OF NINEVEH

IN OUR Museum galleries
   To-day I lingered o'er the prize
Dead Greece vouchsafes to living eyes,—
Her Art for ever in fresh wise
   From hour to hour rejoicing me.
Sighing I turned at last to win
Once more the London dirt and din;
And as I made the swing-door spin
And issued, they were hoisting in
   A wingèd beast from Nineveh.

A human face the creature wore,
And hoofs behind and hoofs before,
And flanks with dark runes fretted o'er.
'Twas bull, 'twas mitred Minotaur,
   A dead disbowelled mystery;
The mummy of a buried faith
Stark from the charnel without scathe,
Its wings stood for the light to bathe,—
Such fossil cerements as might swathe
   The very corpse of Nineveh.

The print of its first rush-wrapping,
Wound ere it dried, still ribbed the thing.
What song did the brown maidens sing,
From purple mouths alternating,
   When that was woven languidly?
What vows, what rites, what prayers preferr'd
What songs has the strange image heard?
In what blind vigil stood interr'd
For ages, till an English word
   Broke silence first at Nineveh?

Oh when upon each sculptured court,
Where even the wind might not resort,—
O'er which Time passed, of like import
With the wild Arab boys at sport,—
   A living face looked in to see:—
Oh seemed it not—the spell once broke—
As though the carven warriors woke,
As though the shaft the string forsook,
The cymbals clashed, the chariots shook,
   And there was life in Nineveh?

On London stones our sun anew
The beast's recovered shadow threw.
(No shade that plague of darkness knew,
No light, no shade, while older grew
   By ages the old earth and sea.)
Lo thou! could all thy priests have shown
Such proof to make thy godhead known?
From their dead Past thou liv'st alone;
And still thy shadow is thine own
   Even as of yore in Nineveh.

That day whereof we keep record,
When near thy city-gates the Lord
Sheltered his Jonah with a gourd,
This sun, (I said) here present, pour'd
   Even thus this shadow that I see.
This shadow has been shed the same
From sun and moon,—from lamps which came
For prayer,—from fifteen days of flame,
The last, while smouldered to a name
   Sardanapalus' Nineveh.

Within thy shadow, haply, once
Sennacherib has knelt, whose sons
Smote him between the altar-stones:
Or pale Semiramis her zones
   Of gold, her incense brought to thee,
In love for grace, in war for aid: . . .
Ay, and who else? . . . till 'neath thy shade
Within his trenches newly made
Last year the Christian knelt and pray'd—
   Not to thy strength—in Nineveh.

Now, thou poor god, within this hall
Where the blank windows blind the wall
From pedestal to pedestal,
The kind of light shall on thee fall
   Which London takes the day to be:
While school-foundations in the act
Of holiday, three files compact,
Shall learn to view thee as a fact
Connected with that zealous tract:
   'Rome,—Babylon and Nineveh.'

Deemed they of this, those worshippers,
When, in some mythic chain of verse
Which man shall not again rehearse,
The faces of thy ministers
    Yearned pale with bitter ecstasy?
Greece, Egypt, Rome,—did any god
Before whose feet men knelt unshod
Deem that in this unblest abode
Another scarce more unknown god
    Should house with him, from Nineveh?

Ah! in what quarries lay the stone
From which this pygmy pile has grown,
Unto man's need how long unknown,
Since thy vast temples, court and cone,
    Rose far in desert history?
Ah! what is here that does not lie
All strange to thine awakened eye?
Ah! what is here can testify
(Save that dumb presence of the sky)
    Unto thy day and Nineveh?

Why, of those mummies in the room
Above, there might indeed have come
One out of Egypt to thy home,
An alien. Nay, but were not some
    Of these thine own 'antiquity'?
And now,—they and their gods and thou
All relics here together,—now
Whose profit? whether bull or cow,
Isis or Ibis, who or how,
    Whether of Thebes or Nineveh?

The consecrated metals found,
And ivory tablets, underground,
Winged teraphim and creatures crown'd
When air and daylight filled the mound,
   Fell into dust immediately.
And even as these, the images
Of awe and worship,—even as these,—
So, smitten with the sun's increase,
Her glory mouldered and did cease
   From immemorial Nineveh.

The day her builders made their halt,
Those cities of the lake of salt
Stood firmly 'stablished without fault,
Made proud with pillars of basalt,
   With sardonyx and porphyry.
The day that Jonah bore abroad
To Nineveh the voice of God,
A brackish lake lay in his road,
Where erst Pride fixed her sure abode
   As then in royal Nineveh.

The day when he, Pride's lord and Man's,
Showed all the kingdoms at a glance
To Him before whose countenance
The years recede, the years advance,
   And said, Fall down and worship me:—
'Mid all the pomp beneath that look,
Then stirred there, haply, some rebuke,
Where to the wind the Salt Pools shook,
And in those tracts, of life forsook,
   That knew thee not, O Nineveh!

Delicate harlot! On thy throne
Thou with a world beneath thee prone
In state for ages sat'st alone;
And needs were years and lustres flown
   Ere strength of man could vanquish thee:
Whom even thy victor foes must bring,
Still royal, among maids that sing
As with doves' voices, taboring
Upon their breasts, unto the King,—
   A kingly conquest, Nineveh!

. . . Here woke my thought. The wind's slow sway
Had waxed; and like the human play
Of scorn that smiling spreads away,
The sunshine shivered off the day:
   The callous wind, it seemed to me,
Swept up the shadow from the ground:
And pale as whom the Fates astound,
The god forlorn stood winged and crown'd:
Within I knew the cry lay bound
   Of the dumb soul of Nineveh.

And as I turned, my sense half shut
Still saw the crowds of kerb and rut
Go past as marshalled to the strut
Of ranks in gypsum quaintly cut.
   It seemed in one same pageantry
They followed forms which had been erst;
To pass, till on my sight should burst
That future of the best or worst
When some may question which was first,
   Of London or of Nineveh.

For as that Bull-god once did stand
And watched the burial-clouds of sand,
Till these at last without a hand
Rose o'er his eyes, another land,
    And blinded him with destiny:—
So may he stand again; till now,
In ships of unknown sail and prow,
Some tribe of the Australian plough
Bear him afar,—a relic now
    Of London, not of Nineveh!

Or it may chance indeed that when
Man's age is hoary among men,—
His centuries threescore and ten,—
His furthest childhood shall seem then
    More clear than later times may be:
Who, finding in this desert place
This form, shall hold us for some race
That walked not in Christ's lowly ways,
But bowed its pride and vowed its praise
    Unto the God of Nineveh.

The smile rose first,—anon drew nigh
The thought: . . . Those heavy wings spread high
So sure of flight, which do not fly;
That set gaze never on the sky;
    Those scriptured flanks it cannot see;
Its crown, a brow-contracting load;
Its planted feet which trust the sod: . . .
 (So grew the image as I trod:)
O Nineveh, was this thy God,—
    Thine also, mighty Nineveh?

DANTE GABRIEL ROSSETTI

IN NO STRANGE LAND

("The Kingdom of God is within you.")

O world invisible, we view thee;
   O world intangible, we touch thee;
O world unknowable, we know thee;
   Inapprehensible, we clutch thee!

Does the fish soar to find the ocean,
   The eagle plunge to find the air—
That we ask of the stars in motion
   If they have rumor of thee there?

Not where the wheeling systems darken,
   And our benumbed conceiving soars!—
The drift of pinions, would we hearken,
   Beats at our own clay-shuttered doors.

The angels keep their ancient places—
   Turn but a stone, and start a wing!
'Tis ye, 'tis your estrangèd faces
   That miss the many-splendored thing.

But (when so sad thou canst not sadder)
   Cry—and upon thy so sore loss
Shall shine the traffic of Jacob's ladder
   Pitched betwixt Heaven and Charing Cross.

Yea, in the night, my Soul, my daughter,
   Cry,—clinging heaven by the hems:
And lo, Christ walking on the water,
   Not of Gennesareth, but Thames!

                         FRANCIS THOMPSON

THE HOUND OF HEAVEN

I FLED Him, down the nights and down the days;
   I fled Him, down the arches of the years;
I fled Him, down the labyrinthine ways
  Of my own mind; and in the mist of tears
I hid from Him, and under running laughter.
    Up vistaed hopes, I sped;
    And shot, precipitated,
  Adown Titanic glooms of chasmèd fears,
From those strong Feet that followed, followed after.
    But with unhurrying chase,
    And unperturbèd pace,
Deliberate speed, majestic instancy,
    They beat,—and a Voice beat
    More instant than the Feet:
"All things betray thee, who betrayest Me."

    I pleaded, outlaw-wise,
By many a hearted casement, curtained red,
  Trellised with intertwining charities;
(For, though I knew His love Who followèd,
    Yet was I sore adread
Lest, having Him, I must have naught beside).

[275]

But, if one little casement parted wide,
   The gust of His approach would clash it to.
   Fear wist not to evade, as Love wist to pursue.
Across the margent of the world I fled,
   And troubled the gold gateways of the stars,
   Smiting for shelter on their clangèd bars;
     Fretted to dulcet jars
And silvern chatter the pale ports o' the moon.
I said to Dawn, Be sudden—to Eve, Be soon:
   With thy young skyey blossoms heap me over
    From this tremendous Lover—
Float thy vague veil about me, lest He see!
   I tempted all His servitors, but to find
My own betrayal in their constancy,—
In faith to Him their fickleness to me,
   Their traitorous trueness, and their loyal deceit.
To all swift things for swiftness did I sue;
   Clung to the whistling mane of every wind.
      But whether they swept, smoothly fleet,
    The long savannahs of the blue;
      Or whether, Thunder-driven,
     They clanged his chariot 'thwart a heaven,
Plashy with flying lightnings round the spurn o' their
      feet:—
   Fear wist not to evade as Love wist to pursue.
     Still with unhurrying chase,
     And unperturbèd pace,
   Deliberate speed, majestic instancy,
     Came on the following Feet,
     And a Voice above their beat—
"Naught shelters thee, who wilt not shelter Me."

I sought no more that after which I strayed
      In face of man or maid;
But still within the little children's eyes
      Seems something, something that replies,
They at least are for me, surely for me!
I turned me to them very wistfully;
But just as their young eyes grew sudden fair
      With dawning answers there,
Their angel plucked them from me by the hair.
"Come then, ye other children, Nature's—share
With me" (said I) "your delicate fellowship;
      Let me greet you lip to lip,
      Let me twine with you caresses,
        Wantoning
      With our Lady-Mother's vagrant tresses,
        Banqueting
      With her in her wind-walled palace,
      Underneath her azured daïs,
      Quaffing, as your taintless way is,
        From a chalice
Lucent-weeping out of the dayspring."
      So it was done:
I in their delicate fellowship was one—
Drew the bolt of Nature's secrecies.
      I knew all the swift importings
      On the wilful face of skies;
      I knew how the clouds arise
      Spumèd of the wild sea-snortings;
        All that's born or dies
      Rose and drooped with; made them shapers
Of mine own moods, or wailful or divine;
      With them joyed and was bereaven.

I was heavy with the even,
When she lit her glimmering tapers
Round the day's dead sanctities.
I laughed in the morning's eyes.
I triumphed and I saddened with all weather,
Heaven and I wept together,
And its sweet tears were salt with mortal mine;
Against the red throb of its sunset-heart
I laid my own to beat,
And share commingling heat;
But not by that, by that, was eased my human smart.
In vain my tears were wet on Heaven's grey cheek.
For ah! we know not what each other says,
These things and I; in sound *I* speak—
Their sound is but their stir, they speak by silences.
Nature, poor stepdame, cannot slake my drouth;
Let her, if she would owe me,
Drop yon blue bosom-veil of sky, and show me
The breasts o' her tenderness:
Never did any milk of hers once bless
My thirsting mouth.
Nigh and nigh draws the chase.
With unperturbèd pace,
Deliberate speed, majestic instancy;
And past those noisèd Feet
A voice comes yet more fleet—
"Lo! naught contents thee, who content'st not Me."

Naked I wait Thy love's uplifted stroke!
My harness piece by piece Thou hast hewn from me,
And smitten me to my knee;
I am defenceless utterly.

[278]

I slept, methinks, and woke,
And, slowly gazing, find me stripped in sleep.
In the rash lustihead of my young powers,
I shook the pillaring hours
And pulled my life upon me; grimed with smears,
I stand amid the dust o' the mounded years—
My mangled youth lies dead beneath the heap.
My days have crackled and gone up in smoke,
Have puffed and burst as sun-starts on a stream.
Yea, faileth now even dream
The dreamer, and the lute the lutanist;
Even the linked fantasies, in whose blossomy twist
I swung the earth a trinket at my wrist,
Are yielding; cords of all too weak account
For earth with heavy griefs so overplussed.
Ah! is Thy love indeed
A weed, albeit an amaranthine weed,
Suffering no flowers except its own to mount?
Ah! must—
Designer infinite!—
Ah! must Thou char the wood ere Thou canst limn
with it?
My freshness spent its wavering shower i' the dust;
And now my heart is as a broken fount,
Wherein tear-drippings stagnate, spilt down ever
From the dank thoughts that shiver
Upon the sighful branches of my mind.
Such is; what is to be?
The pulp so bitter, how shall taste the rind?
I dimly guess what Time in mists confounds;
Yet ever and anon a trumpet sounds
From the hid battlements of Eternity;

[279]

Those shaken mists a space unsettle, then
Round the half-glimpsèd turrets slowly wash again.
      But not ere him who summoneth
      I first have seen, enwound
With glooming robes purpureal, cypress-crowned;
His name I know, and what his trumpet saith.
Whether man's heart or life it be which yields
      Thee harvest, must Thy harvest-fields
      Be dunged with rotten death?

        Now of that long pursuit
        Comes on at hand the bruit;
      That Voice is round me like a bursting sea:
        "And is thy earth so marred,
        Shattered in shard on shard?
      Lo, all things fly thee, for thou fliest Me!
      Strange, piteous, futile thing!
Wherefore should any set thee love apart?
Seeing none but I makes much of naught" (He said),
"And human love needs human meriting:
      How hast thou merited—
Of all man's clotted clay the dingiest clot?
      Alack, thou knowest not
How little worthy of any love thou art!
Whom wilt thou find to love ignoble thee,
      Save Me, save only Me?
All which I took from thee I did but take,
      Not for thy harms,
But just that thou might'st seek it in My arms.
      All which thy child's mistake
Fancies as lost, I have stored for thee at home:
      Rise, clasp My hand, and come!"

Halts by me that footfall:
Is my gloom, after all,
Shade of His hand, outstretched caressingly?
"Ah, fondest, blindest, weakest,
I am He Whom thou seekest!
Thou dravest love from thee, who dravest Me."

FRANCIS THOMPSON

THE RENAISSANCE FUSION

DRAMATIS PERSONAE

THE POPE.
THE CARDINAL OF LORRAINE.
FAUSTUS.
VALDES ⎫
CORNELIUS ⎬ *Friends to Faustus.*
WAGNER, *servant to Faustus.*
AN OLD MAN.
SCHOLARS, FRIARS, AND ATTENDANTS.
LUCIFER.
BELZEBUB.
MEPHISTOPHILIS.
GOOD ANGEL.
EVIL ANGEL.
THE SEVEN DEADLY SINS.
DEVILS.
THE SPIRIT OF HELEN OF TROY.
CHORUS.

[The text of Marlowe's play has been transmitted to our times in imperfect form; some of the more serious scenes were curtailed for stage production, while comic scenes were rewritten and other spectacular scenes added to suit the changing taste of Elizabethan audiences. The present abridgement preserves every scene that has come down to us in approximately the form in which Marlowe wrote it. Several scenes not essential to the plot are omitted, as well as the more frankly comic scenes, which although they show something of the scope of Faustus' ambitions, seem incongruous to the modern reader.—C. A. Z.]

THE TRAGICAL HISTORY OF DOCTOR FAUSTUS

Enter Chorus.

CHORUS. Not marching now in fields of Thrasimene,
Where Mars did mate the Carthaginians;
Nor sporting in the dalliance of love;
In courts of kings where state is overturn'd;
Nor in the pomp of proud audacious deeds,
Intends our Muse to vaunt his heavenly verse:
Only this, gentlemen,—we must perform
The form of Faustus' fortunes, good or bad:
To patient judgements we appeal for plaud,
And speak for Faustus in his infancy.
Now is he born, his parents base of stock,
In Germany, within a town call'd Rhode:
Of riper years, to Wittenberg he went,
Whereas his kinsmen chiefly brought him up.
So soon he profits in divinity,
The fruitful plot of scholarism grac'd,
That shortly he was grac'd with doctor's name,
Excelling all whose sweet disputes delight
In heavenly matters of theology;
Till swoln with cunning, of a self-conceit,
His waxen wings did mount above his reach,

And, melting, heavens conspir'd his overthrow;
For, falling to a devilish exercise,
And glutted now with learning's golden gifts,
He surfeits upon cursèd necromancy;
Nothing so sweet as magic is to him,
Which he prefers before his chiefest bliss:
And this the man that in his study sits.   [*Exit.*

SCENE I.

Enter FAUSTUS *in his Study.*

FAUSTUS.   Settle thy studies, Faustus, and begin
To sound the depth of that thou wilt profess:
Having commenc'd, be a divine in show,
Yet level at the end of every art,
And live and die in Aristotle's works.
Sweet Analytics, 'tis thou hast ravish'd me!
Bene disserere est finis logices.
Is, to dispute well, logic's chiefest end?
Affords this art no greater miracle?
Then read no more; thou hast attain'd that end.
A greater subject fitteth Faustus' wit:
Bid *on kai me on* farewell; Galen come,
Seeing, *Ubi desinit philosophus, ibi incipit medicus:*
Be a physician, Faustus; heap up gold,
And be etèrniz'd for some wondrous cure!
Summum bonum medicinae sanitas:
The end of physic is our body's health.
Why, Faustus, hast thou not attain'd that end?
Is not thy common talk sound aphorisms?
Are not thy bills hung up as monuments,
Whereby whole cities have escap'd the plague,

And thousand desp'rate maladies been eas'd?
Yet art thou still but Faustus, and a man.
Couldst thou make men to live eternally,
Or, being dead, raise them to life again,
Then this profession were to be esteem'd.
Physic, farewell! Where is Justinian? [*Reads.*
Si una eademque res legatur duobus, alter rem, alter valorem rei, &c.

A pretty case of paltry legacies! [*Reads.*
Exhaereditare filium non potest pater, nisi, &c.
Such is the subject of the institute,
And universal body of the law:
His study fits a mercenary drudge,
Who aims at nothing but external trash;
Too servile and illiberal for me.
When all is done, divinity is best:
Jerome's Bible, Faustus; view it well. [*Reads.*
Stipendium peccati mors est. Ha! *Stipendium, &c.*
The reward of sin is death: that's hard. [*Reads.*
Si peccasse negamus, fallimur, et nulla est in nobis veritas:
If we say that we have no sin, we deceive ourselves, and
there's no truth in us.
Why, then, belike we must sin, and so consequently die:
Aye, we must die an everlasting death.
What doctrine call you this, *Che serà, serà:*
What will be, shall be? Divinity, adieu!
These metaphysics of magicians,
And necromantic books are heavenly;
Lines, circles, signs, letters, and characters;
Aye, these are those that Faustus most desires.
O, what a world of profit and delight,
Of power, of honour, of omnipotence,

Is promis'd to the studious artizan!
All things that move between the quiet poles
Shall be at my command: emperors and kings
Are but obeyèd in their several provinces,
Nor can they raise the wind, or rend the clouds;
But his dominion that exceeds in this,
Stretcheth as far as doth the mind of man;
A sound magician is a mighty god:
Here, Faustus, tire thy brains to gain a deity!

Enter WAGNER.

Wagner, commend me to my dearest friends,
The German Valdes and Cornelius;
Request them earnestly to visit me.
    WAGNER. I will, sir.   [*Exit.*
    FAUSTUS. Their conference will be a greater help to me
Than all my labours, plod I ne'er so fast.

Enter the good Angel *and* the evil Angel.

    GOOD ANGEL. O, Faustus, lay that damnèd book aside,
And gaze not on it, lest it tempt thy soul,
And heap God's heavy wrath upon thy head!
Read, read the Scriptures:—that is blasphemy.
    EVIL ANGEL. Go forward, Faustus, in that famous art
Wherein all Nature's treasure is contain'd:
Be thou on earth as Jove is in the sky,
Lord and commander of these elements. [*Exeunt* Angels.
    FAUSTUS. How am I glutted with conceit of this!
Shall I make spirits fetch me what I please,
Resolve me of all ambiguities,
Perform what desperate enterprise I will?
I'll have them fly to India for gold,

Ransack the ocean for orient pearl,
And search all corners of the new-found world
For pleasant fruits and princely delicates;
I'll have them read me strange philosophy,
And tell the secrets of all foreign kings;
I'll have them wall all Germany with brass,
And make swift Rhine circle fair Wittenberg;
I'll have them fill the public schools with silk,
Wherewith the students shall be bravely clad;
I'll levy soldiers with the coin they bring,
And chase the Prince of Parma from our land,
And reign sole king of all our provinces;
Yea, stranger engines for the brunt of war,
Than was the fiery keel at Antwerp's bridge,
I'll make my servile spirits to invent.

Enter VALDES *and* CORNELIUS.

Come, German Valdes, and Cornelius,
And make me blest with your sage conference!
Valdes, sweet Valdes, and Cornelius,
Know that your words have won me at the last
To practise magic and concealèd arts:
Yet not your words only, but mine own fantasy,
That will receive no object; for my head
But ruminates on necromantic skill.
Philosophy is odious and obscure;
Both law and physic are for petty wits;
Divinity is basest of the three,
Unpleasant, harsh, contemptible, and vile:
'Tis magic, magic, that hath ravish'd me.
Then, gentle friends, aid me in this attempt;
And I, that have with concise syllogisms

Gravell'd the pastors of the German church,
And made the flowering pride of Wittenberg
Swarm to my problems, as the infernal spirits
On sweet Musaeus when he came to hell,
Will be as cunning as Agrippa was,
Whose shadows made all Europe honour him.

    VALDES.   Faustus, these books, thy wit, and our experi-
        ence,
Shall make all nations to canónize us.
As Indian Moors obey their Spanish lords,
So shall the subjects of every element
Be always serviceable to us three;
Like lions shall they guard us when we please;
Like Almain rutters with their horsemen's staves,
Or Lapland giants, trotting by our sides;
Sometimes like women, or unwedded maids,
Shadowing more beauty in their airy brows
Than have the white breasts of the queen of love:
From Venice shall they drag huge argosies,
And from America the golden fleece
That yearly stuffs old Philip's treasury;
If learnèd Faustus will be resolute.

    FAUSTUS.   Valdes, as resolute am I in this
As thou to live: therefore object it not.

    CORNELIUS.   The miracles that magic will perform
Will make thee vow to study nothing else.
He that is grounded in astrology,
Enrich'd with tongues, well seen in minerals,
Hath all the principles magic doth require:
Then doubt not, Faustus, but to be renown'd,
And more frequented for this mystery
Than heretofore the Delphian oracle.

The spirits tell me they can dry the sea,
And fetch the treasure of all foreign wrecks,
Aye, all the wealth that our forefathers hid
Within the massy entrails of the earth:
Then tell me, Faustus, what shall we three want?

FAUSTUS.   Nothing, Cornelius. O, this cheers my soul!
Come, show me some demonstrations magical,
That I may conjure in some lusty grove,
And have these joys in full possession.

VALDES.   Then haste thee to some solitary grove,
And bear wise Bacon's and Albertus' works,
The Hebrew Psalter, and New Testament;
And whatsoever else is requisite
We will inform thee ere our conference cease.

CORNELIUS.   Valdes, first let him know the words of
     art;
And then, all other ceremonies learn'd,
Faustus may try his cunning by himself.

VALDES.   First I'll instruct thee in the rudiments,
And then wilt thou be perfecter than I.

FAUSTUS.   Then come and dine with me, and, after
     meat,
We'll canvass every quiddity thereof;
For, ere I sleep, I'll try what I can do:
This night I'll conjure, though I die therefore.

                                        [*Exeunt.*

SCENE III.

Enter FAUSTUS *to conjure.*

FAUSTUS.   Now that the gloomy shadow of the earth,
Longing to view Orion's drizzling look,

Leaps from th' antarctic world unto the sky,
And dims the welkin with her pitchy breath,
Faustus, begin thine incantations,
And try if devils will obey thy hest,
Seeing thou hast pray'd and sacrific'd to them.
Within this circle is Jehovah's name,
Forward and backward anagrammatiz'd,
The breviated names of holy saints,
Figures of every adjunct to the heavens,
And characters of signs and erring stars,
By which the spirits are enforc'd to rise:
Then fear not, Faustus, but be resolute,
And try the uttermost magic can perform.—
Sint mihi dei Acherontis propitii! Valeat numen triplex Jehovae! Ignei, aerii, aquatani spiritus, salvete! Orientis princeps Belzebub, inferni ardentis monarcha, et Demogorgon, propitiamus vos, ut appareat et surgat Mephistophilis. Quid tu moraris? Per Jehovam, Gehennam, et consecratam aquam quam nunc spargo, signumque crucis quod nunc facio, et per vota nostra, ipse nunc surgat nobis dicatus Mephistophilis!

Enter MEPHISTOPHILIS.

I charge thee to return, and change thy shape;
Thou art too ugly to attend on me:
Go, and return an old Franciscan friar;
That holy shape becomes a devil best.

　　　　　　　　　　　　　　[*Exit* MEPHISTOPHILIS.

I see there's virtue in my heavenly words:
Who would not be proficient in this art?
How pliant is this Mephistophilis,
Full of obedience and humility!

Such is the force of magic and my spells:
Now, Faustus, thou art conjuror laureat,
That canst command great Mephistophilis:
Quin regis Mephistophilis fratris imagine.

   Re-enter MEPHISTOPHILIS *like a Franciscan friar.*

MEPHISTOPHILIS. Now, Faustus, what wouldst thou
   have me do?

FAUSTUS. I charge thee wait upon me whilst I live,
To do whatever Faustus shall command,
Be it to make the moon drop from her sphere,
Or th' ocean to overwhelm the world.

MEPHISTOPHILIS. I am a servant to great Lucifer,
And may not follow thee without his leave:
No more than he commands must we perform.

FAUSTUS. Did not he charge thee to appear to me?

MEPHISTOPHILIS. No, I came hither of mine own
   accord.

FAUSTUS. Did not my conjuring speeches raise thee?
   speak.

MEPHISTOPHILIS. That was the cause, but yet *per
   accidens;*
For, when we hear one rack the name of God,
Abjure the Scriptures and his Saviour Christ,
We fly, in hope to get his glorious soul;
Nor will we come, unless he use such means
Whereby he is in danger to be damn'd.
Therefore the shortest cut for conjuring
Is stoutly to abjure the Trinity,
And pray devoutly to the prince of hell.

FAUSTUS. So Faustus hath
Already done; and holds this principle,

There is no chief but only Belzebub;
To whom Faustus doth dedicate himself.
This word 'damnation' terrifies him not,
For he confounds hell in Elysium:
His ghost be with the old philosophers!
But, leaving these vain trifles of men's souls,
Tell me what is that Lucifer thy lord?

    MEPHISTOPHILIS.   Arch-regent and commander of all
        spirits.

    FAUSTUS.   Was not that Lucifer an angel once?

    MEPHISTOPHILIS.   Yes, Faustus, and most dearly lov'd
        of God.

    FAUSTUS.   How comes it, then, that he is prince of
        devils?

    MEPHISTOPHILIS.   O, by aspiring pride and insolence;
For which God threw him from the face of heaven.

    FAUSTUS.   And what are you that live with Lucifer?

    MEPHISTOPHILIS.   Unhappy spirits that fell with
        Lucifer,
Conspir'd against our God with Lucifer,
And are for ever damn'd with Lucifer.

    FAUSTUS.   Where are you damn'd?

    MEPHISTOPHILIS.   In hell.

    FAUSTUS.   How comes it, then, that thou art out of
        hell?

    MEHISTOPHILIS.   Why, this is hell, nor am I out of it:
Think'st thou that I, who saw the face of God,
And tasted the eternal joys of heaven,
Am not tormented with ten thousand hells,
In being depriv'd of everlasting bliss?
O, Faustus, leave these frivolous demands,
Which strike a terror to my fainting soul!

FAUSTUS.   What, is great Mephistophilis so passionate
For being deprivèd of the joys of heaven?
Learn thou of Faustus manly fortitude,
And scorn those joys thou never shalt possess.
Go bear these tidings to great Lucifer:
Seeing Faustus hath incurr'd eternal death
By desp'rate thoughts against Jove's deity,
Say, he surrenders up to him his soul,
So he will spare him four and twenty years,
Letting him live in all voluptuousness;
Having thee ever to attend on me,
To give me whatsoever I shall ask,
To tell me whatsoever I demand,
To slay mine enemies, to aid my friends,
And always be obedient to my will.
Go and return to mighty Lucifer,
And meet me in my study at midnight,
And then resolve me of thy master's mind.

MEPHISTOPHILIS.   I will, Faustus.   [*Exit.*

FAUSTUS.   Had I as many souls as there be stars,
I'd give them all for Mephistophilis.
By him I'll be great emp'ror of the world,
And make a bridge thorough the moving air,
To pass the ocean with a band of men;
I'll join the hills that bind the Afric shore,
And make that country continent to Spain,
And both contributory to my crown:
The Emp'ror shall not live but by my leave,
Nor any potentate of Germany.
Now that I have obtain'd what I desir'd,
I'll live in speculation of this art,
Till Mephistophilis return again.   [*Exit.*

SCENE V.

Enter FAUSTUS *in his Study.*

FAUSTUS. Now, Faustus, must thou needs be damn'd,
and canst thou not be sav'd:
What boots it, then, to think of God or heaven?
Away with such vain fancies, and despair;
Despair in God, and trust in Belzebub:
Now go not backward; no, Faustus, be resolute:
Why waver'st thou? O, something soundeth in mine ears,
'Abjure this magic, turn to God again!'
Aye, and Faustus will turn to God again.
To God? he loves thee not;
The god thou serv'st is thine own appetite,
Wherein is fix'd the love of Belzebub:
To him I'll build an altar and a church,
And offer lukewarm blood of new-born babes.

Enter Good Angel *and* Evil.

GOOD ANGEL. Sweet Faustus, leave that execrable art.
FAUSTUS. Contrition, prayer, repentance—what of
them?
GOOD ANGEL. O, they are means to bring thee unto
heaven!
EVIL ANGEL. Rather illusions, fruits of lunacy,
That makes men foolish that do trust them most.
GOOD ANGEL. Sweet Faustus, think of heaven and heav-
enly things.
EVIL ANGEL. No, Faustus; think of honour and of
wealth.   [*Exeunt* Angels.
FAUSTUS. Of wealth!
Why, the signiory of Emden shall be mine.

When Mephistophilis shall stand by me,
What god can hurt thee, Faustus? thou art safe:
Cast no more doubts.—Come, Mephistophilis,
And bring glad tidings from great Lucifer;—
Is 't not midnight?—come, Mephistophilis,
Veni, veni, Mephistophile!

Enter MEPHISTOPHILIS.

Now tell me what says Lucifer, thy lord?

MEPHISTOPHILIS. That I shall wait on Faustus while
   he lives,
So he will buy my service with his soul.

FAUSTUS. Already Faustus hath hazarded that for thee.

MEPHISTOPHILIS. But, Faustus, thou must bequeath it
   solemnly,
And write a deed of gift with thine own blood;
For that security craves great Lucifer.
If thou deny it, I will back to hell.

FAUSTUS. Stay, Mephistophilis, and tell me, what good
Will my soul do thy lord?

MEPHISTOPHILIS. Enlarge his kingdom.

FAUSTUS. Is that the reason why he tempts us thus?

MEPHISTOPHILIS. *Solamen miseris socios habuisse
   doloris.*

FAUSTUS. Why, have you any pain that torture others?

MEPHISTOPHILIS. As great as have the human souls of
   men.
But tell me, Faustus, shall I have thy soul?
And I will be thy slave, and wait on thee,
And give thee more than thou hast wit to ask.

FAUSTUS. Aye, Mephistophilis, I give it thee.

MEPHISTOPHILIS. Then, Faustus, stab thine arm cour-
ageously,
And bind thy soul, that at some certain day
Great Lucifer may claim it as his own;
And then be thou as great as Lucifer.
FAUSTUS. [*Stabbing his arm*] Lo, Mephistophilis, for
love of thee,
I cut mine arm, and with my proper blood
Assure my soul to be great Lucifer's,
Chief lord and regent of perpetual night!
View here the blood that trickles from mine arm,
And let it be propitious for my wish.
MEPHISTOPHILIS. But, Faustus, thou must
Write it in manner of a deed of gift.
FAUSTUS. Aye, so I will [*Writes*]. But, Mephistophilis,
My blood congeals, and I can write no more.
MEPHISTOPHILIS. I'll fetch thee fire to dissolve it
straight. [*Exit.*
FAUSTUS. What might the staying of my blood portend?
Is it unwilling I should write this bill?
Why streams it not, that I may write afresh?
Faustus gives to thee his soul: ah, there it stay'd!
Why shouldst thou not? is not thy soul thine own?
Then write again, *Faustus gives to thee his soul.*

Re-enter MEPHISTOPHILIS *with a chafer of coals.*

MEPHISTOPHILIS. See, Faustus, here is fire; set it on.
FAUSTUS. So, now the blood begins to clear again;
Now will I make an end immediately. [*Writes.*
MEPHISTOPHILIS. O, what will not I do to obtain his
soul? [*Aside.*

FAUSTUS. *Consummatum est;* this bill is ended,
And Faustus hath bequeath'd his soul to Lucifer.
But what is this inscription on mine arm?
Homo, fuge: whither should I fly?
If unto God, he'll throw me down to hell.
My senses are deceiv'd; here's nothing writ:—
I see it plain; here in this place is writ,
Homo, fuge: yet shall not Faustus fly.

MEPHISTOPHILIS. I'll fetch him somewhat to delight
his mind.   [*Aside, and then exit.*

Re-enter MEPHISTOPHILIS *with* Devils, *giving crowns and rich apparel to* FAUSTUS, *dance, and then depart.*

FAUSTUS. Speak, Mephistophilis, what means this show?

MEPHISTOPHILIS. Nothing, Faustus, but to delight thy
mind withal,
And to show thee what magic can perform.

FAUSTUS. But may I raise up spirits when I please?

MEPHISTOPHILIS. Aye, Faustus, and do greater things
than these.

FAUSTUS. Then there's enough for a thousand souls.
Here, Mephistophilis, receive this scroll,
A deed of gift of body and of soul:
But yet conditionally that thou perform
All articles prescrib'd between us both.

MEPHISTOPHILIS. Faustus, I swear by hell and Lucifer
To effect all promises between us made!

FAUSTUS. Then hear me read them, Mephistophilis.
[*Reads*] *On these conditions following. First, that Faustus
may be a spirit in form and substance. Secondly, that
Mephistophilis shall be his servant, and at his command.*

Thirdly, that Mephistophilis shall do for him, and bring him whatsoever. Fourthly, that he shall be in his chamber or house invisible. Lastly, that he shall appear to the said John Faustus, at all times, in what form or shape soever he please. I, John Faustus, of Wittenberg, Doctor, by these presents, do give both body and soul to Lucifer prince of the East, and his minister Mephistophilis; and furthermore grant unto them that, twenty-four years being expired, the articles above written inviolate, full power to fetch or carry the said John Faustus, body and soul, flesh, blood, or goods, into their habitation wheresoever. By me, John Faustus.

MEPHISTOPHILIS.   Speak, Faustus, do you deliver this as your deed?

FAUSTUS.   Aye, take it, and the devil give thee good on 't.

MEPHISTOPHILIS.   Now, Faustus, ask what thou wilt.

FAUSTUS.   First will I question with thee about hell. Tell me, where is the place that men call hell?

MEPHISTOPHILIS.   Under the heavens.

FAUSTUS.   Aye, so are all things else. But whereabouts?

MEPHISTOPHILIS.   Within the bowels of these elements, Where we are tortur'd and remain for ever: Hell hath no limits, nor is circumscrib'd In one self place; for where we are is hell, And where hell is, there must we ever be: And, to conclude, when all the world dissolves, And every creature shall be purified, All places shall be hell that is not heaven.

FAUSTUS.   Come, I think hell's a fable.

MEPHISTOPHILIS.   Aye, think so still, till experience change thy mind.

FAUSTUS. Why, think'st thou, then, that Faustus shall
   be damn'd?
MEPHISTOPHILIS. Aye, of necessity, for here's the scroll
Wherein thou hast given thy soul to Lucifer.
FAUSTUS. Aye, and body too: but what of that?
Think'st thou that Faustus is so fond to imagine
That, after this life, there is any pain?
Tush, these are trifles and mere old wives' tales.
MEPHISTOPHILIS. But, Faustus, I am an instance to
   prove the contrary;
For I am damnèd, and am now in hell.
FAUSTUS. How! now in hell!
Nay, an this be hell, I'll willingly be damn'd here:
What! sleeping, eating, walking, and disputing!
But leaving off this, let me have a wife,
The fairest maid in Germany, for I
Am wanton and lascivious
And cannot live without a wife.
MEPHISTOPHILIS. Well, Faustus, thou shalt have a wife.

He fetches in a woman-devil, *with fireworks.*

FAUSTUS. What sight is this?
MEPHISTOPHILIS. Now, Faustus, wilt thou have a wife?
FAUSTUS. Here's a hot whore indeed! No, I'll no wife.
MEPHISTOPHILIS. Tut, Faustus,
Marriage is but a ceremonial toy;
If thou lovest me, think no more of it.
She whom thine eye shall like, thy heart shall have,
Be she as chaste as was Penelope,
As wise as Saba, or as beautiful

As was bright Lucifer before his fall.
Hold, take this book, peruse it thoroughly:

[Gives book.

The iterating of these lines brings gold;
The framing of this circle on the ground
Brings whirlwinds, tempests, thunder, and lightning;
Pronounce this thrice devoutly to thyself,
And men in armour shall appear to thee,
Ready to execute what thou desir'st.

FAUSTUS.   Thanks, Mephistophilis; yet fain would I
have a book wherein I might behold all spells and incantations, that I might raise up spirits when I please.

MEPHISTOPHILIS.   Here they are in this book.

[Turns to them.

FAUSTUS.   Now would I have a book where I might see
all characters and planets of the heavens, that I might
know their motions and dispositions.

MEPHISTOPHILIS.   Here they are too.

[Turns to them.

FAUSTUS.   Nay, let me have one book more,—and then
I have done,—wherein I might see all plants, herbs, and
trees, that grow upon the earth.

MEPHISTOPHILIS.   Here they be.

FAUSTUS.   O, thou art deceived.

MEPHISTOPHILIS.   Tut, I warrant thee.

[Turns to them.

SCENE VI.

Enter FAUSTUS *in his Study and* MEPHISTOPHILIS.

FAUSTUS.   When I behold the heavens, then I repent,
And curse thee, wicked Mephistophilis,
Because thou hast depriv'd me of those joys.

MEPHISTOPHILIS. Why, Faustus,
Thinkest thou heaven is such a glorious thing?
I tell thee, 'tis not half so fair as thou,
Or any man that breathes on earth.

FAUSTUS. How prov'st thou that?

MEPHISTOPHILIS. 'Twas made for man, therefore is
man more excellent.

FAUSTUS. If it were made for man, 'twas made for me:
I will renounce this magic and repent.

Enter Good Angel *and* Evil Angel.

GOOD ANGEL. Faustus, repent; yet God will pity thee.

EVIL ANGEL. Thou art a spirit; God cannot pity thee.

FAUSTUS. Who buzzeth in mine ears I am a spirit?
Be I a devil, yet God may pity me;
Aye, God will pity me, if I repent.

EVIL ANGEL. Aye, but Faustus never shall repent.

[*Exeunt* Angels.

FAUSTUS. My heart's so harden'd, I cannot repent:
Scarce can I name salvation, faith, or heaven,
But fearful echoes thunder in mine ears,
'Faustus, thou art damn'd!' Then swords, and knives,
Poison, guns, halters, and envenom'd steel
Are laid before me to dispatch myself;
And long ere this I should have slain myself,
Had not sweet pleasure conquer'd deep despair.
Have not I made blind Homer sing to me
Of Alexander's love and Oenon's death?
And hath not he, that built the walls of Thebes
With ravishing sound of his melodious harp,
Made music with my Mephistophilis?

[303]

Why should I die, then, or basely despair?
I am resolv'd; Faustus shall ne'er repent.—
Come, Mephistophilis, let us dispute again,
And argue of divine astrology.
Tell me, are there many heavens above the moon?
Are all celestial bodies but one globe,
As is the substance of this centric earth?

MEPHISTOPHILIS.   As are the elements, such are the
   spheres,
Even from the moon unto the imperial heaven,
Mutually folded in each other's orb,
And, Faustus,
All jointly move upon one axletree,
Whose terminine is term'd the world's wide pole;
Nor are the names of Saturn, Mars, or Jupiter
Feign'd, but are erring stars.

FAUSTUS.   But, tell me, have they all one motion, both
situ et tempore?

MEPHISTOPHILIS.   All jointly move from east to west
in twenty-four hours upon the poles of the world; but
differ in their motion upon the poles of the zodiac.

FAUSTUS.   Tush,
These slender trifles Wagner can decide:
Hath Mephistophilis no greater skill?
Who knows not the double motion of the planets?
The first is finish'd in a natural day;
The second thus: as Saturn in thirty years; Jupiter in
twelve; Mars in four; the Sun, Venus, and Mercury in a
year; the Moon in twenty-eight days. Tush, these are
freshmen's suppositions. But, tell me, hath every sphere
a dominion or *intelligentia?*

MEPHISTOPHILIS.   Aye.

FAUSTUS. How many heavens or spheres are there?

MEPHISTOPHILIS. Nine; the seven planets, the firmament, and the imperial heaven.

FAUSTUS. But is there not *coelum igneum, et cristallinum?*

MEPHISTOPHILIS. No, Faustus, they be but fables.

FAUSTUS. Well, resolve me in this question: why have we not conjunctions, oppositions, aspects, eclipses, all at one time, but in some years we have more, in some less?

MEPHISTOPHILIS. *Per inaequalem motum respectu totius.*

FAUSTUS. Well, I am answered. Tell me who made the world?

MEPHISTOPHILIS. I will not.

FAUSTUS. Sweet Mephistophilis, tell me.

MEPHISTOPHILIS. Move me not, for I will not tell thee.

FAUSTUS. Villain, have I not bound thee to tell me any thing?

MEPHISTOPHILIS. Aye, that is not against our kingdom; but this is. Think thou on hell, Faustus, for thou art damned.

FAUSTUS. Think, Faustus, upon God that made the world.

MEPHISTOPHILIS. Remember this.   [*Exit.*

FAUSTUS. Aye, go, accursèd spirit, to ugly hell!
'Tis thou hast damn'd distressèd Faustus' soul.
Is 't not too late?

Enter Good Angel *and* Evil Angel.

EVIL ANGEL. Too late.

GOOD ANGEL. Never too late, if Faustus can repent.

[305]

EVIL ANGEL.   If thou repent, devils shall tear thee in
    pieces.

GOOD ANGEL.   Repent, and they shall never raze thy
    skin.   [*Exeunt* Angels.

FAUSTUS.   Aye, Christ, my Saviour,
Seek to save distressèd Faustus' soul!

    Enter LUCIFER, BELZEBUB, *and* MEPHISTOPHILIS.

LUCIFER.   Christ cannot save thy soul, for he is just.
There's none but I have int'rest in the same.

FAUSTUS.   O, who art thou that look'st so terrible?

LUCIFER.   I am Lucifer,
And this is my companion-prince in hell.

FAUSTUS.   O, Faustus, they are come to fetch away thy
    soul!

LUCIFER.   We come to tell thee thou dost injure us;
Thou talk'st of Christ, contráry to thy promise:
Thou shouldst not think of God: think of the devil,
And of his dam too.

FAUSTUS.   Nor will I henceforth: pardon me in this,
And Faustus vows never to look to heaven,
Never to name God, or to pray to him,
To burn his Scriptures, slay his ministers,
And make my spirits pull his churches down.

LUCIFER.   Do so, and we will highly gratify thee.
Faustus, we are come from hell to show thee some pas-
time: sit down, and thou shalt see all the Seven Deadly
Sins appear in their proper shapes.

FAUSTUS.   That sight will be as pleasing unto me,
As Paradise was to Adam, the first day
Of his creation.

[306]

LUCIFER.   Talk not of Paradise nor creation; but mark this show: talk of the devil, and nothing else.—Come away!

Enter the Seven Deadly Sins.

Now, Faustus, examine them of their several names and dispositions.

FAUSTUS.   What art thou, the first?

PRIDE.   I am Pride. I disdain to have any parents. I am like Ovid's flea; I can creep into every corner of a wench; sometimes, like a periwig, I sit upon her brow; or, like a fan of feathers, I kiss her lips; indeed, I do—what do I not? But fie, what a scent is here! I'll not speak another word, except the ground were perfumed, and covered with cloth of arras.

FAUSTUS.   What are thou, the second?

COVETOUSNESS.   I am Covetousness, begotten of an old churl, in an old leathern bag; and, might I have my wish, I would desire that this house and all the people in it were turned to gold, that I might lock you up in my good chest, O my sweet gold!

FAUSTUS.   What art thou, the third?

WRATH.   I am Wrath. I had neither father nor mother: I leapt out of a lion's mouth when I was scarce half-an-hour old; and ever since I have run up and down the world with this case of rapiers, wounding myself when I had nobody to fight withal. I was born in hell; and look to it, for some of you shall be my father.

FAUSTUS.   What art thou, the fourth?

ENVY.   I am Envy, born of a chimney-sweeper and an oyster-wife. I cannot read, and therefore wish all books were burnt. I am lean with seeing others eat. O, that there would come a famine through all the world, that all might die, and I live alone! then thou shouldst see how fat I would be. But must thou sit, and I stand? come down, with a vengeance!

FAUSTUS. Away, envious rascal!—What art thou, the fifth?

GLUTTONY. Who I, sir? I am Gluttony. My parents are all dead, and the devil a penny they have left me, but a bare pension, and that is thirty meals a-day and ten bevers,—a small trifle to suffice nature. O, I come of a royal parentage! my grandfather was a Gammon of Bacon, my grandmother a Hogshead of Claret-wine; my godfathers were these, Peter Pickle-herring and Martin Martlemas-beef; O, but my godmother, she was a jolly gentlewoman, and well beloved in every good town and city; her name was Mistress Margery March-beer. Now, Faustus, thou hast heard all my progeny; wilt thou bid me to supper?

FAUSTUS. No, I'll see thee hanged; thou wilt eat up all my victuals.

GLUTTONY. Then the devil choke thee!

FAUSTUS. Choke thyself, glutton!—What art thou, the sixth?

SLOTH. I am Sloth. I was born on a sunny bank, where I have lain ever since; and you have done me great injury to bring me from thence: let me be carried thither again by Gluttony and Lechery. I'll not speak another word for a king's ransom.

FAUSTUS. What are you, Mistress Minx, the seventh and last?

LECHERY. Who, I, sir? I am one that loves an inch of

raw mutton better than an ell of fried stock-fish; and the
first letter of my name begins with Lechery.

LUCIFER. Away, to hell, to hell!   [*Exeunt the* Sins.]
Now, Faustus, how dost thou like this?

FAUSTUS. O, this feeds my soul!

LUCIFER. Tut, Fastus, in hell is all manner of delight.

FAUSTUS. O, might I see hell, and return again,
How happy were I then!

LUCIFER. Thou shalt; I will send for thee at midnight.
In meantime take this book; peruse it thoroughly,
And thou shalt turn thyself into what shape thou wilt.

FAUSTUS. Great thanks, mighty Lucifer!
This will I keep as chary as my life.

LUCIFER. Farewell, Faustus, and think on the devil.

FAUSTUS. Farewell, great Lucifer. Come, Mephis-
    tophilis.   [*Exeunt omnes.*

Enter the CHORUS.

CHORUS. Learnèd Faustus,
To know the secrets of astronomy
Graven in the book of Jove's high firmament,
Did mount himself to scale Olympus' top,
Being seated in a chariot burning bright,
Drawn by the strength of yoky dragons' necks,
He views the clouds, the planets, and the stars,
The tropic zones, and quarters of the sky,
From the bright circle of the hornèd moon,
E'en to the height of *Primum Mobile:*
And whirling round with this circumference,
Within the concave compass of the pole;
From east to west his dragons swiftly glide,
And in eight days did bring him home again.

Not long he stayed within his quiet house,
To rest his bones after his weary toil,
But new exploits do hale him out again,
And mounted then upon a dragon's back,
That with his wings did part the subtle air,
He now is gone to prove cosmography,
That measures coasts, and kingdoms of the earth:
And, as I guess, will first arrive at Rome,
To see the Pope and manner of his court,
And take some part of holy Peter's feast,
That to this day is highly solemniz'd.   [*Exit.*

SCENE VII. THE POPE'S PRIVY-CHAMBER.

Enter FAUSTUS *and* MEPHISTOPHILIS.

FAUSTUS.   Having now, my good Mephistophilis,
Pass'd with delight the stately town of Trier,
Environ'd round with airy mountain-tops,
With walls of flint, and deep-entrenchèd lakes,
Not to be won by any conquering prince;
From Paris next, coasting the realm of France,
We saw the river Maine fall into Rhine,
Whose banks are set with groves of fruitful vines;
Then up to Naples, rich Campania,
Whose buildings fair and gorgeous to the eye,
The streets straight forth, and pav'd with finest brick,
Quarter the town in four equivalents;
There saw we learnèd Maro's golden tomb,
The way he cut, an English mile in length,
Thorough a rock of stone, in one night's space;
From thence to Venice, Padua, and the rest,
In one of which a sumptuous temple stands,

That threats the stars with her aspiring top,
Whose frame is paved with sundry coloured stones,
And roofed aloft with curious work in gold.
Thus hitherto hath Faustus spent his time:
But tell me now what resting-place is this?
Hast thou, as erst I did command,
Conducted me within the walls of Rome?

MEPHISTOPHILIS. Faustus, I have; and, because we will
not be unprovided, I have taken up his Holiness' privy-
chamber for our use.

FAUSTUS. I hope his Holiness will bid us welcome.

MEPHISTOPHILIS. Tut, 'tis no matter, man; we'll be
bold with his good cheer.
And now, my Faustus, that thou may'st perceive
What Rome containeth to delight thee with,
Know that this city stands upon seven hills
That underprop the groundwork of the same:
Just through the midst runs flowing Tiber's stream,
With winding banks that cut it in two parts;
Over the which four stately bridges lean,
That make safe passage to each part of Rome:
Upon the bridge call'd Ponte Angelo
Erected is a castle passing strong,
Within whose walls such store of ordnance are,
And double cannons fram'd of carvèd brass,
As match the days within one cómplete year;
Besides the gates, and high pyramides,
Which Julius Caesar brought from Africa.

FAUSTUS. Now, by the kingdoms of infernal rule,
Of Styx, of Acheron, and the fiery lake
Of ever-burning Phlegethon, I swear
That I do long to see the monuments

And situation of bright-splendent Rome:
Come, therefore, let's away.

    MEPHISTOPHILIS.   Nay, Faustus, stay: I know you'd
      fain see the Pope,
And take some part of holy Peter's feast,
Where thou shalt see a troop of bald-pate friars,
Whose *summum bonum* is in belly-cheer.

    FAUSTUS. ° Well, I'm content to compass then some
      sport,
And by their folly make us merriment.
Then charm me, that I
May be invisible, to do what I please,
Unseen of any whilst I stay in Rome.

                          [MEPHISTOPHILIS *charms him.*

    MEPHISTOPHILIS.   So, Faustus; now
Do what thou wilt, thou shalt not be discern'd.

  Sound a Sonnet. Enter the POPE *and the* CARDINAL OF
    LORRAINE *to the banquet, with* Friars *attending.*

    POPE.   My Lord of Lorraine, will't please you draw
      near?

    FAUSTUS.   Fall to, and the devil choke you, an you
      spare!

    POPE.   How now! who's that which spake?—Friars,
      look about.

    FIRST FRIAR.   Here's nobody, if it like your Holiness.

    POPE.   My lord, here is a dainty dish was sent me from
the Bishop of Milan.

    FAUSTUS.   I thank you, sir.   [*Snatches the dish.*

    POPE.   How now! who's that which snatched the meat
from me? will no man look?—My lord, this dish was sent
me from the Cardinal of Florence.

FAUSTUS. You say true; I'll ha 't.   [*Snatches the dish.*

POPE. What, again?—My lord, I'll drink to your grace.

FAUSTUS. I'll pledge your grace.   [*Snatches the cup.*

CARDINAL OF LORRAINE. My lord, it may be some ghost, newly crept out of Purgatory, come to beg a pardon of your Holiness.

POPE. It may be so.—Friars, prepare a dirge to lay the fury of this ghost.—Once again, my lord, fall to.

[*The* POPE *crosses himself.*

FAUSTUS. What, are you crossing of yourself?
Well, use that trick no more, I would advise you.

[*The* POPE *crosses himself again.*

Well, there's the second time. Aware the third;
I give you fair warning.

[*The* POPE *crosses himself again, and* FAUSTUS *hits him a box of the ear; and they all run away.*

Come on, Mephistophilis; what shall we do?

MEPHISTOPHILIS. Nay, I know not: we shall be cursed with bell, book, and candle.

FAUSTUS. How! bell, book, and candle,—candle, book, and bell,—
Forward and backward, to curse Faustus to hell!
Anon you shall hear a hog grunt, a calf bleat, and an ass bray,
Because it is Saint Peter's holiday.

Re-enter all the Friars *to sing the Dirge.*

FIRST FRIAR. Come, brethren, let's about our business with good devotion.

They sing.

Cursed be he that stole away his Holiness' meat from the table! maledicat Dominus!

Cursed be he that struck his Holiness a blow on the face! maledicat Dominus!

Cursed be he that took Friar Sandelo a blow on the pate! maledicat Dominus!

Cursed be he that disturbeth our holy dirge! maledicat Dominus!

Cursed be he that took away his Holiness' wine! male-dicat Dominus!

Et omnes Sancti! Amen!

[MEPHISTOPHILIS *and* FAUSTUS *beat the* Friars *and fling fireworks among them; and so exeunt.*

Enter Chorus.

CHORUS. When Faustus had with pleasure ta'en the view
Of rarest things, and royal courts of kings,
He stay'd his course, and so returnèd home;
Where such as bear his absence but with grief,
I mean his friends and near'st companions,
Did gratulate his safety with kind words,
And in their conference of what befell,
Touching his journey through the world and air,
They put forth questions of astrology,
Which Faustus answer'd with such learnèd skill
As they admir'd and wonder'd at his wit.
Now is his fame spread forth in every land.

SCENE XIII. A ROOM IN THE HOUSE OF FAUSTUS.

Enter WAGNER.

WAGNER. I think my master means to die shortly,
For he hath given to me all his goods:

[314]

And yet, methinketh, if that death were near,
He would not banquet, and carouse, and swill
Amongst the students, as even now he doth,
Who are at supper with such belly-cheer
As Wagner ne'er beheld in all his life.
See, where they come! belike the feast is ended.

Enter FAUSTUS *with two or three* Scholars, *and*
MEPHISTOPHILIS.

FIRST SCHOLAR. Master Doctor Faustus, since our conference about fair ladies, which was the beautiful'st in all
the world, we have determined with ourselves that Helen
of Greece was the admirablest lady that ever lived: therefore, Master Doctor, if you will do us that favour, as to
let us see that peerless dame of Greece, whom all the
world admires for majesty, we should think ourselves
much beholding unto you.

FAUSTUS. Gentlemen,
For that I know your friendship is unfeign'd,
And Faustus' custom is not to deny
The just requests of those that wish him well,
You shall behold that peerless dame of Greece,
No otherways for pomp and majesty
Than when Sir Paris cross'd the seas with her,
And brought the spoils to rich Dardania.
Be silent, then, for danger is in words.

[*Music sounds, and* HELEN *passeth over the stage.*
SECOND SCHOLAR. Too simple is my wit to tell her
    praise,
Whom all the world admires for majesty.

THIRD SCHOLAR. No marvel though the angry Greeks
    pursu'd

With ten years' war the rape of such a queen,
Whose heavenly beauty passeth all compare.

    FIRST SCHOLAR. Since we have seen the pride of
        Nature's works,
And only paragon of excellence,
Let us depart; and for this glorious deed
Happy and blest be Faustus evermore!

    FAUSTUS. Gentlemen, farewell: the same I wish to you.
                       [*Exeunt* Scholars *and* WAGNER.

Enter an Old Man.

    OLD MAN. Ah, Doctor Faustus, that I might prevail
To guide thy steps unto the way of life,
By which sweet path thou may'st attain the goal
That shall conduct thee to celestial rest!
Break heart, drop blood, and mingle it with tears,
Tears falling from repentant heaviness
Of thy most vile and loathsome filthiness,
The stench whereof corrupts the inward soul
With such flagitious crimes of heinous sins
As no commiseration may expel,
But mercy, Faustus, of thy Saviour sweet,
Whose blood alone must wash away thy guilt.

    FAUSTUS. Where art thou, Faustus? wretch, what hast
        thou done?
Damn'd art thou, Faustus, damn'd; despair and die!
Hell calls for right, and with a roaring voice
Says, 'Faustus, come; thine hour is almost come';
And Faustus now will come to do thee right.
                 [MEPHISTOPHILIS *gives him a dagger.*

    OLD MAN. Ah, stay, good Faustus, stay thy desperate
        steps!

[316]

I see an angel hovers o'er thy head,
And, with a vial full of precious grace,
Offers to pour the same into thy soul:
Then call for mercy, and avoid despair.

FAUSTUS.   Ah, my sweet friend, I feel
Thy words to comfort my distressèd soul!
Leave me a while to ponder on my sins.

OLD MAN.   I go, sweet Faustus; but with heavy cheer,
Fearing the ruin of thy hopeless soul.   [*Exit.*

FAUSTUS.   Accursèd Faustus, where is mercy now?
I do repent; and yet I do despair:
Hell strives with grace for conquest in my breast:
What shall I do to shun the snares of death?

MEPHISTOPHILIS.   Thou traitor, Faustus, I arrest thy
soul
For disobedience to my sovereign lord:
Revolt, or I'll in piece-meal tear thy flesh.

FAUSTUS.   Sweet Mephistophilis, entreat thy lord
To pardon my unjust presumption,
And with my blood again I will confirm
My former vow I made to Lucifer.

MEPHISTOPHILIS.   Do it, then, quickly, with unfeignèd
heart,
Lest greater danger do attend thy drift.

  [FAUSTUS *stabs his arm, and writes on a paper with*
    his blood.

FAUSTUS.   Torment, sweet friend, that base and crooked
age,
That durst dissuade me from thy Lucifer,
With greatest torments that our hell affords.

MEPHISTOPHILIS.   His faith is great; I cannot touch his
soul;

But what I may afflict his body with
I will attempt, which is but little worth.

    FAUSTUS.   One thing, good servant, let me crave of
    thee,
To glut the longing of my heart's desire,—
That I might have unto my paramour
That heavenly Helen which I saw of late,
Whose sweet embracings may extinguish clean
These thoughts that do dissuade me from my vow,
And keep mine oath I made to Lucifer.

    MEPHISTOPHILIS.   Faustus, this, or what else thou shalt
    desire,
Shall be perform'd in twinkling of an eye.

Re-enter HELEN.

    FAUSTUS.   Was this the face that launch'd a thousand
    ships,
And burnt the topless towers of Ilium?—
Sweet Helen, make me immortal with a kiss.—

                                [Kisses her.

Her lips suck forth my soul: see where it flies!—
Come, Helen, come, give me my soul again.
Here will I dwell, for heaven is in these lips,
And all is dross that is not Helena.
I will be Paris, and for love of thee,
Instead of Troy, shall Wittenberg be sack'd
And I will combat with weak Menelaus,
And wear thy colours on my plumèd crest;
Yes, I will wound Achilles in the heel,
And then return to Helen for a kiss.
O, thou art fairer than the evening air
Clad in the beauty of a thousand stars;

Brighter art thou than flaming Jupiter
When he appear'd to hapless Semele;
More lovely than the monarch of the sky
In wanton Arethusa's azur'd arms;
And none but thou shalt be my paramour!   [*Exeunt.*

Enter the Old Man.

OLD MAN. Accursèd Faustus, miserable man,
That from thy soul exclud'st the grace of heaven,
And fly'st the throne of his tribunal-seat!

Enter the Devils.

Satan begins to sift me with his pride:
As in this furnace God shall try my faith,
My faith, vile hell, shall triumph over thee.
Ambitious fiends, see how the heavens smile
At your repulse, and laugh your state to scorn!
Hence, hell! for hence I fly unto my God.   [*Exeunt.*

SCENE XIV. THE SAME.

Enter FAUSTUS, *with* Scholars.

FAUSTUS. Ah, gentlemen!
FIRST SCHOLAR. What ails Faustus?
FAUSTUS. Ah, my sweet chamber-fellow, had I lived
with thee, then had I lived still! but now I die eternally.
Look, comes he not? comes he not?
SECOND SCHOLAR. What means Faustus?
THIRD SCHOLAR. Belike he is grown into some sickness
by being over-solitary.

FIRST SCHOLAR. If it be so, we'll have physicians to cure him.—'Tis but a surfeit; never fear, man.

FAUSTUS. A surfeit of deadly sin, that hath damned both body and soul.

SECOND SCHOLAR. Yet, Faustus, look up to heaven; remember God's mercies are infinite.

FAUSTUS. But Faustus' offence can ne'er be pardoned: the serpent that tempted Eve may be saved, but not Faustus. Ah, gentlemen, hear me with patience, and tremble not at my speeches! Though my heart pants and quivers to remember that I have been a student here these thirty years, O, would I had never seen Wittenberg, never read book! and what wonders I have done, all Germany can witness, yea, all the world; for which Faustus hath lost both Germany and the world, yea, heaven itself, heaven, the seat of God, the throne of the blessed, the kingdom of joy; and must remain in hell for ever,— hell, ah, hell, for ever! Sweet friends, what shall become of Faustus, being in hell for ever?

THIRD SCHOLAR. Yet, Faustus, call on God.

FAUSTUS. On God, whom Faustus hath abjured! on God, whom Faustus hath blasphemed! Ah, my God, I would weep! but the devil draws in my tears. Gush forth blood, instead of tears! yea, life and soul—O, he stays my tongue! I would lift up my hands; but see, they hold them, they hold them!

ALL. Who, Faustus?

FAUSTUS. Lucifer and Mephistophilis. Ah, gentlemen, I gave them my soul for my cunning!

ALL. God forbid!

FAUSTUS. God forbade it, indeed; but Faustus hath done it: for vain pleasure of twenty-four years hath Faustus lost eternal joy and felicity. I writ them a bill with mine own blood: the date is expired; the time will come, and he will fetch me.

FIRST SCHOLAR. Why did not Faustus tell us of this before, that divines might have prayed for thee?

FAUSTUS. Oft have I thought to have done so; but the devil threatened to tear me in pieces, if I named God, to fetch both body and soul, if I once gave ear to divinity: and now 'tis too late. Gentlemen, away, lest you perish with me.

SECOND SCHOLAR. O, what shall we do to save Faustus?

FAUSTUS. Talk not of me, but save yourselves, and depart.

THIRD SCHOLAR. God will strengthen me; I will stay with Faustus.

FIRST SCHOLAR. Tempt not God, sweet friend; but let us into the next room, and there pray for him.

FAUSTUS. Aye, pray for me, pray for me; and what noise soever ye hear, come not unto me, for nothing can rescue me.

SECOND SCHOLAR. Pray thou, and we will pray that God may have mercy upon thee.

FAUSTUS. Gentlemen, farewell; if I live till morning, I'll visit you; if not, Faustus is gone to hell.

ALL. Faustus, farewell.

       [*Exeunt* Scholars.—*The clock strikes eleven.*

FAUSTUS. Ah, Faustus,
Now hast thou but one bare hour to live,
And then thou must be damn'd perpetually!
Stand still, you ever-moving spheres of heaven,
That time may cease, and midnight never come;
Fair Nature's eye, rise, rise again, and make

Perpetual day; or let this hour be but
A year, a month, a week, a natural day,
That Faustus may repent and save his soul!
O lente, lente currite, noctis equi!
The stars move still, time runs, the clock will strike,
The devil will come, and Faustus must be damn'd.
O, I'll leap up to my God!—Who pulls me down?—
See, see, where Christ's blood streams in the firmament!
One drop would save my soul, half a drop: ah, my
    Christ!—
Ah, rend not my heart for naming of my Christ!
Yet will I call on him: O, spare me, Lucifer!—
Where is it now? 'tis gone: and see, where God
Stretcheth out his arm, and bends his ireful brows!
Mountains and hills, come, come, and fall on me,
And hide me from the heavy wrath of God!
No, no!
Then will I headlong run into the earth:
Earth, gape! O, no, it will not harbour me!
You stars that reign'd at my nativity,
Whose influence hath allotted death and hell,
Now draw up Faustus, like a foggy mist,
Into the entrails of yon lab'ring clouds,
That, when you vomit forth into the air,
My limbs may issue from your smoky mouths,
So that my soul may but ascend to heaven!
                          [The watch strikes.
Ah, half the hour is past! 'twill all be past anon.
O God,
If thou wilt not have mercy on my soul,
Yet for Christ's sake, whose blood hath ransom'd me,
Impose some end to my incessant pain;

[322]

Let Faustus live in hell a thousand years,
A hundred thousand, and at last be sav'd!
O, no end is limited to damnèd souls!
Why wert thou not a creature wanting soul?
Or why is this immortal that thou hast?
Ah, Pythagoras' metempsychosis, were that true,
This soul should fly from me, and I be chang'd
Unto some brutish beast! all beasts are happy,
For, when they die,
Their souls are soon dissolv'd in elements;
But mine must live still to be plagu'd in hell.
Curs'd be the parents that engender'd me!
No, Faustus, curse thyself, curse Lucifer
That hath depriv'd thee of the joys of heaven.

[The clock striketh twelve.

O, it strikes, it strikes! Now, body, turn to air,
Or Lucifer will bear thee quick to hell!

[Thunder and lightning.

O soul, be chang'd into little water-drops,
And fall into the ocean, ne'er be found!

Enter Devils.

My God, my God, look not so fierce on me!
Adders and serpents, let me breathe a while!
Ugly hell, gape not! come not, Lucifer!
I'll burn my books!—Ah, Mephistophilis!

[Exeunt with him.

Enter Chorus.

CHORUS. Cut is the branch that might have grown full
straight,
And burnèd is Apollo's laurel-bough,

[323]

That sometime grew within this learnèd man.
Faustus is gone: regard his hellish fall,
Whose fiendful fortune may exhort the wise,
Only to wonder at unlawful things,
Whose deepness doth entice such forward wits
To practise more than heavenly power permits.

[*Exit.*

Terminat hora diem; terminat author opus.

CHRISTOPHER MARLOWE

FRA LIPPO LIPPI

I AM poor brother Lippo, by your leave!
You need not clap your torches to my face.
Zooks, what's to blame? you think you see a monk!
What, 'tis past midnight, and you go the rounds,
And here you catch me at an alley's end
Where sportive ladies leave their doors ajar?
The Carmine's my cloister; hunt it up,
Do—harry out, if you must show your zeal,
Whatever rat, there, haps on his wrong hole,
And nip each softling of a wee white mouse,
Weke, weke, that's crept to keep him company!
Aha, you know your betters? Then, you'll take
Your hand away that's fiddling on my throat,
And please to know me likewise. Who am I?
Why, one, sir, who is lodging with a friend
Three streets off—he's a certain . . . how d'ye call?
Master—a . . . Cosimo of the Medici,
In the house that caps the corner. Boh! you were best!
Remember and tell me, the day you're hanged,
How you affected such a gullet's-gripe!
But you, sir, it concerns you that your knaves
Pick up a manner nor discredit you.
Zooks, are we pilchards, that they sweep the streets
And count fair prize what comes into their net?

He's Judas to a tittle, that man is!
Just such a face! Why, sir, you make amends.
Lord! I'm not angry! Bid your hang-dogs go
Drink out this quarter-florin to the health
Of the munificent House that harbours me
(And many more beside, lads! more beside!),
And all's come square again. I'd like his face—
His, elbowing on his comrade in the door
With the pike and lantern—for the slave that holds
John Baptist's head a-dangle by the hair
With one hand ("Look you, now," as who should say)
And his weapon in the other, yet unwiped!
It's not your chance to have a bit of chalk,
A wood-coal or the like? or you should see!
Yes, I'm the painter, since you style me so.
What, brother Lippo's doings, up and down,
You know them and they take you? like enough!
I saw the proper twinkle in your eye—
'Tell you, I liked your looks at very first.
Let's sit and set things straight now, hip to haunch.
Here's spring come, and the nights one makes up bands
To roam the town and sing out carnival,
And I've been three weeks shut within my mew,
A-painting for the great man, saints and saints
And saints again. I could not paint all night—
Ouf! I leaned out of window for fresh air.
There came a hurry of feet and little feet,
A sweep of lute-strings, laughs, and whiffs of song—
Flower o' the broom,
Take away love, and our earth is a tomb!
Flower o' the quince,
I let Lisa go, and what good in life since?

Flower o' the thyme—and so on. Round they went.
Scarce had they turned the corner when a titter,
Like the skipping of rabbits by moonlight—three slim
    shapes—
And a face that looked up . . . zooks, sir, flesh and blood,
That's all I'm made of! Into shreds it went,
Curtain and counterpane and coverlet,
All the bed furniture—a dozen knots,
There was a ladder! Down I let myself,
Hands and feet, scrambling somehow, and so dropped,
And after them. I came up with the fun
Hard by St. Laurence, hail fellow, well met—
Flower o' the rose,
If I've been merry, what matter who knows?
And so as I was stealing back again
To get to bed and have a bit of sleep
Ere I rise up tomorrow and go work
On Jerome knocking at his poor old breast
With his great round stone to subdue the flesh,
You snap me of the sudden. Ah, I see!
Though your eye twinkles still, you shake your head—
Mine's shaved—a monk, you say—the sting's in that!
If Master Cosimo announced himself,
Mum's the word naturally; but a monk!
Come, what am I a beast for? tell us, now!
I was a baby when my mother died
And father died and left me in the street.
I starved there, God knows how, a year or two
On fig-skins, melon-parings, rinds, and shucks,
Refuse and rubbish. One fine frosty day
My stomach being empty as your hat,
The wind doubled me up and down I went.

Old Aunt Lapaccia trussed me with one hand
(Its fellow was a stinger as I knew),
And so along the wall, over the bridge,
By the straight cut to the convent. Six words there,
While I stood munching my first bread that month:
"So, boy, you're minded," quoth the good fat father
Wiping his own mouth—'twas refection-time—
"To quit this very miserable world?
Will you renounce" . . . "the mouthful of bread?"
    thought I;
By no means! Brief, they made a monk of me;
I did renounce the world, its pride and greed,
Palace, farm, villa, shop, and banking-house,
Trash, such as these poor devils of Medici
Have given their hearts to—all at eight years old.
Well, sir, I found in time, you may be sure,
'Twas not for nothing—the good bellyful,
The warm serge and the rope that goes all round,
And day-long blessed idleness beside!
"Let's see what the urchin's fit for"—that came next.
Not overmuch their way, I must confess.
Such a to-do! they tried me with their books.
Lord, they'd have taught me Latin in pure waste!
Flower o' the clove,
All the Latin I construe is "amo," I love!
But, mind you, when a boy starves in the streets
Eight years together, as my fortune was,
Watching folk's faces to know who will fling
The bit of half-stripped grape-bunch he desires,
And who will curse or kick him for his pains—
Which gentleman processional and fine,
Holding a candle to the Sacrament,

Will wink and let him lift a plate and catch
The droppings of the wax to sell again,
Or holla for the Eight and have him whipped—
How say I?—nay, which dog bites, which lets drop
His bone from the heap of offal in the street!
Why, soul and sense of him grow sharp alike,
He learns the look of things, and none the less
For admonitions from the hunger-pinch.
I had a store of such remarks, be sure,
Which, after I found leisure, turned to use:
I drew men's faces on my copybooks,
Scrawled them within the antiphonary's marge,
Joined legs and arms to the long music-notes,
Found eyes and nose and chin for A's and B's,
And made a string of pictures of the world
Betwixt the ins and outs of verb and noun,
On the wall, the bench, the door. The monks looked
    black.
"Nay," quoth the Prior, "turn him out, d'ye say?
In no wise. Lose a crow and catch a lark.
What if at last we get our man of parts,
We Carmelites, like those Camaldolese
And Preaching Friars, to do our church up fine
And put the front on it that ought to be!"
And hereupon they bade me daub away.
Thank you! my head being crammed, the walls a blank,
Never was such prompt disemburdening.
First, every sort of monk, the black and white,
I drew them, fat and lean; then folks at church,
From good old gossips waiting to confess
Their cribs of barrel-droppings, candle-ends—
To the breathless fellow at the altar-foot,

Fresh from his murder, safe and sitting there
With the little children round him in a row
Of admiration, half for his beard and half
For that white anger of his victim's son
Shaking a fist at him with one fierce arm,
Signing himself with the other because of Christ
(Whose sad face on the cross sees only this
After the passion of a thousand years),
Till some poor girl, her apron o'er her head
(Which the intense eyes looked through), came at eve
On tiptoe, said a word, dropped in a loaf,
Her pair of earrings, and a bunch of flowers
(The brute took growling), prayed, and then was gone.
I painted all, then cried, " 'Tis ask and have—
Choose, for more's ready!"—laid the ladder flat,
And showed my covered bit of cloister-wall.
The monks closed in a circle and praised loud
Till checked, taught what to see and not to see,
Being simple bodies—"That's the very man!
Look at the boy who stoops to pat the dog!
That woman's like the Prior's niece who comes
To care about his asthma; it's the life!"
But there my triumph's straw-fire flared and funked—
Their betters took their turn to see and say;
The Prior and the learned pulled a face
And stopped all that in no time. "How? what's here?
Quite from the mark of painting, bless us all!
Faces, arms, legs, and bodies like the true
As much as pea and pea! It's devil's-game!
Your business is not to catch men with show,
With homage to the perishable clay,
But lift them over it, ignore it all,

[330]

Make them forget there's such a thing as flesh.
Your business is to paint the souls of men—
Man's soul, and it's a fire, smoke . . . no, it's not . . .
It's vapor done up like a newborn babe—
(In that shape when you die it leaves your mouth)
It's . . . well, what matters talking, it's the soul!
Give us no more of body than shows soul.
Here's Giotto, with his Saint a-praising God!
That sets us praising—why not stop with him?
Why put all thoughts of praise out of our head
With wonder at lines, colours, and what not?
Paint the soul, never mind the legs and arms!
Rub all out, try at it a second time.
Oh, that white smallish female with the breasts,
She's just my niece . . . Herodias, I would say—
Who went and danced and got men's heads cut off—
Have it all out!" Now, is this sense, I ask?
A fine way to paint soul, by painting body
So ill, the eye can't stop there, must go further
And can't fare worse! Thus, yellow does for white
When what you put for yellow's simply black,
And any sort of meaning looks intense
When all beside itself means and looks nought.
Why can't a painter lift each foot in turn,
Left foot and right foot, go a double step,
Make his flesh liker and his soul more like,
Both in their order? Take the prettiest face,
The Prior's niece . . . patron-saint—is it so pretty
You can't discover if it means hope, fear,
Sorrow or joy? Won't beauty go with these?
Suppose I've made her eyes all right and blue,
Can't I take breath and try to add life's flash,

[331]

And then add soul and heighten them threefold?
Or say there's beauty with no soul at all—
(I never saw it—put the case the same—)
If you get simple beauty and nought else,
You get about the best thing God invents—
That's somewhat. And you'll find the soul you have
    missed,
Within yourself, when you return Him thanks!
"Rub all out!" Well, well, there's my life, in short,
And so the thing has gone on ever since.
I'm grown a man no doubt, I've broken bounds—
You should not take a fellow eight years old
And make him swear to never kiss the girls—
I'm my own master, paint now as I please—
Having a friend, you see, in the Corner-house!
Lord, it's fast holding by the rings in front—
Those great rings serve more purposes than just
To plant a flag in, or tie up a horse!
And yet the old schooling sticks—the old grave eyes
Are peeping o'er my shoulder as I work,
The heads shake still—"It's Art's decline, my son!
You're not of the true painters, great and old;
Brother Angelico's the man, you'll find;
Brother Lorenzo stands his single peer.
Fag on at flesh, you'll never make the third!"
Flower o' the pine,
You keep your mistr . . . manners, and I'll stick to mine!
I'm not the third, then; bless us, they must know!
Don't you think they're the likeliest to know,
They, with their Latin? So I swallow my rage,
Clench my teeth, suck my lips in tight, and paint
To please them—sometimes do, and sometimes don't,

For, doing most, there's pretty sure to come
A turn—some warm eve finds me at my saints—
A laugh, a cry, the business of the world—
(Flower o' the peach,
Death for us all, and his own life for each!)
And my whole soul revolves, the cup runs over,
The world and life's too big to pass for a dream,
And I do these wild things in sheer despite,
And play the fooleries you catch me at,
In pure rage! the old mill-horse, out at grass
After hard years, throws up his stiff heels so,
Although the miller does not preach to him
The only good of grass is to make chaff.
What would men have? Do they like grass or no—
May they or mayn't they? all I want's the thing
Settled forever one way. As it is
You tell too many lies and hurt yourself.
You don't like what you only like too much,
You do like what, if given you at your word,
You find abundantly detestable.
For me, I think I speak as I was taught—
I always see the Garden and God there
A-making man's wife—and, my lesson learned,
The value and significance of flesh,
I can't unlearn ten minutes afterwards.

You understand me. I'm a beast, I know.
But see, now—why, I see as certainly
As that the morning-star's about to shine,
What will hap some day. We've a youngster here
Comes to our convent, studies what I do,
Slouches and stares and lets no atom drop—

His name is Guidi—he'll not mind the monks—
They call him Hulking Tom, he lets them talk—
He picks my practice up—he'll paint apace,
I hope so—though I never live so long,
I know what's sure to follow. You be judge!
You speak no Latin more than I, belike—
However, you're my man, you've seen the world
—The beauty and the wonder and the power,
The shapes of things, their colours, lights and shades,
Changes, surprises—and God made it all!
—For what? Do you feel thankful, aye or no,
For this fair town's face, yonder river's line,
The mountain round it, and the sky above,
Much more the figures of man, woman, child,
These are the frame to? What's it all about?
To be passed over, despised? or dwelt upon,
Wondered at? oh, this last, of course, you say.
But why not do as well as say—paint these
Just as they are, careless what comes of it?
God's works—paint any one, and count it crime
To let a truth slip. Don't object, "His works
Are here already—nature is complete.
Suppose you reproduce her—(which you can't)
There's no advantage! you must beat her, then."
For, don't you mark? we're made so that we love
First when we see them painted, things we have passed
Perhaps a hundred times nor cared to see;
And so they are better, painted—better to us,
Which is the same thing. Art was given for that—
God uses us to help each other so,
Lending our minds out. Have you noticed, now,
Your cullion's hanging face? A bit of chalk,

And trust me but you should, though! how much more,
If I drew higher things with the same truth!
That were to take the Prior's pulpit-place,
Interpret God to all of you! Oh, oh,
It makes me mad to see what men shall do
And we in our graves! This world's no blot for us,
Nor blank—it means intensely, and means good;
To find its meaning is my meat and drink.
"Aye, but you don't so instigate to prayer!"
Strikes in the Prior; "when your meaning's plain
It does not say to folks—remember matins—
Or, mind your fast next Friday!" Why, for this
What need of art at all? A skull and bones,
Two bits of stick nailed crosswise, or, what's best,
A bell to chime the hour with, does as well.
I painted a Saint Laurence six months since
At Prato, splashed the fresco in fine style.
"How looks my painting, now the scaffold's down?"
I ask a brother. "Hugely," he returns—
"Already not one phiz of your three slaves
Who turn the Deacon off his toasted side,
But's scratched and prodded to our heart's content,
The pious people have so eased their own
With coming to say prayers there in a rage.
We get on fast to see the bricks beneath.
Expect another job this time next year,
For pity and religion grow i' the crowd—
Your painting serves its purpose!" Hang the fools!

    —That is—you'll not mistake an idle word
Spoke in a huff by a poor monk, God wot,
Tasting the air this spicy night which turns

The unaccustomed head like Chianti wine!
Oh, the church knows! don't misreport me, now!
It's natural a poor monk out of bounds
Should have his apt word to excuse himself.
And hearken how I plot to make amends.
I have bethought me; I shall paint a piece
. . . There's for you! Give me six months, then go, see
Something in Sant' Ambrogio's! Bless the nuns!
They want a cast o' my office. I shall paint
God in the midst, Madonna and her babe,
Ringed by a bowery, flowery angel-brood,
Lilies and vestments and white faces, sweet
As puff on puff of grated orris-root
When ladies crowd to church at midsummer.
And then i' the front, of course a saint or two—
Saint John, because he saves the Florentines,
Saint Ambrose, who puts down in black and white
The convent's friends and gives them a long day,
And Job, I must have him there past mistake,
The man of Uz (and Us without the z,
Painters who need his patience). Well, all these
Secured at their devotions, up shall come
Out of a corner when you least expect,
As one by a dark stair into a great light,
Music and talking, who but Lippo! I!—
Mazed, motionless, and moonstruck—I'm the man!
Back I shrink—what is this I see and hear?
I, caught up with my monk's things by mistake,
My old serge gown and rope that goes all round,
I, in this presence, this pure company!
Where's a hole, where's a corner for escape?
Then steps a sweet angelic slip of a thing

Forward, puts out a soft palm—"Not so fast!"
—Addresses the celestial presence, "Nay—
He made you and devised you, after all,
Though he's none of you! Could Saint John there draw—
His camel-hair make up a painting-brush?
We come to brother Lippo for all that,
Iste perfecit opus!" So, all smile—
I shuffle sideways with my blushing face
Under the cover of a hundred wings
Thrown like a spread of kirtles when you're gay
And play hot cockles, all the doors being shut,
Till, wholly unexpected, in there pops
The hothead husband! Thus I scuttle off
To some safe bench behind, not letting go
The palm of her, the little lily thing
That spoke the good word for me in the nick,
Like the Prior's niece . . . Saint Lucy, I would say.
And so all's saved for me, and for the church
A pretty picture gained. Go, six months hence!
Your hand, sir, and goodby; no lights, no lights!
The street's hushed, and I know my own way back—
Don't fear me! There's the gray beginning. Zooks!

ROBERT BROWNING

THE BISHOP ORDERS HIS TOMB AT ST. PRAXED'S CHURCH

ROME, 15—

Vanity, saith the preacher, vanity!
    Draw round my bed; is Anselm keeping back?
Nephews—sons mine . . . ah God, I know not! Well—
She, men would have to be your mother once,
Old Gandolf envied me, so fair she was!
What's done is done, and she is dead beside,
Dead long ago, and I am Bishop since.
And as she died so must we die ourselves,
And thence ye may perceive the world's a dream.
Life, how and what is it? As here I lie
In this state-chamber, dying by degrees,
Hours and long hours in the dead night, I ask,
"Do I live; am I dead?" Peace, peace seems all.
St. Praxed's ever was the church for peace;
And so, about this tomb of mine. I fought
With tooth and nail to save my niche, ye know.
—Old Gandolf cozened me, despite my care;
Shrewd was that snatch from out the corner south
He graced his carrion with, God curse the same!

[338]

Yet still my niche is not so cramped but thence
One sees the pulpit o' the epistle-side,
And somewhat of the choir, those silent seats,
And up into the aery dome where live
The angels, and a sunbeam's sure to lurk.
And I shall fill my slab of basalt there,
And 'neath my tabernacle take my rest,
With those nine columns round me, two and two,
The odd one at my feet where Anselm stands,
Peach-blossom marble all, the rare, the ripe,
As fresh-poured red wine of a mighty pulse.
—Old Gandolf with his paltry onion-stone,
Put me where I may look at him! True peach,
Rosy and flawless; how I earned the prize!
Draw close. That conflagration of my church
—What then? So much was saved if aught were missed!
My sons, ye would not be my death? Go dig
The white-grape vineyard where the oil-press stood,
Drop water gently till the surface sinks,
And if ye find . . . ah God, I know not, I! . . .
Bedded in store of rotten fig-leaves soft,
And corded up in a tight olive-frail,
Some lump, ah God, of *lapis lazuli*,
Big as a Jew's head cut off at the nape,
Blue as a vein o'er the Madonna's breast—
Sons, all have I bequeathed you, villas, all,
That brave Frascati villa with its bath—
So, let the blue lump poise between my knees,
Like God the Father's globe on both his hands
Ye worship in the Jesu Church so gay,
For Gandolf shall not choose but see and burst!
Swift as a weaver's shuttle fleet our years;

Man goeth to the grave, and where is he?
Did I say basalt for my slab, sons? Black—
'Twas ever antique-black I meant! How else
Shall ye contrast my frieze to come beneath?
The bas-relief in bronze ye promised me,
Those Pans and Nymphs ye wot of, and perchance
Some tripod, thyrsus, with a vase or so,
The Savior at his sermon on the mount,
St. Praxed in a glory, and one Pan
Ready to twitch the Nymph's last garment off,
And Moses with the tables . . . but I know
Ye mark me not! What do they whisper thee,
Child of my bowels, Anselm? Ah, ye hope
To revel down my villas while I gasp
Bricked o'er with beggar's mouldy travertine
Which Gandolf from his tomb-top chuckles at!
Nay, boys, ye love me—all of jasper, then!
'Tis jasper ye stand pledged to, lest I grieve
My bath must needs be left behind, alas!
One block, pure green as a pistachio-nut,
There's plenty jasper somewhere in the world—
And have I not St. Praxed's ear to pray
Horses for ye, and brown Greek manuscripts,
And mistresses with great smooth marbly limbs?
—That's if ye carve my epitaph aright,
Choice Latin, picked phrase, Tully's every word,
No gaudy ware like Gandolf's second line—
Tully, my masters? Ulpian serves his need!
And then how I shall lie through centuries,
And hear the blessed mutter of the Mass,
And see God made and eaten all day long,
And feel the steady candle-flame, and taste

Good strong, thick, stupefying incense-smoke!
For as I lie here, hours of the dead night,
Dying in state and by such slow degrees,
I fold my arms as if they clasped a crook,
And stretch my feet forth straight as stone can point,
And let the bedclothes for a mort-cloth drop
Into great laps and folds of sculptor's-work.
And as yon tapers dwindle, and strange thoughts
Grow, with a certain humming in my ears,
About the life before I live this life,
And this life too, popes, cardinals, and priests,
St. Praxed at his sermon on the mount,
Your tall pale mother with her talking eyes,
And new-found agate urns as fresh as day,
And marble's language, Latin pure, discreet,
—Aha, ELUCESCEBAT quoth our friend?
No Tully, said I, Ulpian at the best!
Evil and brief hath been my pilgrimage.
All *lapis*, all, sons! Else I give the Pope
My villas. Will ye ever eat my heart?
Ever your eyes were as a lizard's quick;
They glitter like your mother's for my soul,
Or ye would heighten my impoverished frieze,
Piece out its starved design, and fill my vase
With grapes, and add a vizor and a Term,
And to the tripod ye would tie a lynx
That in his struggle throws the thyrsus down,
To comfort me on my entablature
Whereon I am to lie till I must ask
"Do I live, am I dead?" There, leave me, there!
For ye have stabbed me with ingratitude
To death—ye wish it—God, ye wish it! Stone—

Gritstone, a-crumble! Clammy squares which sweat
As if the corpse they keep were oozing through—
And no more *lapis* to delight the world!
Well, go! I bless ye. Fewer tapers there,
But in a row. And, going, turn your backs
—Aye, like departing altar-ministrants,
And leave me in my church, the church for peace,
That I may watch at leisure if he leers—
Old Gandolf—at me, from his onion-stone,
As still he envied me, so fair she was!

ROBERT BROWNING

AN HYMNE OF HEAVENLY BEAUTIE

RAPT with the rage of mine own ravisht thought,
Through contemplation of those goodly sights,
And glorious images in heaven wrought,
Whose wondrous beauty breathing sweet delights,
Do kindle love in high conceipted sprights:
I faine to tell the things that I behold,
But feele my wits to faile, and tongue to fold.

Vouchsafe then, O thou most almightie Spright,
From whom all gifts of wit and knowledge flow,
To shed into my breast some sparkling light
Of thine eternall Truth, that I may show
Some litle beames to mortall eyes below,
Of that immortall beautie, there with thee,
Which in my weake distraughted mynd I see.

That with the glorie of so goodly sight,
The hearts of men, which fondly here admyre
Faire seeming shewes, and feed on vaine delight,
Transported with celestiall desyre
Of those faire formes, may lift themselves up hyer,
And learne to love with zealous humble dewty
Th'eternall fountaine of that heavenly beauty.

[343]

Beginning then below, with th'easie vew
Of this base world, subject to fleshly eye,
From thence to mount aloft by order dew,
To contemplation of th'immortall sky,
Of the soare faulcon so I learne to fly,
That flags awhile her fluttering wings beneath,
Till she her selfe for stronger flight can breath.

Then looke who list, thy gazefull eyes to feed
With sight of that is faire, looke on the frame
Of this wyde *universe*, and therein reed
The endlesse kinds of creatures, which by name
Thou canst not count, much lesse their natures aime:
All which are made with wondrous wise respect,
And all with admirable beautie deckt.

First th'Earth, on adamantine pillers founded,
Amid the Sea engirt with brasen bands;
Then th'Aire still flitting, but yet firmely bounded
On everie side, with pyles of flaming brands,
Never consum'd nor quencht with mortall hands;
And last, that mightie shining christall wall,
Wherewith he hath encompassed this All.

By view whereof, it plainly may appeare,
That still as every thing doth upward tend,
And further is from earth, so still more cleare
And faire it growes, till to his perfect end
Of purest beautie, it at last ascend:
Ayre more then water, fire much more then ayre,
And heaven then fire appeares more pure and fayre.

Looke thou no further, but affixe thine eye
On that bright shynie round still moving Masse,
The house of blessed Gods, which men call *Skye,*
All sowd with glistring stars more thicke then grasse,
Whereof each other doth in brightnesse passe;
But those two most, which ruling night and day,
As King and Queene, the heavens Empire sway.

And tell me then, what hast thou ever seene,
That to their beautie may compared bee,
Or can the sight that is most sharpe and keene,
Endure their Captains flaming head to see?
How much lesse those, much higher in degree,
And so much fairer, and much more then these,
As these are fairer then the land and seas?

For farre above these heavens which here we see,
Be others farre exceeding these in light,
Not bounded, not corrupt, as these same bee,
But infinite in largenesse and in hight,
Unmoving, uncorrupt, and spotlesse bright,
That need no Sunne t'illuminate their spheres,
But their owne native light farre passing theirs.

And as these heavens still by degrees arize,
Untill they come to their first Movers bound,
That in his mightie compasse doth comprize,
And carrie all the rest with him around,
So those likewise doe by degrees redound,
And rise more faire, till they at last arive
To the most faire, whereto they all do strive.

Faire is the heaven, where happy soules have place,
In full enjoyment of felicitie,
Whence they doe still behold the glorious face
Of the divine eternall Majestie;
More faire is that, where those *Idees* on hie,
Enraunged be, which *Plato* so admyred,
And pure *Intelligences* from God inspyred.

Yet fairer is that heaven, in which doe raine
The soveraine *Powres* and mightie *Potentates,*
Which in their high protections doe containe
All mortall Princes, and imperiall States;
And fayrer yet, whereas the royall Seates
And heavenly *Dominations* are set,
From whom all earthly governance is fet.

Yet farre more faire be those bright *Cherubins,*
Which all with golden wings are overdight,
And those eternall burning *Seraphins,*
Which from their faces dart out fierie light;
Yet fairer then they both, and much more bright
Be th'Angels and Archangels, which attend
On Gods owne person, without rest or end.

These thus in faire each other farre excelling,
As to the Highest they approch more neare,
Yet is that Highest farre beyond all telling,
Fairer then all the rest which there appeare,
Though all their beauties joynd together were:
How then can mortall tongue hope to expresse,
The image of such endlesse perfectnesse?

Cease then my tongue, and lend unto my mynd
Leave to be thinke how great that beautie is,
Whose utmost parts so beautifull I fynd:
How much more those essentiall parts of his,
His truth, his love, his wisedome, and his blis,
His grace, his doome, his mercy and his might,
By which he lends us of himselfe a sight.

Those unto all he daily doth display,
And shew himselfe in th'image of his grace,
As in a looking glasse, through which he may
Be seene, of all his creatures vile and base,
That are unable else to see his face,
His glorious face which glistereth else so bright,
That th'Angels selves can not endure his sight.

But we fraile wights, whose sight cannot sustaine
The Suns bright beames, when he on us doth shyne,
But that their points rebutted backe againe
Are duld, how can we see with feeble eyne,
The glory of that Majestie divine,
In sight of whom both Sun and Moone are darke,
Compared to his least resplendent sparke?

The meanes therefore which unto us is lent,
Him to behold, is on his workes to looke,
Which he hath made in beauty excellent,
And in the same, as in a brasen booke,
To reade enregistred in every nooke
His goodnesse, which his beautie doth declare,
For all thats good, is beautifull and faire.

[347]

Thence gathering plumes of perfect speculation,
To impe the wings of thy high flying mynd,
Mount up aloft through heavenly contemplation,
From this darke world, whose damps the soule do blynd,
And like the native brood of Eagles kynd,
On that bright Sunne of glorie fixe thine eyes,
Clear'd from grosse mists of fraile infirmities.

Humbled with feare and awfull reverence,
Before the footestoole of his Majestie,
Throw thy selfe downe with trembling innocence,
Ne dare looke up with corruptible eye
On the dred face of that great *Deity*,
For feare, lest if he chaunce to looke on thee,
Thou turne to nought, and quite confounded be.

But lowly fall before his mercie seate,
Close covered with the Lambes integrity,
From the just wrath of his avengefull threate,
That sits upon the righteous throne on hy:
His throne is built upon Eternity,
More firme and durable then steele or brasse,
Or the hard diamond, which them both doth passe.

His scepter is the rod of Righteousnesse,
With which he bruseth all his foes to dust,
And the great Dragon strongly doth represse,
Under the rigour of his judgement just;
His seate is Truth, to which the faithfull trust;
From whence proceed her beames so pure and bright,
That all about him sheddeth glorious light.

Light farre exceeding that bright blazing sparke,
Which darted is from *Titans* flaming head,
That with his beames enlumineth the darke
And dampish aire, wherby al things are red:
Whose nature yet so much is marvelled
Of mortall wits, that it doth much amaze
The greatest wisards, which thereon do gaze.

But that immortall light which there doth shine,
Is many thousand times more bright, more cleare,
More excellent, more glorious, more divine,
Through which to God all mortall actions here,
And even the thoughts of men, do plaine appeare
For from th'eternall Truth it doth proceed,
Through heavenly vertue, which her beames doe breed.

With the great glorie of that wondrous light,
His throne is all encompassed around,
And hid in his owne brightnesse from the sight
Of all that looke thereon with eyes unsound:
And underneath his feet are to be found
Thunder, and lightning, and tempestuous fyre,
The instruments of his avenging yre.

There in his bosome *Sapience* doth sit,
The soveraine dearling of the *Deity*,
Clad like a Queene in royall robes, most fit
For so great powre and peerelesse majesty.
And all with gemmes and jewels gorgeously
Adornd, that brighter then the starres appeare,
And make her native brightnes seem more cleare.

And on her head a crowne of purest gold
Is set, in signe of highest soveraignty,
And in her hand a scepter she doth hold,
With which she rules the house of God on hy,
And menageth the ever-moving sky,
And in the same these lower creatures all,
Subjected to her powre imperiall.

Both heaven and earth obey unto her will,
And all the creatures which they both containe;
For of her fulnesse which the world doth fill,
They all partake, and do in state remaine,
As their great Maker did at first ordaine,
Through observation of her high beheast,
By which they first were made, and still increast.

The fairenesse of her face no tongue can tell,
For she the daughters of all wemens race,
And Angels eke, in beautie doth excell,
Sparkled on her from Gods owne glorious face,
And more increast by her owne goodly grace,
That it doth farre exceed all humane thought,
Ne can on earth compared be to ought.

Ne could that Painter (had he lived yet)
Which pictured *Venus* with so curious quill,
That all posteritie admyred it,
Have purtrayd this, for all his maistring skill;
Ne she her selfe, had she remained still,
And were as faire, as fabling wits do fayne,
Could once come neare this beauty soverayne.

But had those wits the wonders of their dayes
Or that sweete *Teian* Poet which did spend
His plenteous vaine in setting forth her prayse,
Seene but a glims of this, which I pretend,
How wondrously would he her face commend,
Above that Idole of his fayning thought,
That all the world shold with his rimes be fraught?

How then dare I, the novice of his Art,
Presume to picture so divine a wight,
Or hope t'express her least perfections part,
Whose beautie filles the heavens with her light,
And darkes the earth with shadow of her sight?
Ah gentle Muse thou art too weake and faint,
The pourtraict of so heavenly hew to paint.

Let Angels which her goodly face behold
And see at will, her soveraigne praises sing,
And those most sacred mysteries unfold,
Of that faire love of mightie heavens king.
Enough is me t'admyre so heavenly thing,
And being thus with her huge love possest,
In th'only wonder of her selfe to rest.

But who so may, thrise happie man him hold,
Of all on earth, whom God so much doth grace,
And lets his owne Beloved to behold:
For in the view of her celestiall face,
All joy, all blisse, all happinesse have place,
Ne ought on earth can want unto the wight,
Who of her selfe can win the wishfull sight.

For she out of her secret threasury,
Plentie of riches forth on him will powre,
Even heavenly riches, which there hidden ly
Within the closet of her chastest bowre,
Th'eternall portion of her precious dowre,
Which mighty God hath given to her free,
And to all those which thereof worthy bee.

None thereof worthy be, but those whom shee
Vouchsafeth to her presence to receave,
And letteth them her lovely face to see,
Wherof such wondrous pleasures they conceave,
And sweete contentment, that it doth bereave
Their soule of sense, through infinite delight,
And them transport from flesh into the spright.

In which they see such admirable things,
As carries them into an extasy,
And heare such heavenly notes, and carolings,
Of Gods high praise, that filles the brasen sky,
And feele such joy and pleasure inwardly,
That maketh them all worldly cares forget,
And onely thinke on that before them set.

Ne from thenceforth doth any fleshly sense,
Or idle thought of earthly things remaine:
But all that earst seemd sweet, seemes now offense,
And all that pleased earst, now seemes to paine.
Their joy, their comfort, their desire, their gaine,
Is fixed all on that which now they see,
All other sights but fayned shadowes bee.

And that faire lampe, which useth to enflame
The hearts of men with selfe consuming fyre,
Thenceforth seemes fowle, and full of sinfull blame;
And all that pompe, to which proud minds aspyre
By name of honor, and so much desyre,
Seemes to them basenesse, and all riches drosse,
And all mirth sadnesse, and all lucre losse.

So full their eyes are of that glorious sight,
And senses fraught with such satietie,
That in nought else on earth they can delight,
But in th'aspect of that felicitie,
Which they have written in their inward ey;
On which they feed, and in their fastened mynd
All happie joy and full contentment fynd.

Ah then my hungry soule, which long hast fed
On idle fancies of thy foolish thought,
And with false beauties flattring bait misled,
Hast after vaine deceiptfull shadowes sought,
Which all are fled, and now have left thee nought,
But late repentance through thy follies prief;
Ah ceasse to gaze on matter of thy grief.

And looke at last up to that soveraine light,
From whose pure beams al perfect beauty springs,
That kindleth love in every godly spright,
Even the love of God, which loathing brings
Of this vile world, and these gay seeming things;
With whose sweete pleasures being so possest,
Thy straying thoughts henceforth for ever rest.

EDMUND SPENSER

LYCIDAS

In this Monody the author bewails a learned friend, unfortunately drowned in his passage from Chester on the Irish seas, 1637; and by occasion foretells the ruin of our corrupted clergy, then in their height.

YET once more, O ye laurels, and once more
   Ye myrtles brown, with ivy never sere,
I come to pluck your berries harsh and crude,
And with forced fingers rude,
Shatter your leaves before the mellowing year.
Bitter constraint, and sad occasion dear,
Compels me to disturb your season due:
For Lycidas is dead, dead ere his prime,
Young Lycidas, and hath not left his peer.
Who would not sing for Lycidas? He knew
Himself to sing, and build the lofty rhyme.
He must not float upon his watery bier
Unwept, and welter to the parching wind,
Without the meed of some melodious tear.
Begin then, Sisters of the sacred well,
That from beneath the seat of Jove doth spring,
Begin, and somewhat loudly sweep the string.
Hence with denial vain, and coy excuse,
So may some gentle Muse

With lucky words favour my destined urn,
And as he passes turn,
And bid fair peace be to my sable shroud.
For we were nursed upon the self-same hill,
Fed the same flock by fountain, shade, and rill.

Together both, ere the high lawns appeared
Under the opening eyelids of the morn,
We drove afield, and both together heard
What time the gray-fly winds her sultry horn,
Batt'ning our flocks with the fresh dews of night,
Oft till the star that rose, at evening, bright,
Toward heav'n's descent had sloped his west'ring wheel.
Meanwhile the rural ditties were not mute,
Tempered to the oaten flute,
Rough Satyrs danced, and Fauns with cloven heel
From the glad sound would not be absent long,
And old Damœtas loved to hear our song.

But, O the heavy change, now thou art gone,
Now thou art gone, and never must return!
Thee, Shepherd, thee the woods, and desert caves
With wild thyme and the gadding vine o'ergrown,
And all their echoes mourn.
The willows, and the hazel copses green,
Shall now no more be seen,
Fanning their joyous leaves to thy soft lays.
As killing as the canker to the rose,
Or taint-worm to the weanling herds that graze,
Or frost to flow'rs, that their gay wardrobe wear,
When first the white-thorn blows;
Such, Lycidas, thy loss to shepherd's ear.

Where were ye, Nymphs, when the remorseless deep
Closed o'er the head of your loved Lycidas?

For neither were ye playing on the steep,
Where your old Bards, the famous Druids, lie,
Nor on the shaggy top of Mona high,
Nor yet where Deva spreads her wizard stream:
Ay me! I fondly dream!
Had ye been there, for what could that have done?
What could the Muse herself that Orpheus bore,
The Muse herself for her enchanting son,
Whom universal nature did lament,
When by the rout that made the hideous roar,
His gory visage down the stream was sent,
Down the swift Hebrus to the Lesbian shore?
   Alas! what boots it with incessant care
To tend the homely slighted shepherd's trade,
And strictly meditate the thankless Muse?
Were it not better done as others use,
To sport with Amaryllis in the shade,
Or with the tangles of Neæra's hair?
Fame is the spur that the clear spirit doth raise
(That last infirmity of noble mind)
To scorn delights, and live laborious days;
But the fair guerdon when we hope to find,
And think to burst out into sudden blaze,
Comes the blind Fury with the abhorrèd shears,
And slits the thin-spun life. "But not the praise,"
Phœbus replied, and touched my trembling ears;
"Fame is no plant that grows on mortal soil,
Nor in the glist'ring foil
Set off to the world, nor in broad rumour lies;
But lives and spreads aloft by those pure eyes,
And perfect witness of all-judging Jove;
As he pronounces lastly on each deed,

Of so much fame in heav'n expect thy meed."
  O fountain Arethuse, and thou honoured flood,
Smooth-sliding Mincius, crowned with vocal reeds,
That strain I heard was of a higher mood:
But now my oat proceeds,
And listens to the herald of the sea
That came in Neptune's plea;
He asked the waves, and asked the felon winds,
What hard mishap hath doomed this gentle swain?
And questioned every gust of rugged wings
That blows from off each beakèd promontory:
They knew not of his story,
And sage Hippotades their answer brings,
That not a blast was from his dungeon strayed.
The air was calm, and on the level brine
Sleek Panope with all her sisters played.
It was that fatal and perfidious bark,
Built in th' eclipse, and rigged with curses dark,
That sunk so low that sacred head of thine.
  Next Camus, reverend sire, went footing slow,
His mantle hairy, and his bonnet sedge,
Inwrought with figures dim, and on the edge
Like to that sanguine flow'r inscribed with woe.
"Ah! Who hath reft" (quoth he) "my dearest pledge?"
Last came, and last did go,
The pilot of the Galilean lake.
Two massy keys he bore of metals twain,
(The golden opes, the iron shuts amain)
He shook his mitred locks, and stern bespake,
"How well could I have spared for thee, young swain,
Enow of such as for their bellies' sake
Creep, and intrude, and climb into the fold!

Of other care they little reckoning make,
Than how to scramble at the shearers' feast,
And shove away the worthy bidden guest;
Blind mouths! that scarce themselves know how to hold
A sheep-hook, or have learned aught else the least
That to the faithful herdman's art belongs!
What recks it them? What need they? They are sped;
And when they list, their lean and flashy songs
Grate on their scrannel pipes of wretched straw;
The hungry sheep look up, and are not fed,
But swoln with wind, and the rank mist they draw,
Rot inwardly, and foul contagion spread;
Besides what the grim wolf with privy paw
Daily devours apace, and nothing said;
But that two-handed engine at the door
Stands ready to smite once, and smite no more."
    Return, Alpheus, the dread voice is past,
That shrunk thy streams; return, Sicilian Muse,
And call the vales, and bid them hither cast
Their bells, and flow'rets of a thousand hues.
Ye valleys low, where the mild whispers use
Of shades, and wanton winds, and gushing brooks,
On whose fresh lap the swart-star sparely looks:
Throw hither all your quaint enamelled eyes,
That on the green turf suck the honied showers,
And purple all the ground with vernal flowers.
Bring the rathe primrose that forsaken dies,
The tufted crow-toe, and pale jessamine,
The white pink, and the pansy freaked with jet,
The glowing violet,
The musk-rose, and the well-attired woodbine,
With cowslips wan that hang the pensive head,

And every flower that sad embroidery wears.
Bid amaranthus all his beauty shed,
And daffadillies fill their cups with tears,
To strow the laureate hearse where Lycid lies.
For so to interpose a little ease,
Let our frail thoughts dally with false surmise.
Ay me! Whilst thee the shores, and sounding seas
Wash far away, where'er thy bones are hurled,
Whether beyond the stormy Hebrides,
Where thou perhaps under the whelming tide,
Visit'st the bottom of the monstrous world;
Or whether thou to our moist vows denied,
Sleep'st by the fable of Bellerus old,
Where the great vision of the guarded mount
Looks toward Namancos and Bayona's hold.
Look homeward, Angel, now, and melt with ruth:
And, O ye dolphins, waft the hapless youth.

Weep no more, woful Shepherds, weep no more,
For Lycidas your sorrow is not dead,
Sunk though he be beneath the watery floor.
So sinks the day-star in the ocean bed,
And yet anon repairs his drooping head,
And tricks his beams, and with new spangled ore
Flames in the forehead of the morning sky;
So Lycidas sunk low, but mounted high,
Through the dear might of Him that walked the waves,
Where other groves, and other streams along,
With nectar pure his oozy locks he laves,
And hears the unexpressive nuptial song,
In the blest kingdoms meek of joy and love.
There entertain him all the saints above,
In solemn troops, and sweet societies,

That sing, and singing in their glory move,
And wipe the tears for ever from his eyes.
Now, Lycidas, the shepherds weep no more;
Henceforth thou art the Genius of the shore,
In thy large recompense, and shalt be good
To all that wander in that perilous flood.

Thus sang the uncouth swain to th' oaks and rills,
While the still morn went out with sandals gray,
He touched the tender stops of various quills,
With eager thought warbling his Doric lay:
And now the sun had stretched out all the hills,
And now was dropped into the western bay;
At last he rose, and twitched his mantle blue:
To-morrow to fresh woods and pastures new.

JOHN MILTON

SAMSON AGONISTES

A DRAMATIC POEM

"Τραγῳδία μίμησις πράξεως σπουδαίας," etc.
ARISTOT. *Poet*. c. vi.

"Tragœdia et imitatio actionis seriæ, etc., per misericordiam et metum perficiens talium affectuum lustrationem."

OF THAT SORT OF DRAMATIC POEM WHICH IS CALLED TRAGEDY

PREFACE WRITTEN BY MILTON

TRAGEDY, as it was anciently composed, hath been ever held the gravest, moralest, and most profitable of all other poems; therefore said by Aristotle to be of power, by raising pity, and fear, or terror, to purge the mind of those and such-like passions; that is, to temper and reduce them to just measure with a kind of delight, stirred up by reading or seeing those passions well imitated. Nor is Nature wanting in her own effects to make good his assertion, for so in physic, things of melancholic hue and quality are used against melancholy, sour against sour, salt to remove salt humours. Hence philosophers and other gravest writers, as Cicero,

[361]

Plutarch, and others, frequently cite out of tragic poets, both to adorn and illustrate their discourse. The Apostle Paul himself thought it not unworthy to insert a verse of Euripides into the text of Holy Scripture, 1 Cor. xv. 33; and Paræus, commenting on the Revelation, divides the whole book, as a tragedy, into acts, distinguished each by a chorus of heavenly harpings and song between. Heretofore men in highest dignity have laboured not a little to be thought able to compose a tragedy. Of that honour Dionysius the Elder was no less ambitious than before of his attaining to the tyranny. Augustus Cæsar also had begun his "Ajax," but, unable to please his own judgment with what he had begun, left it unfinished. Seneca, the philosopher, is by some thought the author of those tragedies, at least the best of them, that go under that name. Gregory Nazianzen, a Father of the Church, thought it not unbeseeming the sanctity of his person to write a tragedy, which is entitled "Christ Suffering." This is mentioned to vindicate tragedy from the small esteem, or rather infamy, which in the account of many it undergoes at this day with other common interludes; happening through the poet's error of intermixing comic stuff with tragic sadness and gravity, or introducing trivial and vulgar persons, which by all judicious hath been counted absurd, and brought in without discretion, corruptly to gratify the people. And though ancient tragedy use no prologue, yet using sometimes, in case of self-defence, or explanation, that which Martial calls an epistle, in behalf of this tragedy coming forth after the ancient manner, much different from what among us passes for best, thus much beforehand may be epistled: that Chorus is here introduced after the Greek manner, not ancient only but modern, and still in use among the Italians. In the modelling, therefore, of this poem, with good reason, the ancients and Italians are rather followed, as of much more authority and fame. The measure of verse used in the Chorus is of all sorts, called by the Greeks Monostrophic, or rather Apolelymenon, without regard had to Strophe, Antistrophe, or Epode, which were a kind of stanzas framed only for the music then used with the Chorus that sung; not essential to the poem, and therefore not material; or, being divided into stanzas or pauses, they may be called Allœostropha. Division into act and scene referring chiefly to the stage, to which this work never was intended, is here omitted.

It suffices if the whole drama be found not produced beyond the fifth act; of the style and uniformity, and that commonly called the plot, whether intricate or explicit, which is nothing indeed but such economy or disposition of the fable as may stand best with verisimilitude and decorum, they only will best judge who are not unacquainted with Æschylus, Sophocles, and Euripides, the three tragic poets, unequalled yet by any, and the best rule to all who endeavour to write tragedy. The circumscription of time wherein the whole drama begins and ends is, according to ancient rule and best example, within the space of twenty-four hours.

THE ARGUMENT

SAMSON made captive, blind, and now in the prison at
Gaza, there to labour as in a common workhouse, on a
festival-day, in the general cessation from labour, comes
forth into the open air, to a place nigh, somewhat retired,
there to sit a while and bemoan his condition; where he
happens at length to be visited by certain friends and
equals of his tribe, which make the chorus, who seek to
comfort him what they can; then by his old father
Manoah, who endeavours the like, and withal tells him
his purpose to procure his liberty by ransom; and, lastly,
that this feast was proclaimed by the Philistines as a day
of thanksgiving for their deliverance from the hands of
Samson, which yet more troubles him. Manoah then
departs to prosecute his endeavour with the Philistine
lords for Samson's redemption; who in the meanwhile is
visited by other persons; and lastly by a public officer to
require his coming to the feast before the lords and people, to play or show his strength in their presence. He at
first refuses, dismissing the public officer with absolute
denial to come; at length, persuaded inwardly that this
was from God, he yields to go along with him, who came
now the second time with great threatenings to fetch him.
The chorus yet remaining on the place, Manoah returns
full of joyful hope to procure ere long his son's deliver-

ance; in the midst of which discourse a Hebrew comes in haste, confusedly at first, and afterward more distinctly, relating the catastrophe, what Samson had done to the Philistines, and by accident to himself; wherewith the tragedy ends.

THE PERSONS

SAMSON.
MANOAH, *the Father of Samson.*
DALILA, *his Wife.*
HARAPHA *of Gath.*

Public Officer.
Messenger.
Chorus of Danites.

The Scene before the Prison in Gaza.

SAMS. A little onward lend thy guiding hand
To these dark steps, a little further on;
For yonder bank hath choice of sun or shade:
There I am wont to sit, when any chance
Relieves me from my task of servile toil,
Daily in the common prison else enjoined me,
Where I, a prisoner chained, scarce freely draw
The air imprisoned also, close and damp,
Unwholesome draught: but here I feel amends,
The breath of heav'n fresh blowing, pure and sweet,
With day-spring born; here leave me to respire.
This day a solemn feast the people hold
To Dagon, their sea-idol, and forbid
Laborious works; unwillingly this rest
Their superstition yields me; hence, with leave
Retiring from the popular noise, I seek
This unfrequented place to find some ease;

Ease to the body some, none to the mind
From restless thoughts, that, like a deadly swarm
Of hornets armed, no sooner found alone,
But rush upon me thronging, and present
Times past, what once I was, and what am now.
Oh! wherefore was my birth from heav'n foretold
Twice by an angel, who at last in sight
Of both my parents all in flames ascended
From off the altar, where an off'ring burned,
As in a fiery column charioting
His godlike presence, and from some great act
Or benefit revealed to Abraham's race?
Why was my breeding ordered and prescribed
As of a person separate to GOD,
Designed for great exploits, if I must die
Betrayed, captived, and both my eyes put out,
Made of my enemies the scorn and gaze,
To grind in brazen fetters under task
With this heav'n-gifted strength? O glorious strength
Put to the labour of a beast, debased
Lower than bond-slave! Promise was that I
Should Israel from Philistian yoke deliver;
Ask for this great deliverer now, and find him
Eyeless in Gaza at the mill with slaves,
Himself in bonds under Philistian yoke.
Yet stay, let me not rashly call in doubt
Divine prediction: what! if all foretold
Had been fulfilled but through mine own default,
Whom have I to complain of but myself?
Who, this high gift of strength committed to me,
In what part lodged, how easily bereft me,
Under the seal of silence could not keep,

But weakly to a woman must reveal it,
O'ercome with importunity and tears.
O impotence of mind in body strong!
But what is strength without a double share
Of wisdom? Vast, unwieldy, burthensome,
Proudly secure, yet liable to fall
By weakest subtleties, not made to rule,
But to subserve where wisdom bears command.
GOD, when He gave me strength, to show withal
How slight the gift was, hung it in my hair.
But peace! I must not quarrel with the will
Of highest dispensation, which herein
Haply had ends above my reach to know:
Suffices that to me strength is my bane,
And proves the source of all my miseries,
So many, and so huge, that each apart
Would ask a life to wail; but chief of all,
O loss of sight, of thee I most complain!
Blind among enemies, O worse than chains,
Dungeon, or beggary, or decrepit age!
Light, the prime work of GOD, to me's extinct,
And all her various objects of delight
Annulled, which might in part my grief have eased.
Inferior to the vilest now become
Of man or worm, the vilest here excel me;
They creep, yet see; I, dark in light, exposed
To daily fraud, contempt, abuse, and wrong.
Within doors, or without, still as a fool
In power of others, never in my own;
Scarce half I seem to live, dead more than half.
O dark, dark, dark, amid the blaze of noon,
Irrecoverably dark, total eclipse

Without all hope of day!
O first created beam, and thou great Word,
"Let there be light," and light was over all;
Why am I thus bereaved Thy prime decree?
The sun to me is dark
And silent as the moon,
When she deserts the night,
Hid in her vacant interlunar cave.
Since light so necessary is to life,
And almost life itself, if it be true
That light is in the soul,
She all in every part; why was the sight
To such a tender ball as th' eye confined,
So obvious and so easy to be quenched?
And not, as feeling, through all parts diffused,
That she might look at will through every pore?
Then had I not been thus exiled from light,
As in the land of darkness yet in light,
To live a life half dead, a living death,
And buried; but, O yet more miserable!
Myself my sepulchre, a moving grave,
Buried, yet not exempt
By privilege of death and burial
From worst of other evils, pains, and wrongs,
But made hereby obnoxious more
To all the miseries of life,
Life in captivity
Among inhuman foes.
But who are these? for with joint pace I hear
The tread of many feet steering this way;
Perhaps my enemies, who come to stare
At my affliction, and perhaps t' insult,

Their daily practice to afflict me more.
   CHOR. This, this is he; softly a while,
Let us not break in upon him.
O change beyond report, thought, or belief!
See how he lies at random, carelessly diffused.
With languished head unpropped,
As one past hope, abandoned,
As by himself given over;
In slavish habit, ill-fitted weeds
O'er-worn and soiled;
Or do my eyes misrepresent? can this be he,
That heroic, that renowned,
Irresistible Samson? whom unarmed
No strength of man or fiercest wild beast could withstand;
Who tore the lion, as the lion tears the kid,
Ran on imbattled armies clad in iron,
(And, weaponless himself,)
Made arms ridiculous, useless the forgery
Of brazen shield and spear, the hammered cuirass,
Chalybean tempered steel, and frock of mail
Adamantean proof;
But safest he who stood aloof,
When insupportably his foot advanced,
In scorn of their proud arms and warlike tools,
Spurned them to death by troops. The bold Ascalonite
Fled from his lion ramp; old warriors turned
Their plated backs under his heel,
Or grov'lling soiled their crested helmets in the dust.
Then with what trivial weapon came to hand,
The jaw of a dead ass, his sword of bone,
A thousand fore-skins fell, the flower of Palestine,
In Ramath-lechi, famous to this day:

Then by main force pulled up, and on his shoulders bore
The gates of Azza, post and massy bar,
Up to the hill by Hebron, seat of giants old,
No journey of a Sabbath day, and loaded so;
Like whom the Gentiles feign to bear up heav'n.
Which shall I first bewail,
Thy bondage or lost sight,
Prison within prison
Inseparably dark?
Thou art become, O worst imprisonment!
The dungeon of thyself; thy soul,
Which men enjoying sight oft without cause complain,
Imprisoned now indeed,
In real darkness of the body dwells,
Shut up from outward light,
To incorporate with gloomy night:
For inward light, alas!
Puts forth no visual beam.
O mirror of our fickle state,
Since man on earth unparalleled!
The rarer thy example stands,
By how much from the top of wondrous glory,
Strongest of mortal men,
To lowest pitch of abject fortune thou art fall'n;
For him I reckon not in high estate,
Whom long descent of birth
Or the sphere of fortune raises:
But thee, whose strength, while virtue was her mate,
Might have subdued the earth,
Universally crowned with highest praises.

    SAMS. I hear the sound of words, their sense the air
Dissolves unjointed ere it reach my ear.

CHOR. He speaks: let us draw nigh. Matchless in might,
The glory late of Israel, now the grief,
We come, thy friends and neighbours not unknown,
From Eshtaol and Zora's fruitful vale,
To visit or bewail thee; or, if better,
Counsel or consolation we may bring,
Salve to thy sores: apt words have power to swage
The tumours of a troubled mind,
And are as balm to festered wounds.

SAMS. Your coming, friends, revives me, for I learn
Now of my own experience, not by talk,
How counterfeit a coin they are who friends
Bear in their superscription, of the most
I would be understood; in prosperous days
They swarm, but in adverse withdraw their head,
Not to be found, though sought. Ye see, O friends,
How many evils have inclosed me round;
Yet that which was the worse now least afflicts me,
Blindness; for, had I sight, confused with shame,
How could I once look up, or heave the head,
Who, like a foolish pilot, have shipwrecked
My vessel trusted to me from above,
Gloriously rigged; and for a word, a tear,
Fool! have divulged the secret gift of GOD
To a deceitful woman? Tell me, friends,
Am I not sung and proverbed for a fool
In every street? do they not say, How well
Are come upon him his deserts? Yet why?
Immeasurable strength they might behold
In me, of wisdom nothing more than mean:
This with the other should at least have paired;
These two, proportioned ill, drove me transverse.

CHOR. Tax not divine disposal: wisest men
Have erred, and by bad women been deceived;
And shall again, pretend they ne'er so wise.
Deject not then so overmuch thyself,
Who hast of sorrow thy full load besides.
Yet, truth to say, I oft have heard men wonder
Why thou shouldst wed Philistian women rather
Than of thine own tribe fairer, or as fair,
At least of thy own nation, and as noble.

SAMS. The first I saw at Timna, and she pleased
Me, not my parents, that I sought to wed
The daughter of an infidel. They knew not
That what I motioned was of GOD; I knew
From intimate impulse, and therefore urged
The marriage on, that by occasion hence
I might begin Israel's deliverance,
The work to which I was divinely called.
She proving false, the next I took to wife,
O that I never had! fond wish too late!
Was in the vale of Sorec, Dalila,
That specious monster, my accomplished snare:
I thought it lawful from my former act,
And the same end, still watching to oppress
Israel's oppressors. Of what now I suffer
She was not the prime cause, but I myself,
Who, vanquished with a peal of words,—O weakness!—
Gave up my fort of silence to a woman.

CHOR. In seeking just occasion to provoke
The Philistine, thy country's enemy,
Thou never wast remiss, I bear thee witness:
Yet Israel still serves with all his sons.

SAMS. That fault I take not on me, but transfer

[372]

On Israel's governors, and heads of tribes,
Who, seeing those great acts which GOD had done
Singly by me against their conquerors,
Acknowledged not, or not at all considered
Deliverance offered. I, on the other side,
Used no ambition to commend my deeds;
The deeds themselves, though mute, spoke loud the doer.
But they persisted deaf, and would not seem
To count them things worth notice, till at length
Their lords the Philistines with gathered powers
Entered Judea seeking me, who then
Safe to the rock of Ethan was retired,
Not flying, but forecasting in what place
To set upon them, what advantaged best.
Meanwhile the men of Judah, to prevent
The harass of their land, beset me round;
I willingly on some conditions came
Into their hands, and they as gladly yield me
To the uncircumcised a welcome prey,
Bound with two cords: but cords to me were threads
Touched with the flame. On their whole host I flew
Unarmed, and with a trivial weapon felled
Their choicest youth; they only lived who fled.
Had Judah that day joined, or one whole tribe,
They had by this possessed the towers of Gath,
And lorded over them whom now they serve:
But what more oft in nations grown corrupt,
And by their vices brought to servitude,
Than to love bondage more than liberty,
Bondage with ease than strenuous liberty;
And to despise, or envy, or suspect
Whom GOD hath of His special favour raised

As their deliverer? If he aught begin,
How frequent to desert him, and at last
To heap ingratitude on worthiest deeds.

    CHOR. Thy words to my remembrance bring
How Succoth and the fort of Penuel
Their great deliverer contemned,
The matchless Gideon in pursuit
Of Madian and her vanquished kings:
And how ingrateful Ephraim
Had dealt with Jephtha, who by argument,
Not worse than by his shield and spear,
Defended Israel from the Ammonite,
Had not his prowess quelled their pride
In that sore battle, when so many died
Without reprieve adjudged to death,
For want of well pronouncing Shibboleth.

    SAMS. Of such examples add me to the roll.
Me easily indeed mine may neglect,
But GOD's proposed deliverance not so.

    CHOR. Just are the ways of GOD,
And justifiable to men;
Unless there be who think not GOD at all:
If any be, they walk obscure;
For of such doctrine never was there school,
But the heart of the fool,
And no man therein doctor but himself.

    Yet more there be who doubt His ways not just,
And to His own edicts found contradicting,
Then give the reins to wand'ring thought,
Regardless of His glory's diminution;
Till, by their own perplexities involved,
They ravel more, still less resolved,

But never find self-satisfying solution.
  As if they would confine th' Interminable,
And tie Him to His own prescript,
Who made our laws to bind us, not Himself,
And hath full right to exempt
Whomso it pleases Him by choice
From national obstriction, without taint
Of sin, or legal debt;
For with His own laws He can best dispense.
  He would not else, who never wanted means,
Nor in respect of th' enemy just cause
To set His people free,
Have prompted this heroic Nazarite,
Against his vow of strictest purity,
To seek in marriage that fallacious bride,
Unclean, unchaste.
  Down, Reason, then; at least, vain reasonings down;
Though Reason here aver
That moral verdict quits her of unclean:
Unchaste was subsequent, her stain not his.
  But see! here comes thy reverend sire,
With careful step, locks white as down,
Old Manoah; advise
Forthwith how thou ought'st to receive him.

  SAMS. Aye me! another inward grief, awaked
With mention of that name, renews th' assault.

  MAN. Brethren and men of Dan, for such ye seem,
Though in this uncouth place, if old respect,
As I suppose, towards your once gloried friend,
My son, now captive, hither hath informed
Your younger feet, while mine, cast back with age,
Came lagging after; say if he be here.

[375]

CHOR. As signal now in low dejected state
As erst in highest, behold him where he lies.

MAN. O miserable change! is this the man,
That invincible Samson, far renowned,
The dread of Israel's foes, who with a strength
Equivalent to angels' walked their streets,
None offering fight; who single combatant
Duelled their armies ranked in proud array,
Himself an army, now unequal match
To save himself against a coward armed
At one spear's length? O ever-failing trust
In mortal strength! and oh! what not in man
Deceivable and vain! nay, what thing good,
Prayed for, but often proves our woe, our bane?
I prayed for children, and thought barrenness
In wedlock a reproach; I gained a son,
And such a son as all men hailed me happy:
Who would be now a father in my stead?
O wherefore did GOD grant me my request,
And as a blessing with such pomp adorned?
Why are His gifts desirable, to tempt
Our earnest prayers, then, giv'n with solemn hand
As graces, draw a scorpion's tail behind?
For this did the angel twice descend? for this
Ordained thy nurture holy, as of a plant
Select and sacred, glorious for a while,
The miracle of men; then in an hour
Ensnared, assaulted, overcome, led bound,
Thy foes' derision, captive, poor, and blind,
Into a dungeon thrust to work with slaves?
Alas! methinks whom GOD hath chosen once
To worthiest deeds, if he through frailty err,

He should not so o'erwhelm, and as a thrall
Subject him to so foul indignities,
Be it but for honour's sake of former deeds.

    SAMS. Appoint not heav'nly disposition, father:
Nothing of all these evils hath befall'n me
But justly; I myself have brought them on;
Sole author I, sole cause; if aught seem vile,
As vile hath been my folly, who have profaned
The mystery of GOD given me under pledge
Of vow, and have betrayed it to a woman,
A Canaanite, my faithless enemy.
This well I knew, nor was at all surprised,
But warned by oft experience: did not she
Of Timna first betray me, and reveal
The secret wrested from me in her highth
Of nuptial love professed, carrying it straight
To them who had corrupted her, my spies
And rivals? In this other was there found
More faith, who also in her prime of love,
Spousal embraces, vitiated with gold,
Though offered only, by the scent conceived
Her spurious first-born, treason against me?
Thrice she assayed, with flattering prayers and sighs,
And amorous reproaches, to win from me
My capital secret,—in what part my strength
Lay stored, in what part summed, that she might know;—
Thrice I deluded her, and turned to sport
Her importunity, each time perceiving
How openly and with what impudence
She purposed to betray me, and, which was worse
Than undissembled hate, with what contempt
She sought to make me traitor to myself;

[377]

Yet, the fourth time, when, mustering all her wiles,
With blandished parleys, feminine assaults,
Tongue-batteries, she surceased not day nor night
To storm me over-watched and wearied out,
At times when men seek most repose and rest,
I yielded, and unlocked her all my heart,
Who with a grain of manhood well resolved
Might easily have shook off all her snares:
But foul effeminacy held me yoked
Her bond-slave. O indignity! O blot
To honour and religion! servile mind
Rewarded well with servile punishment!
The base degree to which I now am fall'n,
These rags, this grinding, is not yet so base
As was my former servitude, ignoble,
Unmanly, ignominious, infamous,
True slavery; and that blindness worse than this,
That saw not how degenerately I served.

    MAN. I cannot praise thy marriage choices, son,
Rather approved them not; but thou didst plead
Divine impulsion prompting how thou might'st
Find some occasion to infest our foes.
I state not that; this I am sure, our foes
Found soon occasion thereby to make thee
Their captive and their triumph; thou the sooner
Temptation found'st, or over-potent charms
To violate the sacred trust of silence
Deposited within thee; which to have kept
Tacit was in thy power. True: and thou bear'st
Enough and more the burthen of that fault;
Bitterly hast thou paid, and still art paying
That rigid score. A worse thing yet remains:

This day the Philistines a popular feast
Here celebrate in Gaza; and proclaim
Great pomp, and sacrifice, and praises loud
To Dagon, as their god, who hath delivered
Thee, Samson, bound and blind into their hands,
Them out of thine, who slew'st them many a slain.
So Dagon shall be magnified, and GOD,
Besides whom is no GOD, compared with idols,
Disglorified, blasphemed, and had in scorn
By the idolatrous rout amidst their wine;
Which to have come to pass by means of thee,
Samson, of all thy sufferings think the heaviest,
Of all reproach the most with shame that ever
Could have befall'n thee and thy father's house.

   SAMS. Father, I do acknowledge and confess
That I this honour, I this pomp, have brought
To Dagon, and advanced his praises high
Among the heathen round; to GOD have brought
Dishonour, obloquy, and oped the mouths
Of idolists and atheists; have brought scandal
To Israel, diffidence of GOD, and doubt
In feeble hearts, propense enough before
To waver, or fall off, and join with idols;
Which is my chief affliction, shame, and sorrow,
The anguish of my soul, that suffers not
Mine eye to harbour sleep, or thoughts to rest.
This only hope relieves me, that the strife
With me hath end; all the contést is now
'Twixt GOD and Dagon; Dagon hath presumed,
Me overthrown, to enter lists with GOD,
His deity comparing and preferring
Before the GOD of Abraham. He, be sure,

Will not connive, or linger, thus provoked,
But will arise, and His great name assert:
Dagon must stoop, and shall ere long receive
Such a discomfit, as shall quite despoil him
Of all these boasted trophies won on me,
And with confusion blank his worshippers.

    MAN. With cause this hope relieves thee, and these
        words
I as a prophecy receive: for GOD,
Nothing more certain, will not long defer
To vindicate the glory of His name
Against all competition, nor will long
Endure it, doubtful whether GOD be lord,
Or Dagon. But for thee what shall be done?
Thou must not in the meanwhile here forgot
Lie in this miserable loathsome plight
Neglected. I already have made way
To some Philistian lords, with whom to treat
About thy ransom: well they may by this
Have satisfied their utmost of revenge
By pains and slaveries, worse than death, inflicted
On thee, who now no more canst do them harm.

    SAMS. Spare that proposal, father, spare the trouble
Of that solicitation: let me here,
As I deserve, pay on my punishment,
And expiate, if possible, my crime,
Shameful garrulity. To have revealed
Secrets of men, the secrets of a friend,
How heinous had the fact been, how deserving
Contempt and scorn of all; to be excluded
All friendship, and avoided as a blab,
The mark of fool set on his front!

But I God's counsel have not kept, His holy secret
Presumptuously have published, impiously,
Weakly at least, and shamefully; a sin
That Gentiles in their parables condemn
To their abyss and horrid pains confined.
  Man. Be penitent and for thy fault contrite,
But act not in thy own affliction, son;
Repent the sin, but if the punishment
Thou canst avoid, self-preservation bids;
Or th' execution leave to high disposal,
And let another hand, not thine, exact
Thy penal forfeit from thyself; perhaps
God will relent, and quit thee all His debt,
Who evermore approves and more accepts,
—Best pleased with humble and filial submission,—
Him who imploring mercy sues for life,
Than who self-rigorous chooses death as due,
Which argues over-just, and self-displeased
For self-offence, more than for God offended.
Reject not then what offered means: who knows
But God hath set before us, to return thee
Home to thy country and His sacred house,
Where thou may'st bring thy off'rings, to avert
His further ire, with prayers and vows renewed?
  Sams. His pardon I implore; but as for life,
To what end should I seek it? when in strength
All mortals I excelled, and great in hopes
With youthful courage and magnanimous thoughts
Of birth from heav'n foretold, and high exploits,
Full of divine instinct, after some proof
Of acts indeed heroic, far beyond
The sons of Anak, famous now and blazed,

Fearless of danger, like a petty god
I walked about, admired of all and dreaded
On hostile ground, none daring my affront.
Then, swoll'n with pride, into the snare I fell
Of fair fallacious looks, venereal trains,
Softened with pleasure and voluptuous life,
At length to lay my head and hallowed pledge
Of all my strength in the lascivious lap
Of a deceitful concubine, who shore me,
Like a tame wether, all my precious fleece,
Then turned me out ridiculous, despoiled,
Shav'n, and disarmed, among mine enemies.

CHOR. Desire of wine and all delicious drinks,
Which many a famous warrior overturns,
Thou could'st repress, nor did the dancing ruby,
Sparkling out-poured, the flavour or the smell,
Or taste, that cheers the hearts of gods and men,
Allure thee from the cool crystalline stream.

SAMS. Wherever fountain or fresh current flowed
Against the eastern ray, translucent, pure,
With touch etherial of heav'n's fiery rod,
I drank, from the clear milky juice allaying
Thirst, and refreshed; nor envied them the grape,
Whose heads that turbulent liquor fills with fumes.

CHOR. O madness, to think use of strongest wines
And strongest drinks our chief support of health,
When GOD with these forbidden made choice to rear
His mighty champion, strong above compare,
Whose drink was only from the liquid brook.

SAMS. But what availed this temperance, not complete
Against another object more enticing?
What boots it at one gate to make defence,

[382]

And at another to let in the foe,
Effeminately vanquished? by which means,
Now blind, disheartened, shamed, dishonoured, quelled,
To what can I be useful, wherein serve
My nation, and the work from heav'n imposed?
But to sit idle on the household hearth,
A burd'nous drone; to visitants a gaze,
Or pitied object, these redundant locks
Robustious to no purpose clust'ring down,
Vain monument of strength, till length of years
And sedentary numbness craze my limbs
To a contemptible old age obscure?
Here rather let me drudge and earn my bread,
Till vermin or the draff of servile food
Consume me, and oft-invocated death
Hasten the welcome end of all my pains.
  MAN. Wilt thou then serve the Philistines with that
     gift
Which was expressly given thee to annoy them?
Better at home lie bedrid, not only idle,
Inglorious, unemployed, with age outworn.
But GOD, who caused a fountain at thy prayer
From the dry ground to spring, thy thirst to allay
After the brunt of battle, can as easy
Cause light again within thy eyes to spring,
Wherewith to serve Him better than thou hast;
And I persuade me so: why else this strength
Miraculous yet remaining in those locks?
His might continues in thee not for nought,
Nor shall his wondrous gifts be frustrate thus.
  SAMS. All otherwise to me my thoughts portend,
That these dark orbs no more shall treat with light,

Nor the other light of life continue long,
But yield to double darkness nigh at hand:
So much I feel my genial spirits droop,
My hopes all flat, nature within me seems
In all her functions weary of herself,
My race of glory run, and race of shame,
And I shall shortly be with them that rest.

    MAN. Believe not these suggestions, which proceed
From anguish of the mind and humours black,
That mingle with thy fancy. I, however,
Must not omit a father's timely care
To prosecute the means of thy deliverance
By ransom or how else: meanwhile be calm,
And healing words from these thy friends admit.

    SAMS. O that torment should not be confined
To the body's wounds and sores,
With maladies innumerable
In heart, head, breast, and reins,
But must secret passage find
To the inmost mind,
There exercise all his fierce accidents,
And on her purest spirits prey,
As on entrails, joints, and limbs,
With answerable pains, but more intense,
Though void of corporal sense.

    My griefs not only pain me
As a lingering disease,
But, finding no redress, ferment and rage,
Nor less than wounds immedicable
Rankle, and fester, and gangrene,
To black mortification.
Thoughts, my tormentors, armed with deadly stings,

Mangle my apprehensive tenderest parts,
Exasperate, exulcerate, and raise
Dire inflammation, which no cooling herb,
Or medicinal liquor can assuage,
Nor breath of vernal air from snowy Alp.
Sleep hath forsook and given me o'er
To death's benumbing opium as my only cure:
Thence faintings, swoonings of despair,
And sense of heav'n's desertion.

    I was His nursling once, and choice delight,
His destined from the womb,
Promised by heavenly message twice descending:
Under His special eye
Abstemious I grew up and thrived amain;
He led me on to mightiest deeds,
Above the nerve of mortal arm,
Against the uncircumcised, our enemies:
But now hath cast me off as never known,
And to those cruel enemies,
Whom I by His appointment had provoked,
Left me all helpless with the irreparable loss
Of sight, reserved alive to be repeated
The subject of their cruelty and scorn.
Nor am I in the list of them that hope;
Hopeless are all my evils, all remediless;
This one prayer yet remains, might I be heard,
No long petition—speedy death,
The close of all my miseries, and the balm.

    CHOR. Many are the sayings of the wise,
In ancient and in modern books enrolled,
Extolling patience as the truest fortitude;
And to the bearing well of all calamities,

All chances incident to man's frail life,
Consolatories writ
With studied argument, and much persuasion sought,
Lenient of grief and anxious thought:
But with the afflicted in his pangs their sound
Little prevails, or rather seems a tune
Harsh and of dissonant mood from his complaint,
Unless he feel within
Some source of consolation from above,
Secret refreshings, that repair his strength,
And fainting spirits uphold.
   God of our fathers, what is man!
That thou towards him with hand so various,
Or might I say contrarious,
Temper'st thy providence through his short course,
Not evenly, as thou rul'st
The angelic orders and inferior creatures mute,
Irrational and brute.
Nor do I name of men the common rout,
That wandering loose about
Grow up and perish, as the summer fly,
Heads without names no more remembered,
But such as thou hast solemnly elected,
With gifts and graces eminently adorned
To some great work, thy glory,
And people's safety, which in part they effect:
Yet toward these thus dignified, thou oft
Amidst their height of noon,
Changest thy countenance, and thy hand with no regard
Of highest favours past
From thee on them, or them to thee of service.

Nor only dost degrade them, or remit
To life obscured, which were a fair dismission,
But throw'st them lower than thou didst exalt them high,
Unseemly falls in human eye,
Too grievous for the trespass of omission;
Oft leav'st them to the hostile sword
Of heathen and profane, their carcasses
To dogs and fowls a prey, or else captived;
Or to the unjust tribunals, under change of times,
And condemnation of the ingrateful multitude.
If these they 'scape, perhaps in poverty
With sickness and disease thou bow'st them down,
Painful diseases and deformed,
In crude old age:
Though not disordinate, yet causeless suff'ring
The punishment of dissolute days: in fine,
Just or unjust, alike seem miserable,
For oft alike both come to evil end.
So deal not with this once thy glorious champion,
The image of thy strength, and mighty minister.
What do I beg? how hast thou dealt already!
Behold him in this state calamitous, and turn
His labours, for thou canst, to peaceful end.
But who is this? what thing of sea or land—
Female of sex it seems—
That so bedecked, ornate, and gay,
Comes this way sailing
Like a stately ship
Of Tarsus, bound for the isles
Of Javan or Gadire,
With all her bravery on, and tackle trim,
Sails filled, and streamers waving,

Courted by all the winds that hold them play,
An amber scent of odorous perfume
Her harbinger, a damsel train behind?
Some rich Philistian matron she may seem;
And now, at nearer view, no other certain
Than Dalila thy wife.

SAMS. My wife! my traitress! let her not come near me.

CHOR. Yet on she moves, now stands and eyes thee fixed,
About to have spoke, but now, with head declined,
Like a fair flow'r surcharged with dew, she weeps,
And words addressed seem into tears dissolved,
Wetting the borders of her silken veil:
But now again she makes address to speak.

DAL. With doubtful feet and wavering resolution
I came, still dreading thy displeasure, Samson;
Which to have merited, without excuse,
I cannot but acknowledge; yet if tears
May expiate, though the fact more evil drew
In the perverse event than I foresaw,
My penance hath not slackened, though my pardon
No way assured: but conjugal affection,
Prevailing over fear and timorous doubt,
Hath led me on, desirous to behold
Once more thy face, and know of thy estate,
If aught in my ability may serve
To lighten what thou suffer'st, and appease
Thy mind with what amends is in my power,
Though late, yet in some part to recompense
My rash, but more unfortunate, misdeed.

SAMS. Out, out, hyæna! these are thy wonted arts,
And arts of every woman false like thee,
To break all faith, all vows, deceive, betray,

Then, as repentant, to submit, beseech,
And reconcilement move with feigned remorse,
Confess, and promise wonders in her change:
Not truly penitent, but chief to try
Her husband, how far urged his patience bears,
His virtue or weakness which way to assail;
Then with more cautious and instructed skill
Again transgresses, and again submits;
That wisest and best men full oft beguiled,
With goodness principled not to reject
The penitent, but ever to forgive,
Are drawn to wear out miserable days,
Entangled with a pois'nous bosom snake,
If not by quick destruction soon cut off,
As I by thee; to ages an example.
   DAL. Yet hear me, Samson; not that I endeavour
To lessen or extenuate my offence,
But that, on th' other side, if it be weighed
By itself, with aggravations not surcharged,
Or else with just allowance counterpoised,
I may, if possible, thy pardon find
The easier towards me, or thy hatred less.
First granting, as I do, it was a weakness
In me, but incident to all our sex,
Curiosity, inquisitive, importune
Of secrets, then with like infirmity
To publish them, both common female faults:
Was it not weakness also to make known
For importunity, that is, for nought,
Wherein consisted all thy strength and safety?
To what I did thou show'dst me first the way.
But I to enemies revealed, and should not;

Nor should'st thou have trusted that to woman's frailty:
Ere I to thee, thou to thyself wast cruel.
Let weakness then with weakness come to parle,
So near related, or the same of kind,
Thine forgive mine; that men may censure thine
The gentler, if severely thou exact not
More strength from me than in thyself was found.
And what if love, which thou interpret'st hate,
The jealousy of love, powerful of sway
In human hearts, nor less in mine towards thee,
Caused what I did? I saw thee mutable
Of fancy, feared lest one day thou would'st leave me
As her at Timna, sought by all means therefore
How to endear, and hold thee to me firmest:
No better way I saw than by importuning
To learn thy secrets, get into my power
Thy key of strength and safety. Thou wilt say,
"Why then revealed?" I was assured by those
Who tempted me, that nothing was designed
Against thee but safe custody and hold:
That made for me; I knew that liberty
Would draw thee forth to perilous enterprises,
While I at home sat full of cares and fears,
Wailing thy absence in my widowed bed:
Here I should still enjoy thee day and night,
Mine and love's prisoner, not the Philistines',
Whole to myself, unhazarded abroad,
Fearless at home of partners in my love.
These reasons in love's law have passed for good,
Though fond and reasonless to some perhaps:
And love hath oft, well meaning, wrought much woe,
Yet always pity or pardon hath obtained.

Be not unlike all others, not austere
As thou art strong, inflexible as steel.
If thou in strength all mortals dost exceed,
In uncompassionate anger do not so.

    SAMS. How cunningly the sorceress displays
Her own transgressions, to upbraid me mine!
That malice not repentance brought thee hither,
By this appears: I gave, thou say'st, th' example,
I led the way; bitter reproach, but true;
I to myself was false ere thou to me;
Such pardon therefore as I give my folly,
Take to thy wicked deed; which when thou seest
Impartial, self-severe, inexorable,
Thou wilt renounce thy seeking, and much rather
Confess it feigned. Weakness is thy excuse,
And I believe it, weakness to resist
Philistian gold. If weakness may excuse,
What murderer, what traitor, parricide,
Incestuous, sacrilegious, but may plead it?
All wickedness is weakness: that plea therefore
With GOD or man will gain thee no remission.
But love constrained thee! Call it furious rage
To satisfy thy lust. Love seeks to have love:
My love how could'st thou hope, who took'st the way
To raise in me inexpiable hate,
Knowing, as needs I must, by thee betrayed?
In vain thou striv'st to cover shame with shame,
Or by evasions thy crime uncover'st more.

    DAL. Since thou determin'st weakness for no plea
In man or woman, though to thy own condemning,
Hear what assaults I had, what snares besides,
What sieges girt me round, ere I consented,

Which might have awed the best resolved of men,
The constantest, to have yielded without blame.
It was not gold, as to my charge thou lay'st,
That wrought with me. Thou know'st the magistrates
And princes of my country came in person,
Solicited, commanded, threatened, urged,
Adjured by all the bonds of civil duty
And of religion, pressed how just it was,
How honourable, how glorious, to entrap
A common enemy, who had destroyed
Such numbers of our nation: and the priest
Was not behind, but ever at my ear,
Preaching how meritorious with the gods
It would be to ensnare an irreligious
Dishonourer of Dagon. What had I
To oppose against such powerful arguments?
Only my love of thee held long debate,
And combated in silence all these reasons
With hard contest: at length that grounded maxim,
So rife and celebrated in the mouths
Of wisest men, that to the public good
Private respects must yield, with grave authority
Took full possession of me and prevailed;
Virtue, as I thought, truth, duty, so enjoining.
    SAMS. I thought where all thy circling wiles would end:
In feigned religion, smooth hypocrisy.
But had thy love, still odiously pretended,
Been, as it ought, sincere, it would have taught thee
Far other reasonings, brought forth other deeds.
I, before all the daughters of my tribe
And of my nation, chose thee from among
My enemies, loved thee, as too well thou knew'st;

Too well; unbosomed all my secrets to thee,
Not out of levity, but overpowered
By thy request, who could deny thee nothing:
Yet now am judged an enemy. Why then
Didst thou at first receive me for thy husband,
Then, as since then, thy country's foe professed?
Being once a wife, for me thou wast to leave
Parents and country; nor was I their subject,
Nor under their protection, but my own;
Thou mine, not theirs. If aught against my life
Thy country sought of thee, it sought unjustly,
Against the law of nature, law of nations;
No more thy country, but an impious crew
Of men, conspiring to uphold their state
By worse than hostile deeds, violating the ends
For which our country is a name so dear;
Not therefore to be obeyed. But zeal moved thee;
To please thy gods thou didst it; gods unable
To acquit themselves and prosecute their foes
But by ungodly deeds; the contradiction
Of their own deity, gods cannot be;
Less therefore to be pleased, obeyed, or feared.
These false pretexts and varnished colours failing,
Bare in thy guilt how foul must thou appear!
    DAL. In argument with men a woman ever
Goes by the worse, whatever be her cause.
    SAMS. For want of words, no doubt, or lack of breath!
Witness when I was worried with thy peals.
    DAL. I was a fool, too rash, and quite mistaken
In what I thought would have succeeded best.
Let me obtain forgiveness of thee, Samson,
Afford me place to show what recompense

Towards thee I intend for what I have misdone,
Misguided; only what remains past cure
Bear not too sensibly, nor still insist
To afflict thyself in vain. Though sight be lost,
Life yet hath many solaces, enjoyed
Where other senses want not their delights—
At home, in leisure, and domestic ease,
Exempt from many a care and chance to which
Eyesight exposes daily men abroad.
I to the lords will intercede, not doubting
Their favourable ear, that I may fetch thee
From forth this loathsome prison-house, to abide
With me, where my redoubled love and care,
With nursing diligence, to me glad office,
May ever tend about thee to old age,
With all things grateful cheered, and so supplied,
That what by me thou hast lost thou least shalt miss.
    SAMS. No, no; of my condition take no care;
It fits not; thou and I long since are twain;
Nor think me so unwary or accurst,
To bring my feet again into the snare
Where once I have been caught: I know thy trains,
Though dearly to my cost, thy gins, and toils;
Thy fair enchanted cup and warbling charms
No more on me have power, their force is nulled;
So much of adder's wisdom I have learnt,
To fence my ear against thy sorceries.
If in my flower of youth and strength, when all men
Loved, honoured, feared me, thou alone could'st hate me,
Thy husband, slight me, sell me, and forego me;
How would'st thou use me now, blind, and thereby
Deceivable, in most things as a child

Helpless, thence easily contemned, and scorned,
And last neglected? how would'st thou insult,
When I must live uxorious to thy will
In perfect thraldom; how again betray me,
Bearing my words and doings to the lords
To gloss upon, and, censuring, frown or smile?
This gaol I count the house of liberty
To thine, whose doors my feet shall never enter.

DAL. Let me approach at least and touch thy hand.

SAMS. Not for thy life, lest fierce remembrance wake
My sudden rage to tear thee joint by joint.
At distance I forgive thee; go with that,
Bewail thy falsehood, and the pious works
It hath brought forth to make thee memorable
Among illustrious women, faithful wives:
Cherish thy hastened widowhood with the gold
Of matrimonial treason: so farewell.

DAL. I see thou art implacable, more deaf
To prayers than winds and seas; yet winds to seas
Are reconciled at length, and sea to shore:
Thy anger, unappeasable, still rages,
Eternal tempest never to be calmed.
Why do I humble thus myself, and, suing
For peace, reap nothing but repulse and hate,
Bid go with evil omen, and the brand
Of infamy upon my name denounced?
To mix with thy concernments I desist
Henceforth, nor too much disapprove my own.
Fame, if not double-faced, is double-mouthed,
And with contràry blast proclaims most deeds;
On both his wings, one black, the other white,
Bears greatest names in his wild aery flight.

[395]

My name perhaps among the circumcised,
In Dan, in Judah, and the bordering tribes,
To all posterity may stand defamed,
With malediction mentioned, and the blot
Of falsehood most unconjugal traduced.
But in my country, where I most desire,
In Ecron, Gaza, Asdod, and in Gath,
I shall be named among the famousest
Of women, sung at solemn festivals,
Living and dead recorded, who to save
Her country from a fierce destroyer chose
Above the faith of wedlock-bands; my tomb
With odours visited and annual flowers;
Not less renowned than in Mount Ephraim
Jael, who with inhospitable guile
Smote Sisera sleeping through the temples nailed.
Nor shall I count it heinous to enjoy
The public marks of honour and reward
Conferred upon me, for the piety
Which to my country I was judged to have shown.
At this who ever envies or repines,
I leave him to his lot, and like my own.

    CHOR. She's gone, a manifest serpent by her sting,
Discovered in the end, till now concealed.

    SAMS. So let her go: GOD sent her to debase me,
And aggravate my folly, who committed
To such a viper His most sacred trust
Of secrecy, my safety, and my life.

    CHOR. Yet beauty, though injurious, hath strange
        power,
After offence returning, to regain
Love once possessed, nor can be easily

Repulsed, without much inward passion felt
And secret sting of amorous remorse.

    SAMS. Love-quarrels oft in pleasing concord end;
Not wedlock-treachery endangering life.

    CHOR. It is not virtue, wisdom, valour, wit,
Strength, comeliness of shape, or amplest merit,
That woman's love can win or long inherit;
But what it is, hard is to say,
Harder to hit,
Which way soever men refer it,
Much like thy riddle, Samson, in one day
Or seven, though one should musing sit.

    If any of these, or all, the Timnian bride
Had not so soon preferred
Thy paranymph, worthless to thee compared,
Successor in thy bed,
Nor both so loosely disallied
Their nuptials, nor this last so treacherously
Had shorn the fatal harvest of thy head.
Is it for that such outward ornament
Was lavished on their sex, that inward gifts
Were left for haste unfinished, judgment scant,
Capacity not raised to apprehend
Or value what is best
In choice, but oftest to affect the wrong?
Or was too much of self-love mixed,
Of constancy no root infixed,
That either they love nothing, or not long?

    Whate'er it be, to wisest men and best
Seeming at first all heavenly under virgin veil,
Soft, modest, meek, demure,
Once joined, the contrary she proves, a thorn

Intestine, far within defensive arms
A cleaving mischief, in his way to virtue
Adverse and turbulent, or by her charms
Draws him awry enslaved
With dotage, and his sense depraved
To folly and shameful deeds which ruin ends.
What pilot so expert but needs must wreck,
Imbarked with such a steers-mate at the helm?
　　Favoured of heav'n who finds
One virtuous, rarely found,
That in domestic good combines:
Happy that house! his way to peace is smooth;
But virtue, which breaks through all opposition,
And all temptation can remove,
Most shines and most is acceptable above.
　　Therefore GOD's universal law
Gave to the man despotic power
Over his female in due awe,
Nor from that right to part an hour,
Smile she or lour:
So shall he least confusion draw
On his whole life, not swayed
By female usurpation, or dismayed.
　　But had we best retire? I see a storm.
　　SAMS. Fair days have oft contracted wind and rain.
　　CHOR. But this another kind of tempest brings.
　　SAMS. Be less abstruse; my riddling days are past.
　　CHOR. Look now for no enchanting voice, nor fear
The bait of honeyed words; a rougher tongue
Draws hitherward, I know him by his stride,
The giant Harapha of Gath, his look
Haughty as is his pile high-built and proud.

Comes he in peace? what wind hath blown him hither
I less conjecture than when first I saw
The sumptuous Dalila floating this way:
His habit carries peace, his brow defiance.
   SAMS. Or peace or not, alike to me he comes.
   CHOR. His fraught we soon shall know, he now arrives.
   HAR. I come not, Samson, to condole thy chance,
As these perhaps, yet wish it had not been,
Though for no friendly intent. I am of Gath,
Men call me Harapha, of stock renowned
As Og, or Anak, and the Emims old
That Kiriathaim held; thou know'st me now,
If thou at all art known. Much I have heard
Of thy prodigious might and feats performed,
Incredible to me, in this displeased,
That I was never present on the place
Of those encounters, where we might have tried
Each other's force in camp or listed field:
And now am come to see of whom such noise
Hath walked about, and each limb to survey,
If thy appearance answer loud report.
   SAMS. The way to know were not to see, but taste.
   HAR. Dost thou already single me? I thought
Gyves and the mill had tamed thee. O that fortune
Had brought me to the field where thou art famed
To have wrought such wonders with an ass's jaw!
I should have forced thee soon with other arms,
Or left thy carcass where the ass lay thrown;
So had the glory of prowess been recovered
To Palestine, won by a Philistine
From the unforeskinned race, of whom thou bear'st
The highest name for valiant acts: that honour

Certain to have won by mortal duel from thee,
I lose, prevented by thy eyes put out.
   SAMS. Boast not of what thou would'st have done,
      but do
What then thou would'st, thou seest it in thy hand.
   HAR. To combat with a blind man I disdain,
And thou hast need much washing to be touched.
   SAMS. Such usage as your honourable lords
Afford me, assassinated and betrayed,
Who durst not with their whole united powers
In fight withstand me single and unarmed,
Nor in the house with chamber ambushes
Close-banded durst attack me, no, not sleeping,
Till they had hired a woman with their gold,
Breaking her marriage faith to circumvent me.
Therefore, without feigned shifts, let be assigned
Some narrow place inclosed, where sight may give thee,
Or rather flight, no great advantage on me;
Then put on all thy gorgeous arms, thy helmet
And brigandine of brass, thy broad habergeon,
Vant-brass and greaves, and gauntlet, add thy spear,
A weaver's beam, and seven-times-folded shield;
I only with an oaken staff will meet thee,
And raise such outcries on thy clattered iron,
Which long shall not withhold me from thy head,
That in a little time, while breath remains thee,
Thou oft shalt wish thyself at Gath, to boast
Again in safety what thou would'st have done
To Samson, but shalt never see Gath more.
   HAR. Thou durst not thus disparage glorious arms,
Which greatest heroes have in battle worn,
Their ornament and safety, had not spells

And black`enchantments, some magician's art,
Armed thee, or charmed thee strong, which thou from
      heav'n
Feignedst at thy birth was giv'n thee in thy hair,
Where strength can least abide, though all thy hairs
Were bristles ranged like those that ridge the back
Of chafed wild boars or ruffled porcupines.

    SAMS. I know no spells, use no forbidden arts;
My trust is in the living GOD, who gave me
At my nativity this strength, diffused
No less through all my sinews, joints, and bones,
Than thine, while I preserved these locks unshorn,
The pledge of my unviolated vow.
For proof hereof, if Dagon be thy god,
Go to his temple, invocate his aid
With solemnest devotion, spread before him
How highly it concerns his glory now
To frustrate and dissolve these magic spells,
Which I to be the power of Israel's GOD
Avow, and challenge Dagon to the test,
Off'ring to combat thee his champion bold,
With the utmost of his godhead seconded:
Then thou shalt see, or rather to thy sorrow
Soon feel, whose GOD is strongest, thine or mine.

    HAR. Presume not on thy GOD, whate'er He be,
Thee He regards not, owns not, hath cut off
Quite from His people, and delivered up
Into thy enemies' hand; permitted them
To put out both thine eyes, and fettered send thee
Into the common prison, there to grind
Among the slaves and asses, thy comràdes,
As good for nothing else, no better service

[401]

With those thy boisterous locks; no worthy match
For valour to assail, nor by the sword
Of noble warrior, so to stain his honour,
But by the barber's razor best subdued.

SAMS. All these indignities, for such they are
From thine, these evils I deserve and more,
Acknowledge them from GOD inflicted on me
Justly, yet despair not of His final pardon
Whose ear is ever open, and His eye
Gracious to readmit the suppliant;
In confidence whereof I once again
Defy thee to the trial of mortal fight,
By combat to decide whose god is GOD,
Thine, or whom I with Israel's sons adore.

HAR. Fair honour that thou dost thy GOD, in trusting
He will accept thee to defend His cause,
A murderer, a revolter, and a robber!

SAMS. Tongue-doughty giant, how dost thou prove me
these?

HAR. Is not thy nation subject to our lords?
Their magistrates confessed it, when they took thee
As a league-breaker, and delivered bound
Into our hands; for hadst thou not committed
Notorious murder on those thirty men
At Ascalon, who never did thee harm,
Then like a robber strippedst them of their robes?
The Philistines, when thou hadst broke the league,
Went up with armèd powers thee only seeking,
To others did no violence nor spoil.

SAMS. Among the daughters of the Philistines
I chose a wife, which argued me no foe;
And in your city held my nuptial feast:

But your ill-meaning politician lords,
Under pretence of bridal friends and guests,
Appointed to await me thirty spies,
Who, threat'ning cruel death, constrained the bride
To wring from me and tell to them my secret,
That solved the riddle which I had proposed.
When I perceived all set on enmity,
As on my enemies, wherever chanced,
I used hostility, and took their spoil
To pay my underminers in their coin.
My nation was subjected to your lords!
It was the force of conquest; force with force
Is well ejected when the conquered can.
But I, a private person, whom my country
As a league-breaker gave up bound, presumed
Single rebellion, and did hostile acts!
I was no private, but a person raised
With strength sufficient and command from heav'n
To free my country; if their servile minds
Me their deliverer sent would not receive,
But to their masters gave me up for nought,
The unworthier they; whence to this day they serve.
I was to do my part from heav'n assigned,
And had performed it, if my known offence
Had not disabled me; not all your force:
These shifts refuted, answer thy appellant,
Though by his blindness maimed for high attempts,
Who now defies thee thrice to single fight,
As a petty enterprise of small enforce.

    HAR. With thee, a man condemned, a slave enrolled,
Due by the law to capital punishment?
To fight with thee no man of arms will deign.

SAMS. Cam'st thou for this, vain boaster, to survey me,
To descant on my strength, and give thy verdict?
Come nearer; part not hence so slight informed;
But take good heed my hand survey not thee.

HAR. O Baal-zebub! can my ears unused
Hear these dishonours, and not render death?

SAMS. No man withholds thee; nothing from thy hand
Fear I incurable; bring up thy van,
My heels are fettered, but my fist is free.

HAR. This insolence other kind of answer fits.

SAMS. Go, baffled coward, lest I run upon thee,
Though in these chains—bulk without spirit vast—
And with one buffet lay thy structure low,
Or swing thee in the air, then dash thee down
To the hazard of thy brains and shattered sides.

HAR. By Astaroth, ere long thou shalt lament
These braveries in irons loaden on thee.

CHOR. His giantship is gone, somewhat crestfall'n,
Stalking with less unconscionable strides,
And lower looks, but in a sultry chafe.

SAMS. I dread him not, nor all his giant brood,
Though fame divulge him father of five sons,
All of gigantic size, Goliah chief.

CHOR. He will directly to the lords, I fear,
And with malicious counsel stir them up
Some way or other yet further to afflict thee.

SAMS. He must allege some cause, and offered fight
Will not dare mention, lest a question rise
Whether he durst accept the offer or not,
And that he durst not plain enough appeared.
Much more affliction than already felt
They cannot well impose, nor I sustain,

If they intend advantage of my labours,
The work of many hands, which earns my keeping,
With no small profit daily to my owners.
But come what will, my deadliest foe will prove
My speediest friend, by death to rid me hence,
The worst that he can give, to me the best.
Yet so it may fall out, because their end
Is hate, not help to me, it may with mine .
Draw their own ruin who attempt the deed.

    CHOR. Oh, how comely it is, and how reviving
To the spirits of just men long oppressed!
When GOD into the hands of their deliverer
Puts invincible might
To quell the mighty of the earth, the oppressor,
The brute and boisterous force of violent men,
Hardy and industrious to support
Tyrannic power, but raging to pursue
The righteous, and all such as honour truth!
He all their ammunition
And feats of war defeats,
With plain heroic magnitude of mind
And celestial vigour armed,
Their armouries and magazines contemns,
Renders them useless, while
With wingèd expedition,
Swift as the lightning glance, he executes
His errand on the wicked, who, surprised,
Lose their defence, distracted and amazed.

    But Patience is more oft the exercise
Of saints, the trial of their fortitude,
Making them each his own deliverer,
And victor over all

That tyranny or fortune can inflict:
Either of these is in thy lot,
Samson, with might endued
Above the sons of men; but sight bereaved
May chance to number thee with those
Whom Patience finally must crown.

   This idol's day hath been to thee no day of rest,
Labouring thy mind
More than the working day thy hands.
And yet perhaps more trouble is behind,
For I descry this way
Some other tending; in his hand
A sceptre or quaint staff he bears,
Comes on amain, speed in his look.
By his habit I discern him now
A public officer, and now at hand.
His message will be short and voluble.

   OFF. Hebrews, the pris'ner Samson here I seek.

   CHOR. His manacles remark him; there he sits.

   OFF. Samson, to thee our lords thus bid me say:
This day to Dagon is a solemn feast,
With sacrifices, triumph, pomp, and games;
Thy strength they know surpassing human rate,
And now some public proof thereof require
To honour this great feast and great assembly;
Rise therefore with all speed and come along,
Where I will see thee heartened and fresh clad
To appear as fits before th' illustrious lords.

   SAMS. Thou know'st I am an Hebrew; therefore tell
      them
Our law forbids at their religious rites
My presence; for that cause I cannot come.

OFF. This answer, be assured, will not content them.

SAMS. Have they not sword-players, and ev'ry sort
Of gymnic artists, wrestlers, riders, runners,
Jugglers and dancers, antics, mummers, mimics,
But they must pick me out, with shackles tired,
And over-laboured at their public mill,
To make them sport with blind activity?
Do they not seek occasion of new quarrels,
On my refusal, to distress me more,
Or make a game of my calamities?
Return the way thou camest; I will not come.

OFF. Regard thyself; this will offend them highly.

SAMS. Myself? my conscience and internal peace.
Can they think me so broken, so debased
With corporal servitude, that my mind ever
Will condescend to such absurd commands?
Although their drudge, to be their fool or jester,
And in my midst of sorrow and heart-grief
To show them feats, and play before their god,
The worst of all indignities, yet on me
Joined with extreme contempt? I will not come.

OFF. My message was imposed on me with speed,
Brooks no delay. Is this thy resolution?

SAMS. So take it with what speed thy message needs.

OFF. I am sorry what this stoutness will produce.

SAMS. Perhaps thou shalt have cause to sorrow indeed.

CHOR. Consider, Samson, matters now are strained
Up to the height, whether to hold or break.
He's gone, and who knows how he may report
Thy words by adding fuel to the flame?
Expect another message more imperious,
More lordly thundering than thou well wilt bear.

[407]

SAMS. Shall I abuse this consecrated gift
Of strength, again returning with my hair
After my great transgression, so requite
Favour renewed, and add a greater sin
By prostituting holy things to idols;
A Nazarite in place abominable,
Vaunting my strength in honour to their Dagon?
Besides, how vile, contemptible, ridiculous,
What act more execrably unclean, profane?
   CHOR. Yet with this strength thou servest the Philis-
      tines,
Idolatrous, uncircumcised, unclean.
   SAMS. Not in their idol-worship, but by labour
Honest and lawful to deserve my food
Of those who have me in their civil power.
   CHOR. Where the heart joins not, outward acts defile
      not.
   SAMS. Where outward force constrains, the sentence
      holds;
But who constrains me to the temple of Dagon,
Not dragging? the Philistian lords command;
Commands are no constraints. If I obey them,
I do it freely, venturing to displease
GOD for the fear of man, and man prefer,
Set GOD behind: which in His jealousy
Shall never, unrepented, find forgiveness.
Yet that He may dispense with me or thee
Present in temples at idolatrous rites
For some important cause, thou need'st not doubt.
   CHOR. How thou wilt here come off surmounts my
      reach.

SAMS. Be of good courage, I begin to feel
Some rousing motions in me, which dispose
To something extraordinary my thoughts.
I with this messenger will go along,
Nothing to do, be sure, that may dishonour
Our law, or stain my vow of Nazarite.
If there be aught of presage in the mind,
This day will be remarkable in my life
By some great act, or of my days the last.
    CHOR. In time thou hast resolved; the man returns.
    OFF. Samson, this second message from our lords
To thee I am bid say. Art thou our slave,
Our captive, at the public mill our drudge,
And darest thou at our sending and command
Dispute thy coming? come without delay;
Or we shall find such engines to assail
And hamper thee, as thou shalt come of force,
Though thou wert firmlier fastened than a rock.
    SAMS. I could be well content to try their art,
Which to no few of them would prove pernicious.
Yet knowing their advantages too many,
Because they shall not trail me through their streets
Like a wild beast, I am content to go.
Masters' commands come with a power resistless
To such as owe them absolute subjection;
And for a life who will not change his purpose?
So mutable are all the ways of men!
Yet this be sure, in nothing to comply
Scandalous or forbidden in our law.
    OFF. I praise thy resolution: doff these links;
By this compliance thou wilt win the lords
To favour, and, perhaps, to set thee free.

[409]

SAMS. Brethren, farewell; your company along
I will not wish, lest it perhaps offend them
To see me girt with friends; and how the sight
Of me as of a common enemy,
So dreaded once, may now exasperate them
I know not. Lords are lordliest in their wine;
And the well-feasted priest then soonest fired
With zeal, if aught religion seem concerned;
No less the people on their holy-days
Impetuous, insolent, unquenchable:
Happen what may, of me expect to hear
Nothing dishonourable, impure, unworthy
Our GOD, our law, my nation, or myself;
The last of me or no I cannot warrant.

   CHOR. Go, and the Holy One
Of Israel be thy guide
To what may serve His glory best, and spread His name
Great among the heathen round;
Send thee the Angel of thy birth, to stand
Fast by thy side, who from thy father's field
Rode up in flames after his message told
Of thy conception, and be now a shield
Of fire; that Spirit that first rushed on thee
In the camp of Dan
Be efficacious in thee now at need.
For never was from heaven imparted
Measure of strength so great to mortal seed,
As in thy wondrous actions hath been seen.
But wherefore comes old Manoah in such haste
With youthful steps? much livelier than ere while
He seems; supposing here to find his son,
Or of him bringing to us some glad news?

MAN. Peace with you, brethren! my inducement hither
Was not at present here to find my son,
By order of the lords new parted hence,
To come and play before them at their feast.
I heard all as I came; the city rings,
And numbers thither flock; I had no will,
Lest I should see him forced to things unseemly.
But that which moved my coming now was chiefly
To give ye part with me what hope I have
With good success to work his liberty.

CHOR. That hope would much rejoice us to partake
With thee; say, reverend Sire, we thirst to hear.

MAN. I have attempted one by one the lords,
Either at home or through the high street passing,
With supplication prone and father's tears,
To accept of ransom for my son their pris'ner.
Some much averse I found, and wondrous harsh,
Contemptuous, proud, set on revenge and spite;
That part most reverenced Dagon and his priests:
Others more moderate seeming, but their aim
Private reward, for which both GOD and State
They easily would set to sale: a third
More generous far and civil, who confessed
They had enough revenged, having reduced
Their foe to misery beneath their fears,
The rest was magnanimity to remit,
If some convenient ransom were proposed.—
What noise or shout was that? it tore the sky.

CHOR. Doubtless the people shouting to behold
Their once great dread, captive and blind before them,
Or at some proof of strength before them shown.

MAN. His ransom, if my whole inheritance

[411]

May compass it, shall willingly be paid
And numbered down: much rather I shall choose
To live the poorest in my tribe, than richest,
And he in that calamitous prison left.
No, I am fixed not to part hence without him.
For his redemption all my patrimony,
If need be, I am ready to forego
And quit: not wanting him, I shall want nothing.

CHOR. Fathers are wont to lay up for their sons;
Thou for thy son are bent to lay out all:
Sons wont to nurse their parents in old age;
Thou in old age car'st how to nurse thy son,
Made older than thy age through eyesight lost.

MAN. It shall be my delight to tend his eyes,
And view him sitting in the house, ennobled,
With all those high exploits by him achieved,
And on his shoulders waving down those locks,
That of a nation armed the strength contained:
And I persuade me GOD hath not permitted
His strength again to grow up with his hair,
Garrisoned round about him like a camp
Of faithful soldiery, were not His purpose
To use him further yet in some great service,
Not to sit idle with so great a gift
Useless, and thence ridiculous, about him.
And since his strength with eyesight was not lost,
GOD will restore him eyesight to his strength.

CHOR. Thy hopes are not ill-founded, nor seem vain,
Of his delivery, and thy joy thereon
Conceived, agreeable to a father's love;
In both which we, as next, participate.

MAN. I know your friendly minds, and—O what noise!

Mercy of heav'n, what hideous noise was that?
Horribly loud, unlike the former shout.
CHOR. Noise call you it, or universal groan,
As if the whole inhabitation perished?
Blood, death, and deathful deeds are in that noise,
Ruin, destruction at the utmost point.
MAN. Of ruin indeed methought I heard the noise.
Oh, it continues: they have slain my son!
CHOR. Thy son is rather slaying them; that outcry
From slaughter of one foe could not ascend.
MAN. Some dismal accident it needs must be:
What shall we do, stay here, or run and see?
CHOR. Best keep together here, lest running thither
We unawares run into danger's mouth.
This evil on the Philistines is fallen;
From whom could else a general cry be heard?
The sufferers then will scarce molest us here;
From other hands we need not much to fear.
What if his eyesight (for to Israel's GOD
Nothing is hard), by miracle restored,
He now be dealing dole among his foes,
And over heaps of slaughtered walk his way?
MAN. That were a joy presumptuous to be thought.
CHOR. Yet GOD hath wrought things as incredible
For His people of old; what hinders now?
MAN. He can, I know, but doubt to think He will;
Yet hope would fain subscribe, and tempts belief.
A little stay will bring some notice hither.
CHOR. Of good or bad so great, of bad the sooner;
For evil news rides post, while good news baits.
And to our wish I see one hither speeding,
An Hebrew, as I guess, and of our tribe.

MESSENGER. O whither shall I run, or which way fly
The sight of this so horrid spectacle,
Which erst my eyes beheld, and yet behold?
For dire imagination still pursues me.
But Providence or instinct of nature seems,
Or reason, though disturbed and scarce consulted,
To have guided me aright, I know not how,
To thee first, reverend Manoah, and to these
My countrymen, whom here I knew remaining,
As at some distance from the place of horror,
So in the sad event too much concerned.

MAN. The accident was loud, and here before thee
With rueful cry, yet what it was we hear not;
No preface needs, thou seest we long to know.

MESS. It would burst forth, but I recover breath,
And sense distract, to know well what I utter.

MAN. Tell us the sum, the circumstance defer.

MESS. Gaza yet stands, but all her sons are fallen,
All in a moment overwhelmed and fallen.

MAN. Sad; but thou know'st to Israelites not saddest
The desolation of a hostile city.

MESS. Feed on that first, there may in grief be surfeit.

MAN. Relate by whom.

MESS. By Samson.

MAN. That still lessens
The sorrow, and converts it nigh to joy.

MESS. Ah! Manoah, I refrain too suddenly
To utter what will come at last too soon;
Lest evil tidings with too rude irruption
Hitting thy agèd ear should pierce too deep.

MAN. Suspense in news is torture, speak them out.

MESS. Take then the worst in brief, Samson is dead.

[4¹4]

MAN. The worst indeed! Oh, all my hopes defeated
To free him hence! but death, who sets all free,
Hath paid his ransom now and full discharge.
What windy joy this day had I conceived
Hopeful of his delivery, which now proves
Abortive as the first-born bloom of spring
Nipt with the lagging rear of winter's frost!
Yet, ere I give the reins to grief, say first,
How died he? death to life is crown or shame.
All by him fell, thou say'st; by whom fell he?
What glorious hand gave Samson his death's wound?
    MESS. Unwounded of his enemies he fell.
    MAN. Wearied with slaughter, then, or how? explain.
    MESS. By his own hands.
    MAN. Self-violence? what cause
Brought him so soon at variance with himself
Among his foes?
    MESS. Inevitable cause
At once both to destroy and be destroyed:
The edifice, where all were met to see him,
Upon their heads and on his own he pulled.
    MAN. O lastly over-strong against thyself!
A dreadful way thou took'st to thy revenge.
More than enough we know; but, while things yet
Are in confusion, give us, if thou canst,
Eye-witness of what first or last was done,
Relation more particular and distinct.
    MESS. Occasions drew me early to this city,
And as the gates I entered with sunrise,
The morning trumpets festival proclaimed
Through each high street. Little I had dispatched,
When all abroad was rumoured, that this day

Samson should be brought forth to show the people
Proof of his mighty strength in feats and games;
I sorrowed at his captive state, but minded
Not to be absent at that spectacle.
The building was a spacious theatre,
Half-round, on two main pillars vaulted high,
With seats, where all the lords and each degree
Of sort might sit in order to behold;
The other side was open, where the throng
On banks and scaffolds under sky might stand;
I among these aloof obscurely stood.
The feast and noon grew high, and sacrifice
Had filled their hearts with mirth, high cheer, and wine,
When to their sports they turned. Immediately
Was Samson as a public servant brought,
In their state livery clad; before him pipes
And timbrels, on each side went armèd guards,
Both horse and foot, before him and behind
Archers, and slingers, cataphracts, and spears.
At sight of him the people with a shout
Rifted the air, clamouring their god with praise,
Who had made their dreadful enemy their thrall.
He patient, but undaunted, where they led him,
Came to the place, and what was set before him,
Which without help of eye might be assayed,
To heave, pull, draw, or break, he still performed,
All with incredible stupendous force,
None daring to appear antagonist.
At length, for intermission sake, they led him
Between the pillars; he his guide requested,
For so from such as nearer stood we heard,
As over-tired, to let him lean awhile

With both his arms on those two massy pillars,
That to the arched roof gave main support.
He, unsuspicious, led him; which when Samson
Felt in his arms, with head awhile inclined,
And eyes fast fixt he stood, as one who prayed,
Or some great matter in his mind revolved:
At last, with head erect, thus cried aloud:
"Hitherto, lords, what your commands imposed
I have performed, as reason was, obeying,
Not without wonder or delight beheld:
Now of my own accord such other trial
I mean to show you of my strength, yet greater;
As with amaze shall strike all who behold."
This uttered, straining all his nerves, he bowed.
As with the force of winds and waters pent,
When mountains tremble, those two massy pillars
With horrible convulsion to and fro
He tugged, he shook, till down they came, and drew
The whole roof after them, with burst of thunder,
Upon the heads of all who sat beneath,
Lords, ladies, captains, counsellors, or priests,
Their choice nobility and flower, not only
Of this, but each Philistian city round,
Met from all parts to solemnize this feast.
Samson, with these immixed, inevitably
Pulled down the same destruction on himself;
The vulgar only 'scaped who stood without.
    CHOR. O dearly-bought revenge, yet glorious!
Living or dying, thou hast fulfilled
The work for which thou wast foretold
To Israel, and now liest victorious
Among thy slain, self-killed

Not willingly, but tangled in the fold
Of dire necessity, whose law in death conjoined
Thee with thy slaughtered foes in number more
Than all thy life had slain before.

    1 SEMICHOR. While their hearts were jocund and
        sublime,
Drunk with idolatry, drunk with wine,
And fat regorged of bulls and goats,
Chanting their idol, and preferring
Before our living Dread who dwells
In Silo His bright sanctuary:
Among them He a spirit of frenzy sent,
Who hurt their minds,
And urged them on with mad desire
To call in haste for their destroyer;
They, only set on sport and play,
Unweetingly importuned
Their own destruction to come speedy upon them.
So fond are mortal men,
Fall'n into wrath divine,
As their own ruin on themselves to invite,
Insensate left, or to sense reprobate,
And with blindness internal struck.

    2 SEMICHOR. But he, though blind of sight,
Despised and thought extinguished quite,
With inward eyes illuminated,
His fiery virtue roused
From under ashes into sudden flame,
And as an evening dragon came,
Assailant on the perchèd roosts
And nests in order ranged
Of tame villatic fowl; but as an eagle

His cloudless thunder bolted on their heads.
So virtue, given for lost,
Depressed and overthrown, as seemed,
Like that self-begotten bird
In the Arabian woods imbost,
That no second knows nor third,
And lay ere while a holocaust,
From out her ashy womb now teemed;
Revives, reflourishes, then vigorous most
When most unactive deemed;
And though her body die, her fame survives
A secular bird ages of lives.
   MAN. Come, come, no time for lamentation now,
Nor much more cause: Samson hath quit himself
Like Samson, and heroically hath finished
A life heroic, on his enemies
Fully revenged; hath left them years of mourning,
And lamentation to the sons of Caphtor
Through all Philistian bounds. To Israel
Honour hath left and freedom, let but them
Find courage to lay hold on this occasion;
To himself and father's house eternal fame;
And, which is best and happiest yet, all this
With GOD not parted from him, as was feared,
But favouring and assisting to the end.
Nothing is here for tears, nothing to wail
Or knock the breast; no weakness, no contempt,
Dispraise, or blame; nothing but well and fair,
And what may quiet us in a death so noble.
Let us go find the body where it lies
Soaked in his enemies' blood, and from the stream
With lavers pure and cleansing herbs wash off

The clotted gore. I, with what speed the while
Gaza is not in plight to say us nay,
Will send for all my kindred, all my friends,
To fetch him hence, and solemnly attend
With silent obsequy and funeral train
Home to his father's house: there will I build him
A monument, and plant it round with shade
Of laurel ever green, and branching palm,
With all his trophies hung, and acts inrolled
In copious legend, or sweet lyric song.
Thither shall all the valiant youth resort,
And from his memory inflame their breasts
To matchless valour and adventures high:
The virgins also shall on feastful days
Visit his tomb with flowers, only bewailing
His lot unfortunate in nuptial choice,
From whence captivity and loss of eyes.
   CHOR. All is best, though we oft doubt,
What the unsearchable dispose
Of Highest Wisdom brings about,
And ever best found in the close.
Oft He seems to hide His face,
But unexpectedly returns,
And to His faithful champion hath in place
Bore witness gloriously; whence Gaza mourns,
And all that band them to resist
His uncontrollable intent:
His servants He, with new acquist
Of true experience from this great event,
With peace and consolation hath dismissed,
And calm of mind, all passion spent.

JOHN MILTON